THE SEA SWALLOWS

Campaigning In the South Vietnam Delta with Chinese Catholic Exiles

Colonel Henry F. Dagenais

DEDICATED TO

The Co-Vans of South East Asia

1958 - 1973

CONTENTS

PART I

Chapters

PART II

AUTHOR'S NOTES

From the time I first arrived in Vietnam to when I put pen to paper to begin this account, 30 years had lapsed. Another 12 passed before I sat down to finish my attempt to provide a record of the first of two tours of duty with local and indigenous military forces. Eight months of the first year were spent with the exiled Chinese Catholics known as the Sea Swallows and the last four months as the District Senior Advisor for the district in which the Chinese enclave was located.

Sometimes the events seem dim and long past, other times like they happened yesterday, or now. The characters are real: I have made no attempt to disguise the identity of anyone; when I remembered names I used them; when memory failed or a name was never known, I gave one. The names of locations, villages, and hamlets are as they were known at the time. I have used both English and Vietnamese when referring to places, titles, and military rank that are common throughout the book. I have used the metric system for distances and measurements except when referring to airports or landing strips, which are expressed in feet. The sequence of events is as accurate as memory and some old notes serve me. With the exception of a biography of Father Hoa, no other records or official government documents have been consulted in writing of these experiences. I have made no attempt to ensure my account coincides with what anyone else has written. It is as I remember events, from my position on the ground at the time.

ACKNOWLEDGEMENTS

The writing of this narrative would not have come to fruition without the help and encouragement of family and friends. A review by Lieutenant Colonel Helen Fournier of the military terms and jargon used insured that a reader would have a clear understanding of the situation and environment being described. Kathleen Silloway's deep edit recommended drastic changes to the overall structure of the original manuscript. Comments on selective chapters by Colonel Chris Evangelos and Lieutenant Colonel Dave Mahalik, officers who had served in the advisory effort provided back to earth reality to my recollection of events. Steve Satler took forty five year old slides and produced photographs that appeared to have been taken yesterday. Phil Marcus, lawyer, published author, and college professor shepherded me throughout the preparation of my manuscript and the wickets of the publishing business. My daughter, Jennifer Dagenais Starks, was both my tutor of the Word program and severest critic from start to finish. And last but certainly not least was the constant encouragement and continual push to keep going from my wife Ann. My thanks to all.

Aerial view of Hai Yen.

The author and
Father Augustine Nguyễn Lạc Hóa
1967

PROLOGUE

In the late1980s, several years after I had retired from active duty, I received a notice of the quarterly dinner of the local chapter of the Retired Officers Association at Fort Meade, Maryland. There was always a guest speaker and I sometimes attended. At this particular dinner, the speaker was Mr. Bernard Yoh, Director of Communications for the watch-dog group Accuracy in Media. A short description of his background mentioned that he had been a general in the Chinese National Army and had received the surrender of Shanghai from the Japanese in 1945, the largest city they had ever captured. He was a key supporter of the Chinese priest Father Hoa and the Sea Swallows in their battle to survive in a Viet Cong controlled area in the Mekong Delta. Intrigued by anyone who supported the Sea Swallows, I mailed in my reservation. A few days later I received a call from the president of the chapter, asking if I knew Mr. Yoh. I replied that I did not but had served as the Senior Advisor to the Sea Swallows in 1967/68. I was then informed that I would be seated at the head table with Mr.Yoh and that he would be told of my presence.

While dressing for that evening, I attached to my lapel a small triangular pin depicting a swallow flying over a palm tree and the sea. This insignia had been designed by Father Hoa and reportedly represented a bird that migrates south and returns to China annually. It became the symbol of the exiled Chinese who adopted the name Sea Swallows. It was worn as a shoulder patch and as a regimental crest of the type traditionally seen on military uniforms in most armies throughout the world. It also became their organizational flag that was flown on holidays and during formal military ceremonies.

The night of the event my wife and I had arrived early and were enjoying a cocktail when Mr.Yoh entered the banquet room and was

13

led in my direction. Upon spying the Sea Swallow pin on my jacket, Yoh presented his hand asking, "You were with the Sea Swallows; you know Father Hoa?"

"Yes," I replied, shaking his offered hand.

"We must talk," Yoh stated.

That began, for me, an intense dialogue that dominated Mr.Yoh's visit. Our discussion had to be interrupted for dinner and again for him to address the attendees. It was evident that the saga of Father Hoa and the Sea Swallows was a passionate episode in his life. Our discussion, which in fact consisted mostly of me listening and Yoh speaking, covered the Swallows' arduous journey escaping from China to the establishment of Hai Yen in the hamlet of Binh Hung, deep in the delta of South Vietnam. Through the efforts of Mr. Yoh and Major General (then Colonel) Edward Landsdale, a rather shadowy counter-insurgency expert, President Diem agreed to allow the United States to provide support to Father Hoa. (I was aware of how difficult the struggle to survive was before the U.S. support via the CIA was received.) That support--consisting of weapons, ammunition, communication equipment, building supplies, boats and outboard motors, individual equipment, uniforms, and funds--enabled Father Hoa to build an anti-communist enclave in Viet Cong territory with a military force of approximately a thousand soldiers.

Hearing first-hand from one of the two most influential individuals responsible for the establishment and success of the Sea Swallows not only gave credence to my discussions with Father Hoa but also supported what I knew from serving with the Sea Swallows.

These three remarkable men are all now deceased--Father Hoa at a monastery in Taiwan in 1989; General Landsdale in McLean,

14

Virginia, in1987; and Bernard Yoh in Bethesda, Maryland, in 1996. I consider myself fortunate to have met them all.

INTRODUCTION

I spent a total of two years in Vietnam assigned to the Military Assistance Command Vietnam (MACV). From September 1967 to September 1968, I was a District and Special Sub Sector Advisor in An Xuyen Province, IV Corps. Then from February 1971 until February 1972, I was assigned to a number of positions in Vinh Binh Province, IV Corps. I first arrived there to fill the position of Senior Regional Force/Popular Force (RF/PF) Advisor for the Province, but because of the draw-down of U.S. forces, I held for short periods of time the positions of Deputy for Plans and Operations (DPO), the S3 Operations Officer, and for a few weeks I acted as the Province Senior Advisor (PSA). However this story is concerned with my first tour, the time spent with the exiled Chinese Catholics known as the Sea Swallows and as Senior Advisor to Cai Nuoc District.

In order to set the scene and provide a background for understanding a rather unusual political and military scenario, a brief explanation of the Vietnamese civil and military structure and the supporting American advisory effort is appropriate. The Republic of South Vietnam was comprised of 44 provinces, 4 special zones and several autonomous cities. The country was divided into Regions (later called Corps or Zones) numbered I through IV running from north to south. The I Corps, the most northern, bordered North Vietnam (the Democratic Peoples' Republic of Vietnam). II Corps was the largest and included the cities of Dong Ha, Hue, and Da Nang. III Corps included Saigon, the capital of South Vietnam, and stretching to the end of the country was IV Corps, commonly referred to as "the delta" because of the mouths of the Mekong River. At the far southern end of the country was the Ca Mau Peninsula, location of An Xuyen Province and its capital Ca Mau.

Each province was divided into several districts, each district into two or more villages, and each village into a number of hamlets.

(The military designation for provinces was sectors and for districts, sub sectors. This political structure provided government control down to the smallest population centers. Compared to the United States, a province would equate to a state, a district to a county, a village to a ward or county district, and a hamlet to an unincorporated town or rural community. The Province Chiefs were appointed by the Vietnamese president and approved by the National Assembly. The District Chiefs were appointed by the Province Chief and approved by the president. Village Chiefs were appointed by the District Chiefs and approved by the Province Chiefs, and Hamlet Chiefs were appointed by the Villages and approved by the District Chiefs. In better times, these officials were civilian and elected by the population of the areas for which they were responsible. However, in the ongoing battle against the Vietnamese Communists (Viet Cong), military leaders were generally put in control. Each level had its own civil and military staff to carry out the functions of government and to process the struggle against the Viet Cong.

MACV, one of the two major U.S. military commands in Vietnam, was responsible for both the military and civil advisory efforts to the Republic of South Vietnam. The U.S. Army Vietnam (USARV) commanded all U.S. military forces engaged in combat operations and was subordinate to COMUSMACV (Commander U.S. Military Advisory Command Vietnam) as were other services and allied forces. The advisory effort under the command of CORDS (Civil Operations and Revolutionary Development Support) was projected down through the Vietnamese military and civil chains to the lowest level. Teams of military advisors were assigned to ARVN (Army of the Republic of Vietnam) corps, divisions, regiments, and battalions. Special teams operated at training centers, military schools, logistical bases, and administrative/finance units. On the civil side, advisors served at region, province, district, and in some instances at the village levels. Special teams were also assigned to selected cities.

17

The Province and District Teams are of the most concern in this account. The Province Team, normally commanded by a Colonel or Foreign Service Officer, consisted of a mix of military and State Department personnel. Advisors were assigned to the civil side of the province in the Departments of Public Health, Public Safety, Agriculture, Finance, Sanitation, Power, Refugee Control, etc. On the military side, the Province Team advised on combat planning and operations, training, intelligence, administration, and logistics. Advisors mirrored the Vietnamese staff in all positions, participated in combat operations, and as much as the Vietnamese commander would permit were involved in all facets of the military effort. At the district level, "the cutting edge," a five to seven-man team commanded by a major, provided both military and civil advisory support to the District Chief and his staff. The mission at the district level varied greatly depending on the level of Viet Cong activity. Some districts in strongly controlled government areas had little combat activity. Teams assigned to those areas were able to become heavily engaged in building schools and health stations, providing electric power, clean water, new strains of rice and swine all programs that were considered "nation building." At the other end of the spectrum were districts almost entirely involved in combat operations where "nation building" virtually did not exist. Cai Nuoc District and Hai Yen Special Sub Sector, An Xuyen Province, were definitely in the latter category. My first tour of duty in Vietnam was spent exclusively in that environment and is the basis of my experiences.

REPUBLIC OF VIETNAM

SOUTH CHINA SEA

GULF OF THAILAND

Saigon

Ax Xyuen

Hai Yen

AN XYUEN PROVINCE

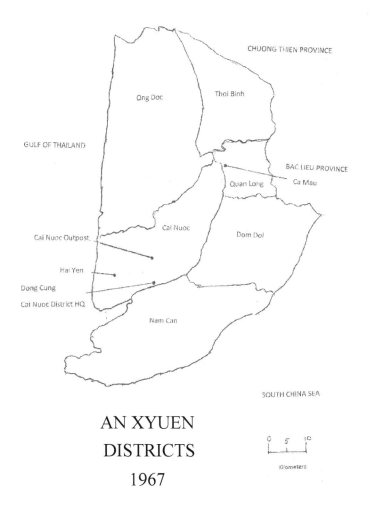

CHUONG THIEN PROVINCE

Ong Doc

Thoi Binh

GULF OF THAILAND

BAC LIEU PROVINCE

Quan Long

Ca Mau

Cai Nuoc

Dom Doi

Cai Nuoc Outpost

Hai Yen

Dong Cung

Cai Nuoc District HQ

Nam Can

SOUTH CHINA SEA

AN XYUEN
DISTRICTS
1967

0   5   10
Kilometers

FREQUENTLY MENTIONED LOCATIONS

Saigon - the capital of the Republic of South Vietnam, 200 kilometers north of An Xyuen Province

Can Tho - largest city in the delta, location of IV Corps Headquarters

Ca Mau - capital of An Xyen Province and location of the Province U.S. Advisory Team

Cai Nuoc District - 50 kilometers south of Ca Mau

Cai Nuoc Outpost – old location of Cai Nuoc District Headquarters

Dong Cung Hamlet – relocated site of Cai Nuoc District Headquarters

Hai Yen – Special Sub Sector, Chinese Catholic Enclave located in Cai Nuoc District

Tan Hung Tay Village – located in Cai Nuoc District and bordering on Gulf of Thailand

Cai Doi Ngen Village – 4 kilometers north of Hai Yen in Cai Nuoc District

Binh Hung Hamlet - Cai Nuoc District location of Hai Yen

Cai Bot Village - Viet Cong base area east of Hai Yen

Quan Pho – Viet Cong base area, northeast of Hai Yen

Nan Cam District – Southernmost district in An Xyuen Province and the Republic of South Vietnam, borders on Cai Nuoc District

Dom Doi District – Borders Cai Nuoc District to the south east.

Song Ong Doc District – Borders Cai Nuoc District to the north.

Song Bay Hop – Major river border of Cai Nuoc and Nan Cam Districts, empties into Gulf of Thailand

PRINCIPLE PERSONNEL

MG Eckhart – IV Corps Senior Advisor

LTC Gilland – Province Senior Advisor (PSA) – An Xyuen Province

LTC Culpepper – Deputy Province Senior Advisor (DPSA) - An Xyuen Province

LTC Wright – Deputy for Plans and Operations (DPO) – An Xyuen Province

MAJ Dagenais – District Senior Advisor (DSA) – Cai Nuoc District

LT Bates – Deputy District Senior Advisor – (DDSA) – Cai Nuoc District

LT Harris – Deputy District Senior Advisor – (DDSA) – Cai Nuoc District

Platoon SGT Brown –NCO Operations Advisor

Platoon SGT Johnson – NCO Intelligence Advisor

Platoon SGT Bailey – Senior NCO Medical Advisor

Airman First Class Moates – USAF NCO Medical Advisor

SGT Hai- ARVN Interpreter

Corporal First Class Phong – Bodyguard (Vietnamese)

Father Hoa – Spiritual and Military Leader of the Sea Swallows (Chinese Catholic refugees)

Major Nuoc – Vietnamese Military Commander, Hai Yen

Captain Thinh – Vietnamese Deputy Commander, Hai Yen

Captain Hy – District Chief, Cai Nuoc District

LT Hong – Deputy District Chief, Cai Nuoc District

PART I

CHAPTER 1

DEPARTURE AND ARRIVAL

Saying goodbye to my family again after such a short time was difficult. My daughter Jennifer was only six years old and didn't really comprehend the significance of my departure. After all, I had returned from Korea only 19 months ago and during the time state side I had been on TDY (temporary duty) to a number of schools. My wife Ann and Jennifer had moved with me to the various school locations despite the difficulties in finding housing for such short durations because we knew I was soon leaving on another overseas tour where a full-fledged shooting war was going on and we wanted to have as much time together as possible. So off we went from the Infantry Officers Career Course at Fort Benning, Georgia, to Fort Knox, Kentucky, to the Vietnam Advisor's Course at Fort Gordon, Georgia, and finally to the Defense Language Institute's 15-week Vietnam Language Course at Biggs Field, El Paso, Texas.

I settled Ann and Jennifer back in Chestertown, Maryland, for the duration of my tour and on the 14th of September 1967 left the Baltimore Friendship International Airport bound for the Oakland Army Terminal and Travis Air Force Base, the point of departure for The Republic of South Vietnam.

At Oakland there were several days of processing and the usual hurry up and wait that the army seems always to go through. Eventually, we were bused to Travis Air Base and boarded our flight to Vietnam. Our plane was a Continental Airlines charter flight, which was certainly more comfortable than a USAF MAC (Military Air Command) flight. I was a captain at the time, on the promotion list to major and expecting to be promoted soon, possibly while en route to my new assignment. As there were a number of more senior officers on the flight, I was not assigned any responsibility pertaining to the troops. Just before take-off there was a scurry caused by the absence of two soldiers. After a short search of the terminal we loaded up and left with the two men listed as 'Missing Movement," a rather serious offence.

First stop on our flight was Hawaii, where we had a 90-minute layover, which gave us just enough time to guzzle down a couple of drinks at an airport bar before reloading. Again we were missing two men; after a very short delay we flew on, joking that if there were enough stops the plane would be empty when we arrived in Vietnam. The plane quieted down as everyone grew tired of talking and dozed off to sleep. There was one more stop, Clark Field in the Philippines. This time all passengers were watched closely and no one disappeared. Upon take off, we were fed again and then fell back to sleep.

A now familiar voice came over the intercom: "This is the captain again. We are about 10 minutes off the coast of South Vietnam and about 20 minutes from touchdown at Bien Hoa. We will be going in rather high and will make a steep descent. The VC mortared the field about an hour ago."

A hubbub of noise spread throughout the plane as men roused from the stupor borne of long hours of inactivity--sleeping, eating, talking until hoarse, and then sleeping again.

Again the intercom, the soft voice of a flight attendant reminding us to "please fasten your seat belts and extinguish all smoking materials."

Most of the 160 plus soldiers on the plane, myself included, were on their first tour in a combat zone and wondering what was in store for them – and reacting in a dozen different ways. Some laughed nervously; some tried to act as if landing in Vietnam was old hat and feigned a look of boredom. Others were obviously excited, chattering, eyes bright. Those next to windows peered into the darkness trying to see something, anything. I gathered up my things, a book and small leather bag. The plane took a sharp drop, seeming to lurch sideways. We were descending rapidly, then gradually. A screech of rubber as the wheels touched the runway and a reversal of the engines signaled that we were on the ground in the Republic of South Vietnam.

Flanked by gun jeeps, the plane taxied down the runway to a lighted area and came to a stop. As usual, everyone crowded into the aisles to deplane and waited impatiently, holding bags and making unfunny jokes. An Army captain appeared in the front: "Welcome to Vietnam!" His greeting was received with sarcastic yells and cat calls.

"Gentlemen, you will depart the aircraft at once and follow the guides to the lighted area. Bring your hand baggage; your other bags will be brought to the briefing area. At the briefing area you will be broken down into groups according to your unit of assignment. You will receive a very short orientation while your baggage is off loaded. You will then board buses or trucks and be transported to your respective in-processing areas. Now deplane and good luck."

The captain disappeared down the steps and the passengers began to shuffle forward. Two of the flight attendants were at the front bidding their traditional farewells and smiles. I had not spoken to any of the attendants other than to order drinks or food and to give a few thank yous. Some of the troops, however, had run a continuous flirtation with the women thoughout the flight. The women were used to the play and, understanding the reason for it, handled it well, responding with light teasing and laughter.

As I approached the plane's front exit, I could hear an attendant repeating, "Good bye, good bye now, bye, good bye." It was dark but the dim light from the plane's interior revealed the fixed smiles on the women's faces. I reached the doorway, and as I stepped through I said, "Good bye and thank you."

As I passed the attendant, she reached out and placed her hand on my arm, stopping me. I hesitated and turned back to her.

She said, "Now you be careful, promise?"

I stared at her for a moment. I had not spoken to her during the 20-hour flight except perhaps to thank her for a cup of coffee. She had had long laughing exchanges with some of the other younger soldiers.

I smiled and said, "I will."

She smiled back with an "Okay" and took her hand from my arm and I went on.

I have wondered over the years why, of all the men on board, she stopped me. She had not stopped anyone ahead of me. What possessed her to speak to me with such concern in her voice? Did I remind her of a brother, a friend? I am sure I will never know.

We were led to an area at the side of a corrugated tin building, dimly lit and covered with canvas. There we proceeded to load onto various vehicles. A Non-Commissioned Officer (NCO) singled out the advisors, some 20 or more, and had us board a blue military bus. We loaded our bags, took seats, and waited impatiently for the next leg of our journey to get underway. After a few moments, the young sergeant who led us to the bus sprang into the bus, followed by another soldier who slid into the driver's seat,

"Gentlemen," he announced, "we are on our way to the Kolper Compound in Saigon where you will be in-processed. You can expect to be there several days getting briefed and drawing equipment prior to moving out to your duty station. It will take about an hour to an hour and a half to get to the compound, so just sit back and enjoy the scenery."

With that he nodded to the driver, who shut the door, shoved the bus in gear, and lurched off down a newly graded dirt road to a gate guarded by air police wearing berets and camouflaged uniforms.

It was now daylight, and with the sun came a rise in the heat which we already thought was unbearable. We also experienced a variety of unfamiliar odors that drifted in the windows as we drove along what was the main road from Bien Hoa to Saigon. The bus was not air conditioned, and the windows were covered with a heavy mesh so that a passing Viet Cong could not casually toss a grenade into the bus. Everyone strained to get their first glimpse of the Vietnamese people. The roadside was lined with shacks with people standing out brushing their teeth, eating soup at small stands, and watching the traffic. Between and behind the shacks--which were oviously housing refugees from the war zone--were masonry buildings with tile roofs and unkempt yards. Everywhere was a bright green lush of vegetation and puddles of dirty water. Traffic was heavy with a mix of military vehicles, old buses and cars, bicycles, and an occasional ox cart. Movement was slow, and everyone blew their horn. Frequently an overpowering odor would flood the bus prompting various comments.

"What the hell is that smell?"

"That's nuoc mam," stated the sergeant, "fish sauce. The Vietnamese eat it on rice, made from rotten fish. You had better learn to like it."

How correct he was I would later find out. As we entered Saigon, you could see the effects of the French: wide boulevards with stately trees, walled villas, and gardens that spoke of a once easy and comfortable life for the wealthy. Now the streets and sidewalks held ramshackle buildings and stalls selling everything imaginable, from black market items from the U.S. military Post Exchange (PX) to clothes, food, and souvenirs spread on the sidewalks with hawkeyed vendors ready to take your money. The air was blue with the exhaust from military and civilian cars and trucks, motor bikes, scooters, and small blue taxis. Bicycles, cyclos, and pedicabs rounded out the hodgepodge of vehicles on the streets, all blowing their horns and jockeying for position to be able to proceed. The Vietnamese military vehicle drivers held their horns down and just bulled their way through by sheer threat of running over anything in their way. A mixture of uniforms and native dress could be seen, including children of all ages in various stages of dress. Small children walked around with nothing on but a short shirt, urinating and defecating whenever the urge hit them; I could see the surprise and disgust on the faces of some of the troops on the bus. Newbies! Those of us who had been in Vietnam or Korea before did not find it surprising. Finally, we pulled up to a walled villa; the driver honked his horn, and the gates opened. We had arrived at Kolper Compound, the in and out processing site for MACV advisors.

CHAPTER 2

KOLPER COMPOUND

In the days before Camp Alpha (which was the gigantic installation for the reception and departure of U.S. troops), a leased villa near the center of Saigon was used for in/out processing and providing administrative and logistic support for MACV field advisors. It was named for the first advisor killed in Vietnam. From here, new arrivals were briefed, equipped, assigned, and dispatched out to the field. The villa, like most in Saigon, was built by the French and enclosed by a masonry wall. It was square, three stories high with walkway-style balconies on each floor from which entry was gained into small individual rooms. It had been supplemented by temporary wooden buildings serving a number of uses--mess hall, supply, club, maintenance, and storage. My recollection of the villa itself is vague. There was a warren of small rooms on the first floor used for administration and processing personnel. There must have been at least one large room that held 20 to 25 personnel and where briefings and classes were held. A stairway in the center of the building was the only access to the floors above. On each floor, the stairs opened on a lounge area with some chairs and tables. From this area, one exited onto the balcony and went right or left to reach one's assigned room. There was no entry into the rooms except by the balcony. The rooms were small and equipped with two sets (two beds each) of GI bunks like you often find in Basic Training units. A small latrine with a shower so positioned that you could sit on the toilet and shower at the same time completed the décor. Wine or soda bottles containing potable water for drinking or brushing of teeth were provided. The rooms were so small that the four officers assigned to each could not all stand up in the room at one time. Someone had to get in a bunk or stand out on the balcony. Exhaust fumes from generators below running 24 hours a day kept you with a constant headache. The noise also prevented any type of restful sleep.

Upon assignment to a room, I proceeded to the third floor. In the lobby-like lounge were several women sitting, squatting around a low table, loading .30 caliber carbine magazines from a crate of ammunition. I proudly spoke to them in my recently acquired Vietnamese. They responded "Chao Dai- uy" (hello Captain) and chattered away without me understanding a word they said.

"My God," I thought. "there goes several months of language training down the drain!" I made this comment to my roommate a few minutes later when I found my assigned quarters. "Oh don't worry, they were speaking in Chinese. There are a lot of Chinese in Saigon" I then felt a little better.

Briefings were conducted on security, cultural taboos, the organization of the Vietnamese civil government, military structure, and the advisor's roles and responsibilities. We were given a driving test and issued Driver's Permits. On the last day, we drew weapons and equipment. Company grade officers (Lieutenants and Captains) were required to draw a.30 caliber carbine. Field grade (Majors through Colonels) had the choice of a .45 caliber pistol or a carbine. I took both. Some of the normal issue items were not available, ig, hammocks, two quart canteens, and the round "boonie hats." Field advisors were issued a two-pack emergency survival kit consisting of a variety of items not issued to troops in regular units.

Two incidents come to mind concerning our briefings. On the morning after arrival, one of the first briefings was conducted by a young Specialist in a starched and pressed khaki uniform with a single row of ribbons on his chest: the National Defense, the Vietnam Service, and the Vietnam Campaign medals. He proceeded to preach to us on how dangerous it was to wander around Saigon. He advised us not to leave the compound except on official business. It sounded like the VC were waiting outside the gate to ambush us. The food in the Mess Hall was terrible. Needless to say, that evening and every one thereafter while we were there we were out and about in the city. We were within walking distance of the center of American presence, the Rex and the Brinks hotels with BOQs, offices, Field Ration Messes, and Officer Clubs. The Carville Hotel, where most of the news media people stayed, was across the street, and the Continental Hotel--made famous by Graham Greene's book --was only a block or two away. Immediately after each day's classes were over, we would troop out the gate and away to the Rex, where everything was going on. We would walk up Tu Do Street, known for its bars, brothels, massage parlors, and black market activities. The streets were teeming with people selling everything you could imagine. At that time, you were required to wear a Class A uniform and forbidden to carry weapons when off duty (although I was always armed). In a few months that would change drastically with the arrival of the Tet Offensive.

The second item concerned personal weapons. Some of us had brought our own side arms with us to Vietnam. I had previously taken a Smith and Weston .357 Magnum revolver to Korea and had brought with me a .32 caliber Berretta, a model that was issued to Italian military officers. In one of our early briefings, a Marine Lieutenant Colonel (Lt. Col.) from the MACV Provost Marshal's Office told us that if we had brought any personal firearms in country to turn them in to the arms room there at Kolper Compound and we could retrieve them when we left Vietnam next year. He also said that all that would happen for disobeying orders concerning privately owned weapons was that a Letter of Reprimand would be forwarded to our Command for action deemed appropriate. No one budged although I knew that several besides me had personal side arms. I don't believe that they really expected anyone to turn a weapon in : We were all going out into the countryside where an additional pistol might save our life.

On the next to the last day, they posted our assignments on a bulletin board. I already knew that I was being assigned as a District Senior Advisor (DSA), but not where. We crowded around the list and

I found my name beside Cai Nuoc District, An Xuyen Province, IV Corps.

An old NCO standing beside me looked at my assignment and said, "Stop by the club later and I will buy you a drink." An Xuyen was the southernmost and the largest province in IV Corps, and the government only held Ca Mau, the province capital and several district towns. The majority of the countryside was controlled by the VC.

We had to make our own arrangements to get to our assigned areas. I had to fly out of Tan Son Nhut via the 8th Aerial Port, the unit responsible for in-country flights. I checked the schedules and found that there were routine daily Caribou flights to each of the province capitals. I booked a seat and arrived at first light the next morning at the air terminal. The 8th Aerial Port was a large wooden building, open on all sides with a mass of humanity--all trying to get on flights to everywhere in the country. I was to find out later that there were always people at airports and strips waiting to go somewhere, in many cases anywhere. People waited for days to crowd aboard military or civilian aircraft, sometimes causing a small riot. I had a 0700 hour departure time but waited all day and was told to come back the next morning. Flight schedules were subject to changes hourly. Enemy action, planes diverted to other locations, higher priority routing, and a dozen other reasons caused delays or cancellations. So a return to the Compound for the night and out to Tan Son Nhut at 0 dark thirty again. Luck! I got on a flight at 1030 hours that would eventually stop at Ca Mau, the capital of An Xuyen Province.

After a bumpy ride and several stops, we arrived in Bac Lieu, capital of the province next to An Xuyen. I was then told that the plane was not going on to Ca Mau but was being diverted to pick up some U.S. bodies and return to Saigon. I could stay aboard and return with them to Saigon or get off and hope to catch some transport to Ca Mau by air or road. There was only one road connecting Bac Lieu and Ca

Mau, and people traveled in daylight with care and not at all at night although it was only 20 kilometers. I decided to lay over in Bac Lieu. The ARVN (Army of Vietnam) 21st Division was headquartered there and I thought I could stay with their U.S. Advisors until I got a hop to Ca Mau. I caught a ride from the air strip to the Advisory Team's headquarters, where they were glad to put me up for the night. I bunked in with two advisors to an ARVN ranger battalion, one of whom I knew slightly from Ft. Benning. The quarters were tent sites with wooden sides about three feet high with screening from there to a canvas roof. After chow, I bedded down and sometime later was awakened by several loud explosions. My first mortar attack! There was a lot of noise and confusion, firing, yelling, and running about. In that I had no idea what was going on, I flopped down in a ditch between the tents and lay there until things quieted down. I was told later that it was the first mortar attack on the Division Headquarters in a year. As far as I know, there were no casualties, but everyone was up the rest of the night as a ground attack was possible, if not probable. After morning chow, I got a ride out to the air strip dragging along my personal clothing and equipment. A Caribou came in about mid-morning going on to Ca Mau, and I crawled aboard. In a few minutes we were circling the city, which looked pretty from a few thousand feet up. The main airfield was an asphalt strip about 2,500 feet in length and in fair shape and about three or four kilometers out of town on the road between Ca Mau and Bac Lieu. I could see a wooden building with a couple of trucks and Jeeps and, as usual, a large number of people.

After we taxied in, a quartermaster captain--the S4 (supply officer) for the province team met the plane with a truck for the expected incoming supplies. He was surprised to see me; indeed, he had not been told of my arrival. No wonder, with the many unexpected incidents that were daily occurrences affecting traveling around Vietnam, a country in the throes of war. Well, I was in Ca Mau, and thus ended the first of several treks by air in Vietnam.

CHAPTER 3

CA MAU

An Xyuen Province was the largest and southernmost province in IV corps (the delta). Ca Mau, its capital, had a population of approximately 30,000. The province population living in six districts was estimated to be around 240,000. Less than 30 percent of the province was considered to be under government control. An Xyuen was approximately 200 kilometers south of Saigon, as the crow flies. The only serviceable roads in use in the province were the streets in town and the National Road (interprovince) that connected Ca Mau with Bac Lieu to the east. There was no road network in the province since they had been either destroyed by the VC or allowed to fall in such disrepair that they were unusable. And as the countryside was controlled by the VC, road maintenance was not possible. The only district capital that could be reached by road was Quan Long, the district in which Ca Mau was located and which the road to Bac Lieu passed through.

The Province Advisory Team was set up in an old villa on the eastern edge of town. It sat next to the Headquarters of a regiment from the 21st ARVN Division . The main building had been enlarged, and a number of single-story wooden and aluminum structures had been added as well. These served as offices, quarters, mess, and supply for the team. A squat communications bunker, an Air Force radar site, and some defensive positions were included within the compound area. A small air strip capable of handling light aircraft and helicopters was six or seven hundred meters from the compound and was home to two each U.S. Army and two USAF FACs (Forward Air Controllers) Cessna single engine aircraft. Their call signs were Shotgun and David respectively. This strip was the operational center of air support to the districts and field units. Aircraft positioned here to provide re-supply, medevac, and troop movement within the province. The air field outside of town was the hub for larger aircraft coming and going out of the province and staging for large combat missions that could not be conducted out of the smaller strip.

Of the six districts in the province only four had Advisory Teams assigned. Cai Nuoc, my assignment, and Nam Can, the southernmost and furthest from Ca Mau, did not have teams in place, thanks to the remoteness of the region and the strength of the Viet Cong in the areas. Nam Can District, only about 20 kilometers from the southern end of the country, was garrisoned by two RF (Regional Forces) Companies that could only hold the town. Cai Nuoc District Town had been overrun several times, and the seat of government was later moved 10 kilometers south to Dong Cung, a hamlet on the Song Bay Hop (Bay Hop River). Three RF companies were located there. One company had been left at Cai Nuoc, which was now known as Cai Nuoc Outpost. The location on the Song Bay Hop was now known as Cai Nuoc and was the government headquarters for the District. It was here I was supposed to establish my team. It was approximately 55 kilometers from Ca Mau and the Province Advisory Team.

Upon arrival, I was greeted by the DPO, (Deputy for Plans and Operations) a major whose name I cannot recall. He rotated home soon thereafter. I noted at the time and thought it strange that he wore side arms at all times in the compound. Unless under attack, personnel were not normally armed in the compound unless they were on guard duty. He gave me a short briefing and saw that I got quartered. Later in the day I met the PSA (Province Senior Advisor) Lt. Col. James Gilland, Corps of Engineers, and the DPSA (Deputy Senior Advisor) Lt. Col. Culpepper, a Marine officer who was on an assignment to the State Department. Normally the DPSA provided advice and support to the civil operations, i.e., public health, public safety, refugee control, agriculture, electrification, and other nation building efforts in the province. However, Culpepper was usually seen in a flight suit, carrying an AK-47, and out on military operations. I met with both

Gilland and Culpepper that evening and received some unexpected news. I was not going to Cai Nuoc!

Wow! Was I surprised! Lt. Col. Gilland informed me that there was a change in plans. I would still be assigned as the DSA for Cai Nuoc District and would assemble the District Team as the personnel arrived, but we would be located in Hai Yen. Hai Yen,located in the hamlet of Binh Hung a politically established Special Sub Sector within the Cai Nuoc District, was an enclave of mostly old Nationalist Chinese led by a Catholic priest. Hai Yen was the Chinese name of the camp and was used generally to identify where they located and the area for which they were responsible. The area approximated the political sub division of a Canton, an old level of government between the district and village level and in little use. Cai Nuoc had two cantons. The one in which Hai Yen had been established was comprised of two villages, Phu My and Tan Hung Tay. The area was about 21 kilometers wide and 24 kilometers long, without any roads, and 55 kilometers from the province capital of Ca Mau.

There were two reasons presented for the change in assignments. First was that the district town had been under constant attack and the government was moving the district seat of government about 10 kilometers south to the hamlet of Dong Cung on the Song Bay Hop. It too, however, was under attack and it was not known if the government would maintain the district headquarters there. The second reason and I believe the most paramount was that a Special Forces A Team with a contingent of Civilian Irregular Defense Group (CIDG) mercenaries had been ordered out of Hai Yen by MACV.It was therefore decided that some form of support and advice was needed to fill the gap. The intent was that the District Team would be located there until such time it was thought feasible to move them to wherever the Cai Nuoc District Headquarters was permanently established. A smaller team would remain in Hai Yen. Same job, new place, but with a different set of challenges.

After this illuminating briefing, I busied myself trying to find out what I could on the relationship between the Vietnamese civil and military at the province and Hai Yen. I soon found out that support from the Vietnamese was sadly lacking. I also spent time becoming acquainted with the reporting responsibilities and what I could expect in support from the Province Team. I was waiting for my team personnel, who were due to arrive shortly. The team was authorized a total of six US personnel and a Vietnamese interpreter: One major, DSA; one captain, DDSA; three NCOs in the rank of Platoon Sergeant; and one Specialist E4 radio operator. The career field of two of the sergeants was infantry and they would be working in operations and intelligence. The remaining one was a medic and would be responsible for the health of the team plus assisting the medical personnel in the advised units. Being senior NCOs, they had a wealth of training and experience in subjects related to combat operations. A Captain Bates, who had been assigned to headquarters for another District, was being assigned as my deputy. (Later circumstances indicated that I should have asked more questions concerning his reassignment.) During this time, I went out with the Province Team operations section and observed nothing of any significance, just some troop redeployments. I also spent a few days with the district team assigned to Quan Long District and visited some RF outposts.

I was anxious to go to Hai Yen and meet the Special Forces A Team and the Vietnamese Commander. I wanted to get the A Team's opinion on the situation, both operational and internal. I had heard that there was friction between the Chinese troops and the Vietnamese officer that was in command. One of my sergeants, PSGT. Brown, arrived and became my Team Sgt.

We flew to Hai Yen—the only way of reaching it-- to get oriented and to discuss the departure of the A Team and our arrival. Hai Yen had an air strip built by the Chinese that was about 1,500 feet in length and was surfaced with PSP (punched steel plate). We flew there in an Otter (a Dehaviland built, single engine, fixed wing plane capable of carrying 6 to 8 passengers and some cargo) that was supposed to service Hai Yen twice a week but rarely did. We were met by Lt. Matalic, the A Team Deputy Leader. An A Team is normally 12 men and commanded by a captain. Their commander, Captain Medavets, had been medevaced because of wounds, however, and the team was down to a strength of 7. They had under their command one company of CIDG and a Combat Reconnaissance Platoon (CRP), for a total strength of approximately 140 Vietnamese, Cambodians, and Nungs (Vietnam-born Chinese). Upon their departure the government forces would lose that increment of combat power in the area.

Sergeant Brown and I were briefed on the operations of the SF team. They actually provided little support to the local troops on combat operations except to try to coordinate locations so that they would not be engaging each other in a fire fight. They were helpful in providing some supplies, but relations were not always good between the CIDG and the local troops. Differences in pay and the lack of female companionship for the CIDG were some of the problems. (All the women in camp were the wives or daughters of the Hai Yen soldiers.) Matalic and I made some agreements that he would leave us ammunition, rations, and some uniforms. We also met Major Nuoc, the Vietnamese officer in command in Hai Yen. He was from the northern part of the country, which was by then the Democratic People's Republic of Vietnam (North Vietnam). He was rather tall, thin, and spoke not only Vietnamese but also English, French, and some Chinese. He was relieved a few months after I arrived and replaced by a younger officer who came from commanding a Vietnamese Ranger Battalion, which greatly improved the relationship between the Advisors and the Hai Yen Commander.

After two days, we returned to Ca Mau. The one of the other NCOs had arrived, and we were also still short a radio man. Captain Bates and the interpreter were on board, so I decided to make the move

41

to Hai Yen and overlap with the Special Forces Team a few days before their departure. Lieutenant Colonel Gilland and I went to Can To (IV Corps Headquarters) to brief Brigadier General Desobry, the IV Corps Senior Advisor. While there, I was able to meet some members of the SF B Team, the parent unit of the A Team, and they assured us of their full cooperation on the move. We returned to Ca Mau the next day and continued our planning.

Captain Bates, Sgt. Brown, and I visited Hai Yen again to complete the coordination for our arrival. The A Team would depart within two weeks once we were in place. Their relocation was a little more complicated as they were moving out 140-plus men and supporting supplies and equipment, whereas we were coming in with six men and minimum gear. While we were there, the A Team ran two operations, which Sgt. Brown and I accompanied to get a feel for the area. After our return to Ca Mau, the word came down from Corps to proceed with the move. Target date was no later than 10 November. I and my team (minus our medic) --Capt. Bates, Sgts. Brown and Johnson, and the Vietnamese interpreter Sgt Cao--moved into Hai Yen to stay on the 26th of October, 1967.

CHAPTER 4

HAI YEN

Hai Yen, also known as Binh Hung, was to be my home and base of operations for perhaps as much as 10 months, so therefore detailed descriptions of its location, residents, surrounding environs, and the political and military situations are in order. Hai Yen, a Special Sub Sector, was some 50 kilometers from the province capital and the supporting U.S. Advisory Team. It was bound on the north by Ong Doc District, on the west by the Gulf of Thailand, on the east by the remaining area of Cai Nuoc District, and on the south by the District of Nam Can, which extended to the end of the country and the juncture of the South China Sea and the Gulf of Thailand.

The terrain was mainly tidal flats laced with streams and canals, both natural and man-made. Heavy vegetation ran alongside most natural waterways and unpopulated or abandoned cultivated areas. Tidal mangrove swamps lined the coasts and were almost impenetrable to observation from the air. Movement by foot was slow and hampered by dense foliage and water levels often up to the waist. Leaches and mosquitoes abounded. Line of sight was often only a few feet. In inhabited areas, movement was by foot on trails and paths. The main means of transportation was by sampan and by boats on the larger canals and streams. There were no usable roads--they had been either destroyed by the Viet Cong, been obliterated by the rapid growth of vegetation in a tropical environment, or had disintegrated into footpaths used by the local population.

The population was sparse and located in the villages and hamlets. The few plantations once owned by the French or absentee Vietnamese elite had been destroyed by the VC. The remnants of some of the houses and structures were occupied by local farmers, who scratched out a meager existence from the abandoned fields and paddies. These areas were not under government control, and the VC frequently used the old plantation villas and buildings.

The main occupations were fishing and farming. The majority of the villages and hamlets were built along the canals, which were their source of personal and commercial transportation. The waterways eventually led to open water and to potential markets outside the province. Rice, coconuts, bananas, some pineapples, and other local fruits and vegetables were grown and harvested from the abandoned plantations. Fish and crabs could be caught in almost every stream and l arge shrimp in the gulf. The plantations exported goods, but most of what was the farmers produced remained in An Xuyen and neighboring provinces.

Although villages and hamlets had appointed or elected officials, there was little civilian control existing outside the immediate limits of the communities. Communications with the District Headquarters was by radio only. Support from the Province bypassed the District and was channeled through the Hai Yen military commander, which was concerned mainly with refugee control and collection of taxes. The Vietnamese officer in command of the Hai Yen Territorial Forces (RF/PF troops) exercised limited authority and reported to the Province Chief. The District had no jurisdiction or control over the Hai Yen forces.

CHAPTER 5

THE SEA SWALLOWS

I begin the story of the Sea Swallows with Father Augustine Nguyen Lac Hoa. Father Hoa was born in Kwangtung Province, China, near the Gulf of Tongkin in 1908 as the eldest son of a fisherman. He was fortunate in that he was sent to school and at age 19 decided to study for the priesthood. In 1933, he completed his studies and was ordained in 1935 in Hong Kong. He was assigned as an assistant parish priest in a village on the Luichow Peninsula. In the spring of 1939, China drafted the eldest son of every family in their war against the Japanese. Father Hoa was drafted and, since there was no chaplain system in the Nationalist Army, became a private in the ranks.

When it was discovered that he was educated, he was sent to train as a guerrilla leader. Assigned as a Lieutenant in 1940, he held the rank of major when the Japanese surrendered in 1945. He was retained in the army to fight the Chinese Communists for the next three and a half years and resigned from his position as a Lieutenant Colonel when the communists took control of the country.

Soon after resuming his duties as a priest, he was arrested by the new government. In December 1950, with the help of members of his parish, he managed to escape in a small boat to French controlled northern Vietnam. There, Father Hoa became engaged in assisting persecuted Chinese Catholics in fleeing from the communists. With the help of a small group of his parishioners, he was able to bring out 450 families--a total of 2,174 men, women, and children.

He found himself now fully responsible for the welfare of the refugees, and set out to provide a new home for them. The French controlled the delta area of northern Vietnam, but Ho Chi Mien's communists were gaining in the mountains and much of the

45

countryside in the south. With help from the French and local groups, Father Hoa was able to provide shelter, food, and some employment while he sought a more permanent home for his refugees. He traveled throughout much of Indo China searching for an area that would accept the homeless band of Chinese. South Vietnam in 1951 was full of communist subverters and religious sects with private armies all vying for power. Continuing his search through Thailand, Laos, and Cambodia, he selected Cambodia as the most amenable location. The French, who still controlled both Vietnam and Cambodia, airlifted 2,100 refugees to an area near Snoul in Kratie Province, some 40 miles from the Cambodian-Vietnamese border. There for seven years they eked out a meager living, working mainly on French-owned rubber plantations.

During this time, Cambodia continued to drift toward neutralism, allowing the communist guerrillas to expand, and in 1958 Cambodia formally recognized the People's Republic of China (Communist China). Realizing that a homeless band of Nationalist refugees might be in harm's way, the refugees unanimously agreed to pull up roots again. Those who could afford it made the long trip to Taiwan. Father Hoa intensified his search for a permanent home for his remaining people and looked again at what was now the Republic of South Vietnam (RVN), which, though still challenged by the private armies of the Cao Dais, Hoa Haos, Bin-Xuyen, and the growing communist movement, still appeared to be gaining control of the country.

In July 1958, a Chinese friend and ex-guerrilla leader, Bernard Yoh, arranged for Father Hoa to meet with President Diem, who was sympathetic to the plight of the Catholic Chinese refugees and welcomed them to his new Republic. He offered facilities for migration, food, temporary lodging, and full citizenship, which would entitle them to benefits under the Land Reform Program. Three locations were offered, and Father Hoa selected the one he thought would provide the best land for cultivation even though it was the most dangerous: at the tip of the Ca Mau peninsula in An Xuyen Province.

This land in many areas was deep in water during the monsoons and parched dry clay during the dry season, making it one of the least habitable areas in the country. But rice would grow well due to the fertility of the soil being renewed annually by the silt-laden flood waters, and the canals and streams were teeming with fish. Four hundred fifty refugees, comprising 100 families, were transported by car and truck to Saigon, then to Ca Mau, and from there by sampan to the area intended to be their new home, arriving there on 17 March 1958. They were greeted by a land covered by water and clouds of mosquitoes. Two large and five small huts, some farming tools, and a little rice seed had been provided by the Land Development Administration. In the distance were visible mangrove forests and a small village. This was to be their new home!

The story of the development of these homeless Chinese refugees from a destitute to a vibrant social community supporting a well-disciplined military force, known as the Sea Swallows in a period of less than six years is a saga in itself and needs to be told. Their power and prominence peaked in 1964 but began to wane with the death of President Diem. For the time being, it suffices to be able to refer back to this period at various times during this narrative of my experiences with Father Hoa's Sea Swallows.

CHAPTER 6

ORGANIZATIONAL STRUCTURE

The troops in Hai Yen were a mix, with Chinese still at that time in the majority. The Chinese were first formed into Self Defense and Civil Guard units and later became part of the Territorial Forces, which were comprised of the Regional (RF) and Popular Forces (PF). Regional Force units, which were organized as both battalion and separate companies, were normally recruited, trained and deployed within the province where they were recruited. Popular Force platoons were recruited and usually operated within a home district. In that Hai Yen was not a province or a district and mainly Chinese, this organizational structure was somewhat modified.

In 1964, Vietnamese officers and NCOs were assigned and placed in command of the newly formed 47th RF Battalion (Bn). To convert Father Hoa's soldiers from an unpaid group of civilians to an organized and paid military force, rosters of the names and dates of birth of all the Chinese men were submitted to the ARVN for the purpose of recruitment. There was no on-site muster or verification of numbers or ages of the soldiers by Vietnamese military officials. Reportedly, the ages of some of the older Chinese who had been with Father Hoa from the early days were lowered to insure they would be accepted and thereby on the payroll.

At the time, I was assigned as the Senior Advisor to Hai Yen; seven RF Companies and four PF Platoons along with a Headquarters Staff were authorized. An RF company's authorized strength was 128, and a PF platoon 32, but units were rarely up to strength. In addition to the ARVN assigned to Hai Yen, Father Hoa had recruited Chinese who had been born in RVN. In addition, some local Vietnamese had enlisted, making a hodgepodge force that created command problems.

There were three categories of officers: Chinese who had been appointed by Father Hoa (Sea Swallows), RF appointed by the Province, and Vietnamese officers assigned by the ARVN. Many of the Chinese resented Vietnamese being placed in command over them, and some of the Vietnamese did not trust the Chinese. In an attempt to alleviate this problem, companies were organized with the majority of Chinese troops commanded by Chinese who fled from China with Father Hoa, later known as the Sea Swallows; others were commanded by either ARVN or RF officers, with the PF Platoons led by local PF NCOs. The Command Group was, as far as I knew, all ARVN. This did not make for a smooth-running military force. There were a number of instances that arose because of distrust, disregarding orders, or outright disobedience.

I carried a small spiral pocket notebook that had several pages covered with a jumble of figures representing my efforts to ascertain the actual number of troops available to conduct offensive operations. I knew (or thought I knew) the authorized strength of our forces, but determining the Assigned, Present for Duty, and Present for Operations Strengths was a task that I was never able to complete to my own satisfaction. The Authorized Strength, as best I could determine, was 1,035, representing the RF companies, PF Platoons, and a Headquarters Detachment. That was the total based on the authorized strength levels at the particular time I inquired. The Assigned Strength was 878, and I recognized that could change frequently with incoming replacements and out-going reassignments, discharges, combat losses (KIAs), and absences without leave (AWOLs). Present for Duty (PFD) strength at that time was 713. This number could also change daily with soldiers on leave, wounded, and in medical facilities or away in training.

That left me with the last category and the one that I was most concerned with: Present for Operations (PFO). This was the number of troops I could expect to be available to conduct multiple-day offensive operations and was determined after providing for security of the camp in the absence of the main body, men that were coming in from night patrols and ambushes, and those needed for routine administrative and logistic support. The number was 335, about 47 percent of those present for duty. Total strength numbers included those troops that were located at the four outposts; unless the operation was being conducted in their area, they could not contribute to multi-unit operations. About 50 percent of the assigned strength was the normal number of troops available for operations that were more than one day in duration. Multiple-day operations were usually two or three days in length, although operations with lesser numbers of troops sometimes would be out for four or five days.

When I first arrived, I thought the short duration of these operations was not productive and that the commanders, for whatever reason, were not serious enough in pursuing the enemy. I soon learned that my assumption was incorrect. The commanders were dedicated to the destruction of the VC forces. After some thought, the concerns I had over the number of troops involved and the length of time an operation ran were somewhat lessened. However, conducting operations with 50 percent or more of the troops available for any extended length of time was a risk that commanders did not want to take. Sufficient forces had to be left in Hai Yen and the outposts to insure that they would not be overrun by one VC unit while the main body was attempting to locate and engage another. The VC would soon know the size of the Sea Swallows force in the field and could possibly attack what they might consider a weakly defended position like a platoon-sized outpost.

All locations had to maintain patrolling and ambushes to insure the security of their own unit. VC strongholds were not that distant from Hai Yen. A few hours' movement could put friendly forces in contact with VC units and in reverse could place undermanned government positions under attack. If the units in the field were in contact and an outpost or village came under attack, they would likely be on their own. There would likely be no unit that could assist them; fire support from aircraft would be doubtful unless an advisor was on site. There would be no reserve. No assistance could be expected from outside of Hai Yen Sub Sector, from the Province or ARVN. Unless the operational force in the field was in contact with the VC and the majority of the enemy units were present, the commander had to recognize that an attack elsewhere was not only possible but probable. The longer the force stayed in the field, the greater the risk became. Past experiences were that if the units were absent for more than three nights, there was a 90 percent chance that an outpost or hamlet under government control would come under attack.

Daily operations consisted of patrolling outlying hamlets and known areas of VC activities such as tax collecting and recruiting. Patrols were usually platoon size, 15 to 25 men, and had the mission of gathering intelligence and providing assistance and protection for the local population. In the approximately 500 square kilometers of the area of operations, Hai Yen Special Sub Sector, the main military force at Hai Yen itself, and the four outposts actually controlled less than 20 percent of the area. The VC could move rather freely throughout large portions of the area with little interference from government forces.

The troops were armed mainly with U.S. World War II and Korean War vintage weapons. Individual arms were the M1 .30 caliber Garrand (M1 Rifle), the M1 or M2 .30 caliber carbine, and the .45 caliber Colt pistol. A few of the new M79 Grenade Launchers were in use, and Browning Automatic Rifles and Thompson sub-machine guns completed the available small arms. There were a small number of other weapons being carried that had been obtained in the past and favored by some of the Chinese. These were mostly Browning 9 millimeter pistols and Swedish K 9 mm sub-machine guns. Rifle and hand grenades were in abundance.

Crew-served weapons included .30 caliber Browning Machine Guns, 60 and 81 mm. mortars, and two 57 mm Recoilless Rifles. A 4.2 inch mortar and a 105 mm howitzer provided camp defense and support to troops in the field.

Advisors were armed with the M2 carbine and the .45 caliber pistol while their brothers in arms in U.S. units were issued the more modern M14 or M16 rifle and M60 7.62 Machine Gun. Some advisors supplemented their weaponry with the U.S. 45 caliber Grease Gun and, although unauthorized, a variety of side arms. With all this different weaponry, a problem of re-supply of ammunition existed. The U.S. logistical planners had to maintain dual supply chains--one for the U.S. Army and another for the Vietnamese and advisors. Shortage of ammunition did occur at times but was normally quickly rectified.

The troops were provided the normal issue of clothing and field equipment, including helmets and Korean War vintage flak (protective) vests. On several occasions when all troops in Hai Yen were ordered to stand a muster for the purpose of ascertaining the accountability of individuals and equipment, I was able to note that the soldiers had most of what had been issued to them. What they carried or took with them on operations, however, was a different story.

Readers who remember the pre-World War II and World War II comic strip "Terry and the Pirates" would easily identify the Hai Yen troops. During one of the first operations that I and my NCOs took part in, while watching the soldiers passing by me in single file along a canal bank, it struck me that the soldiers looked just like those in that comic strip! One soldier would be wearing a complete uniform including a helmet, cartridge belt, and other appropriate web gear. The next one might be wearing only shorts, sandals, and a baseball cap. Another may be barefooted and wearing a T-shirt, shorts, and a campaign-style broad-brimmed hat. All were heavily armed, except some were carrying loaded magazines for the BARs and a pistol or grenade hanging around their neck. Most of the uniforms were the OD (Olive Drab) as worn by the majority of the ARVN and Advisors. There were some units such as Ranger Battalions that wore a tiger striped camouflage uniform, and there were other designs, all which seemed to be present within the ranks in Hai Yen. It did not appear to be any guidance as to what a soldier wore or carried on combat operations as long as he was armed. We soon found out that they were proficient with whatever weapons they carried regardless of their appearance.

The majority of the soldiers had their families with them, many of whom had made the long journey from China. A few of the younger soldiers had married local Vietnamese women. The women and children all appeared to accept the U.S. Advisors and were friendly and helpful. Many knew a few words of English and used them whenever they had the opportunity to chat with the Team members. The wives and mothers sought medical care from our medics but, as we found out later, frequently, would consult their own healers after visiting our medics, which Sgt Bailey and Airman Moats referred to as "witch doctors". There was no friction between the Team and the residents of Hai Yen. I thought that it was possibly because we were "all in it together."

I must note, however, one incident that I was involved in that created some ill will for a time. Along the main walkway through the center of the camp, a soldier had erected a pole approximately three meters high with a small platform attached on the top. To it he had tethered a monkey that he had captured or purchased. The monkey was a nasty creature. It would sit on the platform and spit or hurl feces at people passing by. At times it would run down the pole and rush a person, appearing about to attack them. The animal's disposition was made worse by some soldiers teasing and baiting it. One morning when walking to the dispensary building to visit the wounded and ill, I heard a child scream and, as I approached where the monkey was chained, I

53

saw that a small girl had been bitten by the monkey. As I and others ran to the child, the monkey scampered up the pole where he sat dripping blood from his mouth and chattering. It had bit a chunk of flesh from the arm of the child who lay on the ground screaming. I looked up at it, snarling and chattering at us and, pulling my pistol from my holster, shot the monkey off the platform. It fell to the base of the pole, kicked its legs once or twice in convulsions and died. A soldier picked up the little girl and ran to the dispensary, where the medics immediately began treatment.

The soldier began complaining about me shooting his pet but was quickly silenced by several others that had gathered. A few moments later, one of the Chinese officers appeared, admonished the soldier, dispersed the group standing by, and walked away shaking his head. That ended the incident. There was no animosity displayed by others concerning my killing the monkey.

The next day I visited the child to see how she was doing. She had a fever and her arm had swollen to more than twice its normal size. The medics were concerned that she might lose the use of the arm. Fortunately, treatment for the infection was effective, and the child returnedto normal health in a short time.

CHAPTER 7

THE CAMP

Hai Yen was an enclave installed in Cai Nuoc District by refugee Nationalist Chinese Catholics in an area of approximately 500 square kilometers. In 1959, Father Augustine Nguyen Lac Hoa led a group of about 100 families into one of three areas in South Vietnam offered by President Diem. All of these areas were heavily contested by the Viet Minh (later known Viet Cong).

The site selected for the camp was located at Binh Hung, an agriculture development area. (I use the term "camp" because basically it was a military installation with dependents and very few if any civilians.) Hai Yen base was rectangular, with the long axis approximately 700 meters and the short axis 350 meters. The western end of the camp bordered on a natural stream (the Rach Cai Doi), which flowed approximately six kilometers to the Gulf of Thailand. A man-made canal a main form of transportation that connected with the Rach Cai Doi, ran straight through the middle of the camp and out for about another kilometer. A mud wall with several small watch towers and a moat-like ditch surrounded the perimeter. Houses, built of a combination of wood, aluminum, and thatch, lined the canal. There were two more rows of buildings, mostly homes for the soldiers and their families, behind those located on the canal; these were closer to the perimeter walls. Several larger buildings, including a headquarters and a church, also faced on the canal. At the western end of the camp was a more permanent structure which served as a hospital.

Realizing that they must have some way of reaching Ca Mau and other locations, Father Hoa built an air strip on the northern side of the camp. The strip was 1,500 feet in length, built of mud, and surfaced with PSP (punched steel plate), commonly used for temporary air fields. (There was a problem, however; the strip was perpendicular to the prevailing winds, making takeoff and landing for small fixed-wing air craft difficult.) There was an opening through the wall and ditch to the air strip to facilitate receiving cargo and boarding aircraft.

There were several other gates from which personnel could enter or depart the camp. Two were at the west end and allowed passage out onto footpaths along the main stream. There was one on the opposite side of the camp from the air strip entrance, and two near the southeast end of the camp. The southeast quarter of the camp held no buildings or structures. The vegetation was kept cut, and there were several lines of barbed wire running diagonally across with the purpose of canalizing enemy attackers that might breach the wall in a night attack. The thought was that enemy troops running toward the center of the camp and the Headquarters would hit the wire and follow along it looking for a gate. A gap was provided and covered by automatic weapons and claymore mines, thus providing a killing zone.

I had looked at Hai Yen from the air, walked the perimeter, been in and out of most of the buildings, and passed in and out through the various entrances to and from the camp. Now I wanted to take a good look at the static defense measures--walls, ditches, bunkers, watch towers, and fighting positions. I was also concerned with the deployment of automatic weapons, mines, fields of fire, communications when under attack, supporting fires, and the composition, size of, and location of a reserve. I wanted to do this first without any of the Vietnamese/Chinese leaders.

Sergeant Brown and I started one morning by walking the perimeter wall and recording all our observations. Things did not look good. It had been a long time since Hai Yen had suffered a ground attack and several months since receiving any mortar or artillery fire. The condition of the perimeter of the camp reflected the lack of urgency normally fostered by frequent enemy attacks. The mud walls, which were about 10-12 feet above the bottom of the ditch or moat which was created by building the wall, were in fair shape. There were, however, a few places where some repair was needed to replace erosion. The sandbags reinforcing the fighting positions on the wall needed repair, as sandbags filled with mud (there was no sand) lasted only a few months. Only about one-quarter of the positions were being maintained by the soldiers on normal guard duty. Positions that would be necessary to man under a general attack had been allowed to deteriorate. They needed to be cleaned out of mud and have new sandbags filled and placed.

The positions used as watch towers were in a little better shape; – however, in front of each of these positions, claymore mines were deployed. Claymores were command-detonated anti-personnel mines that could be fired electrically or by tripwires. The claymore is about ten inches in length, eight inches in height, and slightly curved so as to create a fan pattern killing zone for the projectiles when fired. Each mine had small folding stakes that acted as legs when placed on the ground. Each mine had several feet of electrical wire and a magneto-charged device that could be fired by a soldier in a protected or hidden position. These mines were deadly when used in a defensive position and could be placed so that their impact areas would overlap. The problem we saw, however, was that a number of the mines had been allowed to tilt forward in the ditch and, if fired, would just fire into the mud! They clearly needed to be repositioned so that they faced forward.

In addition, some of the electrical wires were buried in the mud. I asked how often the soldiers responsible for firing the claymores disconnected the wires and tried the hand chargers to see that they were in working order and check the wires to insure that the electrical charge would fire the mine. The answer was "sometimes, maybe." Brown and I estimated that only 25 percent of the claymores would be effective if fired in their present condition. The machine guns and BARs on the wall appeared to be in reasonable condition, and ammunition was kept clean and available.

My next concern was fields of fire. Vegetation in Vietnam grew at an alarming rate. Because of the heat and frequent rain, grasses, reeds, bushes, and some trees seemed to grow almost overnight. Keeping clear fields of fire was imperative for direct fire weapons, i.e., rifles, machine guns, shoulder-fired rockets, and grenade launchers. Additionally, uncut vegetation provided the enemy with concealment and would allow them to approach the Camp's defenses without being detected until the last moment. Cutting down grasses and bushes was a never ending task.

Anti-personnel mines and grenade traps were used in areas that were difficult to keep clear. On the north side of the perimeter, the air strip was about 40 meters from the wall and moat. It was 1,500 feet in length and 150 feet wide and ran alongside a ditch thirty or more meters wide that was full of water during the wet season. Both the air strip and the ditch provided a clear field of fire. The western end of the Camp bordered on a natural canal that was the main egress to the local hamlet and beyond by boat or on foot and that was heavily guarded. Its line of sight, however, was limited.

The southern side of the Camp presented a different problem. Immediately outside the wall and moat were high grasses and reeds. There was no buffer such as created by the air strip and ditch. Keeping an area 700 meters by 200 or more meters wide clear of all growth was a monumental task. To alleviate some of the clearing, mines of any type and size that were acquired from any source available had been sown without any plan or design over a period of time on that side of the camp. Clearing became a dangerous task and was all but terminated. In each dry season they burned off the area, which also set off an occasional mine. The enemy also knew that that side of camp was heavily mined and rarely tried to infiltrate or attack that side.

Defoliant (Agent Orange) had not been used at Hai Yen, although it was in use elsewhere in the Province.

The fortifications at the east end of the camp, wall, moat, watchtowers, and individual fighting positions were in reasonable shape; the vegetation had been cut back over a period of times so that it was mostly grasses and was clear for about a hundred meters. This end of the camp, although shorter (350 meters) when compared to the north and south sides, was the most vulnerable to attack. VC strongholds lay to the east and southeast, and attacks were normally received from that direction. Because of that, the commander had increased the manning in this section of the camp. The eastern-most quarter had few structures and was designed to entrap and kill enemy forces that might breach the defenses in that area.

Next I needed to find out the plan for supporting fires and if there was an internal reserve force designated to counterattack and restore any breakthroughs of the camp's defenses. For this information I needed to talk with the Hai Yen Commander. After completing our inspection, Brown and I returned to the team house and I requested to meet with Major Nuoc the following morning.

This is one of the times an advisor earns his money. When approaching your counterpart to discuss a situation that needs to be improved, corrected or scrapped, one must be careful not to make comments perceived to be criticizing the counterpart's leadership ability or judgment when rendering decisions or issuing orders. The advisor must learn to couch his words so that any recommendations he may make can be construed to be the ideas of his counterpart and supported by his advice. No one likes to be criticized, but I found that the Asian "losing face" syndrome was prevalent among Vietnamese officers, and that criticism was the quickest way of driving a wedge between an advisor and his counterpart. I have found that some Vietnamese officers were cold and aloof with their Advisors, while

59

others were amenable and a congenial working relationship developed. Major Nuoc was one of the former.

That next morning, I met with Major Nuoc and, after some tea, broached the subject of the condition of the defenses, walls, claymore mines, fields of fires, and the importance of keeping the vegetation under control. I then asked about planned supporting fires and reserves. He had apparently been kept aware of what I was doing and was prepared for me. He placed on a table an enlarged drawing of Hai Yen and an overlay showing mortar and artillery concentrations and target areas. There were a number of targets for the 60 and 81mm mortars, with some of the 60s very close in to the walls. There were also concentrations planned for the 4.2 inch mortar and the 105 mm howitzer on known possible assembly points and routes of movement. All was prepared in accordance with the current procedures for conducting defensive supporting fires.

It was interesting to note that they planned to place 60 mortar fire inside the Camp in the easternmost quadrant if the VC breached the wall at that end. The planning was acceptable, and the execution would be tested when we were next attacked. A reserve force was designed and consisted of one PF Platoon and the HQs personnel. It was located in the left center of the Camp and would be led by Major Nuoc's Deputy or the Operations Officer.

Major Nuoc agreed that the walls and claymores needed attention and that clearing fields of fire would continue. He did complain that he did not have enough men to carry out all the tasks he had -- ambushes, patrols to nearby hamlets, daily operations, plus camp defense. He claimed this kept all of his men busy. I didn't see it that way but felt like I had not been there long enough to comment.

After my meeting with Major Nuoc on camp defenses, I called the team to brief them on our discussion. Sergeant Brown had already told them some of the problems we had noted. I had not informed the team of duty assignments if we were attacked in camp as I had not known exactly what the actions of the Command would be. Now that I had some idea of the defense plan, I was able to make decisions on who would go where and do what. I would join Major Nuoc, accompanied by Sgt Cao. Captain Bates and the three NCOs would go to our bunker to establish and maintain communications with the Province TOC (Tactical Operations Center). Sergeant Bailey would be prepared to join his medical counterpart for the treatment of the wounded. Captain Bates would be prepared to join Captain Thinh on my order, and Sgt. Brown would remain in the bunker as our link to higher Headquarters. Sergeant Johnson would stay with Brown unless directed otherwise by myself or Captain Bates. In the event that I or Bates were wounded or killed, the normal assumption of command by seniority would be exercised.

We discussed actions to be taken if we were overrun before any help reached us. A standing order was in effect that if higher headquarters (Province) did not hear from us in a 24-hour period without prior knowledge, they would dispatch an aircraft for a VR (vertical reconnaissance) and take appropriate action based on the pilot's report. If we were overrun, there were two locations, grid coordinates, on the coast of the gulf of Thailand to which we were to try to E&E (Escape and Evade) for rescue. I had not asked what the troops and their families would do if Hai Yen was taken by the VC. Dom Doi, another district town in the Province, was overrun once and Nam Can, which did not have an Advisory Team, was also taken by the VC. Cai Nuoc District town had been overrun and the District Headquarters was moved to Dong Cung (where eight months later I would be assigned).

CHAPTER 8

THE ADVISORY TEAM

Headquarters, MACV prescribed the mission and an organization to accomplish advising and assisting a typical district. Even though the Vietnamese structure, both military and civil, for governing a district was pretty much standard, it actually varied greatly from Province to Province. This was caused by many factors, first and foremost being security -- how much of the district did the government control? Although our team was designed to provide assistance to a district chief, Hai Yen was not a district but rather a military sub sector within a district.

The Advisory Team was authorized six members: two officers (a major and a captain), three non-commissioned officers, and a PFC or Specialist 4 radio operator. An interpreter was provided by ARVN. There was also an addition to our team, a bodyguard. Soon after our arrival Major Nuoc brought a young soldier to me and announced that he was to be my bodyguard. I politely refused his offer but he insisted that I needed one. The few days that I was visiting with the Special Forces A Team, they too assigned a soldier to me as a bodyguard.

The Major explained that there was a price on my head, a reward by the VC to anyone who killed or captured an Advisor, and that he felt responsible for my safety. After I reluctantly agreed to accept the bodyguard, he was introduced as Ha-si Nhut (Corporal First Class) Phong. Major Nuoc stated that he had been wounded once, was brave, and would not steal. His duties were to accompany and protect me wherever I went. He was armed with a U.S. carbine. We had acquired some other weapons, a Thompson .45 caliber sub-machine gun, a .45 caliber "grease gun," and a Swedish K 9 mm sub- machine gun plus the Team's BAR. He had the option of carrying one of those in lieu of his carbine whenever he wished.

He was to accompany me any time I left the camp, clean and maintain the extra weapons we had, and be available when I needed him. His English was limited but he spoke a little French, so communicating with him was not a problem. He did his job well, and on at least two occasions his actions prevented me from being wounded or killed. He cheerfully accepted the additional task of cleaning our weapons. The additional weapons that we had accumulated were at various times were carried by the team members. All in all Phong was an asset, but I recognized that he was also a conduit for Major Nuoc on conversations and comments among the team members. Based on that possibility, I cautioned the team to be careful when discussing any problems or actions related to the performance of the troops. That warning was even more so applicable to Sgt. Cao, our interpreter.

Administrative and logistical support was supposed to flow down to the District Teams from MACV through the Province Teams. Tactical support, artillery, and close air support could come from both ARVN and U.S. assets; in that we were not within the range of any friendly artillery; we were dependent on US Army gunships and USAF Tactical Air support (Tac Air). The USAF also made air drops of large caliber ammunition to Hai Yen.

There was, at that time, no rations support. We were expected to eat with the local troops or live off the land, so to speak. This was the case even at the Province level, where the team could easily number 60 or more personnel. At Hai Yen, the five (later six) of us pooled our money and started a mess fund from which local food, rice, fish, crabs shrimp, chickens, fruit, and some greens were purchased. C rations and American food were scrounged from any source available whenever a team member went out to Province, Corps, or Saigon. This resulted in some really strange meals, like snakes, chicken feet or 100 day old eggs!

The team also became heir to the hired help that the SF A team had employed around the team house to support the day-to-day housekeeping activities. (SF teams always seem to have more than adequate funds, a luxury we did not possess.) Our predecessors had two women to do laundry and another two to clean the team house, wash the dishes, and mix drinks for the SF Team when they returned from an operation. There was also a cook, a Chinese Corporal First Class, who had been cooking for Americans since the early days of the CIA. Our team, which received no funds for support, had to buy our food and other sundries and pay someone to cook, clean, and handle the household chores. Therefore, decisions about household personnel were made. The cook, nicknamed Bake, was retained. Two of the women were dismissed and the remaining two did the laundry in addition to their other chores. The requirement to mix drinks was scrapped. Each soldier cleaned his own sleeping quarters, made his bed, and cleaned his own weapons. Of course there were many days and nights that all the team was not in camp but on operations or at some hamlet or outpost.

The team house sat astride the canal that ran lengthwise through the camp and was a wooden structure 24 meters in length and 8 wide with a corrugated metal roof. It was high enough above the canal that a sampan could actually pass under it. It was built by the CIA, used by the SF A Team, and became our headquarters and living area. It was divided into one large central room, which took up about one-half the building, several small sleeping areas at one end, and at the other end partition marked off a kitchen area and a latrine with a shower fed by a 50-gallon barrel of water on the roof heated by the sun. The kitchen held a propane gas stove and a reefer (freezer) powered by a diesel generator, which was operated a few hours each night for lighting and to keep the freezer cold. There were window openings along the walls but no windows. The openings were covered with screen to keep out the mosquitoes and mesh to prohibit someone from tossing in a grenade. The roof eaves were about four feet wide, thus proving protection from rain. Four doors, two on each side, all entering the main room from outside the team house, provided entrances and exits. A layer of sand bags were placed between the roofing and ceiling. A few feet out of one door was a bunker built of sandbags and steel plates; this area was used for command, control, and shelter when under attack.

The main room had two large round tables and a smaller rectangle one, all homemade of lumber from packing crates. Chairs were of the folding type or homemade also. A two-foot-high enclosure fenced off what would be called an administrative area or orderly room containing the usual gray steel desk, a secure file cabinet (with thermite grenade placed on top, designed to burn and destroy all contents including the cabinet), radio receivers, a portable typewriter , maps, code books, etc. A work bench at the end of the room was used for cleaning weapons and other routine chores associated with both living and operations. Illumination was provided by elements of an army light set when the generator was running and by gasoline lanterns and oil lamps when it was not. Each team member had an individual sleeping area furnished with a standard army cot, a chair, a small table with an oil lamp, and some shelving. There were sheets and a pillow. Each man used his issue poncho liner for a spread or blanket, and everyone had mosquito netting. Other furnishings and niceties such as pots, pans, and dishes were passed on to us from the previous team.

It was pretty easy to assign primary tasks to the team. As the Senior District Advisor, I was the counterpart to the Hai Yen Commander, who was an ARVN major. The Deputy District Senior Advisor (DDSA), Captain Bates was to command the team in my absence and work with the Vietnamese/Chinese staff. My two infantry NCOs were supposed to occupy intelligence/operations and weapons advisory positions. I appointed Sgt. Brown as my weapons training NCO, and Team Sgt. Sergeant Johnson filled the Intelligence and Operations slot. Both men had come from long assignments in basic training units, which somewhat hindered them in the more advanced duties for which they would be responsible.

Sergeant Bailey was our medic and was older than either than Brown or Johnson. He was a Korean War Veteran and had been a combat medic assigned to an infantry unit during that war. He was the most all-around qualified of the three, having worked in various headquarters and medical facilities during his career. I often found him helping the other two with administrative tasks. Bailey was also in charge of our food service to see that Bake didn't kill us with some stuff such as palm tree grubs or chicken feet.

As we did not have a radio operator and never received one, everyone had to stand radio watch and code or decode messages as necessary. Bailey was senior of the three NCOs, but as a medic it was more appropriate for one of the infantry sergeants to be the Team NCO. Administrative tasks, oh yes we had some, and required reports, yes we had those too, were normally prepared by Captain Bates and Sgt. Johnson. Other routine tasks were picked up by whoever seemed most qualified or who was comfortable with the duty.

I immediately established some never-to-be-broken rules: There will always be someone on the radio in the team house. There will always be at least two men on an operation. No American will go out alone. There will be no fraternization with any female in the camp (they were all wives or children of the soldiers). No one will get drunk! There will be no gambling between officers and NCOs. Daily routines were put in place: time to get up, meal times when in camp, when and how long to run the generator, radio watch, and maintenance of team equipment. Some of these routines would change as we became acclimated to our duties and surroundings. Reactions to attacks were priority and could not be determined if effective until it actually happened. Also we had to learn to live and work together in a close group, isolated from other Americans. It had been 13 days since we had arrived to stay. Sergeant Brown and I spent about two weeks here before that getting acquainted with the SF A Team, which had now departed, and meeting some of the Hai Yen leaders. I was satisfied with our progress. We had gone along on two operations with the A Team, had an initial briefing with Major Nuoc, surveyed the camp defenses, established our routine duties, and began establishing working relationships with our counterparts.

Some friendships developed based on like skills or interests. Sergeant Brown, who in his spare time back in the States worked in a garage, could be found working with a Chinese Master Sgt. named Ming Wi. Ming Wi was in charge of the Hai Yen maintenance, which included repair of boat motors, generators, pumps, and fabrication of items that were unavailable but needed; he also was responsible for keeping the air strip PSP in serviceable condition. Sergeant Bailey was known as Bac-Si (Vietnamese for doctor) and was greeted fondly by all. Sergeant Jackson, an always smiling friendly man, seemed to be a favorite among the soldiers and their families.

My relationship with Major Nuoc was purely business. He never mentioned his family or military background. I knew he was married and originally from the north, but that was about all I knew and rarely saw him unless I requested to meet with him or vice versa. Captain Bates did not bond with the local troops; he wanted to go strictly by the book, was abrasive, and was not liked by the young Vietnamese officers or our own NCOs. This would cause a serious problem in the near future.

Our daily activities when in camp fell into a dull routine. The two women whom we had hired, Poke and Lang, were soldier's wives. Poke was older and one of the Chinese who fled China and followed Father Hoa. Lang was younger and pregnant. Both spoke reasonable English. They did the laundry, cleaned the team house, and helped with serving the meals and cleaning up afterward. The women and Bake, the cook whom we also retained, agreed on a monthly salary of 3,000 piaster each. This was probably less that the SF was paying them, but we had no access to any funds outside of our own pockets. Everyone, however, seemed to be satisfied with the arrangement. Three hours a day was the average time that they spent on their work. Our administrative duties were light; monitoring our two radios, keeping our radio and daily logs, and reporting enemy activity and contacts were the majority of our routine required duties. Requests for combat air support, medevacs and re-supply were our highest priority when contacting the Province Team.

The highlights of the week were the scheduled twice-a-week visits by the Otter, a Dehaviland-built single engine fixed-wing plane originally designed for use in the Canadian bush. It had a crew of two, could carry six to eight passengers plus cargo, and land and take off from rough and rather short landing strips. It was our major source of transport between Hai Yen and the Province Team at Ca Mau. It was also the only one that we had any say in determining what and who would be transported from the province to Hai Yen. The Province Team did have two assigned O1 Army aircraft, single engine Cessnas, but they were utilized only for vertical reconnaissance, artillery adjustment, and courier duties. However they would be used to ferry someone between Hai Yen and the Province when no other means was immediately available.

At times, there were other means of transportation, such as when other organizations visited Hai Yen in pursuit of their own missions, e.g., refugee control, intelligence, RVN military and civil government officials' visits, and security briefings. They always came by chopper, rarely stayed overnight, and usually had room for a passenger or two who we needed to get out. They were also normally requested by the Province Team to take either some light cargo or a passenger or two into Hai Yen with them. This was fortunate, since there were times when the Otter did not make its scheduled visits. Only once a week was not unusual, and subsequent to the Tet Offensive it was several weeks before we saw the Otter return to Hai Yen.

CHAPTER 9

ESTABLISHING RAPPORT

Establishing rapport with your counterpart was probably the most important and crucial step in accomplishing our mission. We had to learn to respect the Vietnamese, their culture, and their experience, and to identify with their expected outcome of the war. We had to understand that our government's goals may not coincide with theirs or with the Vietnamese national leadership. American military personnel who were assigned to an Asian host country that had been at war for a number of years and expected to provide advice on training a competent military force, conducting successful combat operations, and nation building were indeed facing an enormous challenge. Foremost among those challenges was the difference between the western/American and the eastern cultures. Second was the language barrier, as few Americans had any proficiency in Vietnamese. Officers assigned as advisors received some language training varying in length from 8 to 51 weeks. I had completed a 15- week course before departing for Vietnam. A plus for some advisors was that almost all Vietnamese officers and civil government officials spoke fluent French and a few could speak a little English. And third was our troops' lack of experience.

A young captain would come to Vietnam fresh from the Infantry School in Fort Benning, Georgia, with no combat experience or previous service in the far east. He would be assigned to a Vietnamese battalion and be expected to be an advisor to a commander, normally older than he, who may have had years of combat experience and lived his whole life in a country at war. This did not present a good scenario for either one. The success of this relationship depended almost solely on the ability of the advisor to gain the confidence and trust of his counterpart.

Another important challenge, but certainly not the least, was understanding the Vietnamese culture. The lack of knowledge of the many religions, the national beliefs, the history, the taboos, routines, and daily life of the various classes of the Vietnamese people could be a barrier to establishing a good relationship with a counterpart. As an example, an advisor might have suggested a course of action to his counterpart, who would respond with a nod and an affirmative answer-- but who had no intent of accepting the advisor's suggestion. The advisor would then become frustrated after seeing no results and again suggest the same action. Again the Vietnamese officer would seem to agree but then not initiate the action discussed. The U.S. advisor would now be disgusted and perhaps angry. After all, his counterpart had agreed but then did nothing.

Frequently, the problem was not a lack of understanding or communication but one of cultural courtesy on the part of the Vietnamese officer. If he was lower in rank or younger than his counterpart, he would be reluctant to disagree with him even if he had no intentions of adopting the recommendation. Almost all advisors ran into this problem. They soon learned that recommendations had to be couched in such a fashion that their Vietnamese counterpart would consider them to be his own ideas or concepts. In addition, giving credit to the Vietnamese officer for positive results aided in establishing a smooth working relationship. In places where U.S. advisors had been present for longer periods of time and the officers were of higher rank, the failure to speak out against an advisor's recommendations was a much smaller problem.

Cultural beliefs also presented different perceptions that affected operations in the field. The old Chinese in Hai Yen believed in numerology and predictions. An elderly soldier considered to be one who could predict future events was consulted on almost all operations. He used a chart of figures and numbers along with reading the positions of objects tossed on a square of cloth containing various symbols. From

71

these readings he would predict if it was to be a "lucky" or "unlucky" day. On two occasions while on operations I saw decisions made based on if it were a lucky or unlucky day. The soldier-soothsayer was also consulted regularly by the Chinese women concerning births, health, and other family concerns.

There were some additional factors that complicated installing a MACV advisory team in Hai Yen. For one thing, it was not a district; it was a Special Sub Sector within Cai Nuoc District. There was no civil government apparent in Hai Yen. The District Chief (Commander) was located at the town of Dong Cung on the Song (river) Bay Hop some 18 kilometers to the southeast that, because of enemy presence, was unreachable by land. If he exerted any influence on the Village and Hamlet government officials in the Hai Yen area, I was unaware of it, although I was sure there was some system of tax collection going on.

CHAPTER 10

FIRST BRIEFING

At the time when I had first met Major Nuoc, he welcomed me to Hai Yen and offered any help that he might provide. He said that he would brief me on the military situation and activities when I was settled in. I was now ready to see what I had gotten into. I made an appointment for our initial briefing and indicated to him that I would be accompanied by my Deputy and Team Sgt. I correctly suspected that our first discussion would be formal to establish our relationships and that subsequent ones would be less so. After offering tea, Nuoc politely started the conversation by allowing me to ask questions concerning the troop units, their designations, strengths, locations, and missions.

I already knew that there were seven RF companies and four PF platoons and a Headquarters (HQs). I now was told that four companies, 315,473, 475 and 985, were stationed in Hai Yen itself. In addition, the 43 and 44 PF Platoons were in the base camp. The 967 RF Company was manning an outpost in the hamlet of Tan Hung Tau on the Rach (stream) Cai Doi about two kilometers from the Gulf of Thailand. The 474 Company and 42 PF Platoon were located at the village of Cai Doi Ngon three kilometers north-northeast of Hai Yen at the juncture of Rach Cai Doi and Lung (stream) Con Trang. Lung Con Trang flowed to the east and met Rach Quan Phu flowing further east to Nga Ba Dinh where 471 Company was garrisoned.

Nga Ba Dinh was a hamlet at the westward end of the Provincial Road 105. The road no longer existed, having been abandoned some years past because of enemy presence and lack of maintenance. The unit at Nga Ba Dinh had the mission of interdicting VC movement of personnel and supplies by water from the south to the north. Nga Ba Dinh sat at the confluence of the Kinh (manmade navigable canal) Dong Cung, the Rach Dong Cung, and the stream from Quan Phu. The Rach Dong Cung connected with the Song Bay Hop, which was a wide and deep river flowing westward to the Gulf of Thailand. Supplies and equipment was offloaded from North Vietnamese and Chinese vessels at night in the Gulf, traveled up the Bay Hop, and then flowed into the Rach Dong Cung and north as far as the District of Ong Doc. Supplies were also offloaded in the South China Sea and transported by a myriad of small canals and streams to the Song Bay Hop - a distance of about 20 kilometers - and on to the established route aforementioned.

The importance of the Nga Ba Dinh outpost was obvious. I was to find out that the Quan Phu area between Nga Ba Dinh and Cai Doi Ngon was strongly contested by the enemy. Conducting operations in Quan Phu with fewer than 300 was usually a mistake. Therefore, the troops at Nga Ba Dinh were quite isolated. The remaining PF Platoon, 41, was located on the Rach Cai Doi about halfway between Hai Yen and Cai Doi Ngon at the juncture of a canal that flowed eastward to the Gulf of Thailand and to the southwest to Cai Bot lake, a VC stronghold. The area between Cai Doi Ngon, the Village Headquarters, and Hai Yen along Rach Cai Doi was heavily populated and considered friendly. It was possible to travel in daylight between Hai Yen and the village by sampan or on foot in small lightly armed groups.

The disposition of the units was practical. The largest body of troops were located at the main garrison, two companies had the mission to interdict enemy movement from the seas to bases inland, and one protected the only village under friendly control and provided security along the much traveled route between Hai Yen and the village. I already had maps indicating the location of our forces, and now I knew the reason why they were there.

We then discussed the routine operations of the troops, the defense of Hai Yen Camp, the use of patrols, ambushes both planned and ones left in place, offensive operations--single unit daily and

74

multicompany ones lasting several days. It appeared that large operations utilizing 300-plus men were only conducted every 10 to 15 days. Major Nuoc stated that was the best they could do with the forces available. I asked if he would include me in the planning; he readily agreed and said that my team could assist him the most by getting air assets, fire support, medevacs, and supplies. I got the feeling that he did not want me or my team involved in the planning or preparation for any offensive operations. I asked him from whom did he receive orders and what kind of guidance and support could he expect. His response was, as I expected, the Province Chief. I told him that an advisor team would go on every company level operation out of Hai Yen. I also asked his permission for my team members to work with his staff. He then ended the meeting and said we would meet again soon to work together on our efforts to defeat the VC.

I gathered the team together to brief everyone on the meeting with Major Nuoc. As there were only five U.S. members and three of us were at the meeting, it meant that I only had to bring Sgts. Bailey and Johnson up to date. Later we would add one more team member Sgt. Moats USAF, a Rural Medical Technician who came with some restrictions in how I could employ him.

As we went over the meeting, I outlined the interfacing by which we would try to get ourselves accepted by the troops we were to work with. My deputy was to counterpart with the Executive Officer, Captain Thinh, an ex-ranger who was second in command, spoke English well, trained under the French, and had recently been assigned to Hai Yen. Sergeants Brown and Johnson would be working with the operations NCOs to include intelligence and communications. Sergeant Bailey, our medic, would of course work with the Hai Yen medics, which included . The Command did not have a medical officer. There was a Warrant Officer (Chinese) and 16 medics spread throughout the units. The Warrant and about six or seven of them were located at Hai Yen proper, and the others were with the units at the outposts. A masonry building, which had been built as a hospital and seen better times, served as the Camp medical facility. The sick and wounded were treated there, plus any civilian appearing at the morning sick call. This location was Bailey's normal duty station, along with the Warrant Officer, his counterpart.

I cautioned them again to be careful what they said when working with the troops, especially the Officers and NCOs plus our cook, hired help, interpreter, and my body guard. They all could be conduits of information for Major Nuoc. I decided that we would go along on all company-level operations out of Hai Yen. We would normally operate in teams of two - one officer and one NCO. Bailey would not go on operations unless they were Medcap," which were patrols to friendly villages or hamlets for the purpose of providing medical care for the civilians located there. It was MACV policy that Senior Advisors would only go on operations when their counterpart did, but I disregarded this policy because Major Nuoc seldom went on offensive operations. Captain Thinh led most of the multi-unit ones, and I accompanied many of the company-sized ones and some raids.

There would be and were some multi-unit operations where it was necessary to take four advisors to the field, thereby leaving only Bailey back in camp. As his duties were in the hospital, my radio and operator would become the only links to higher HQs. We discussed the fact that we knew problems would arise and that we would have to address them at the time they occurred. We were in a new environment with both political and internal issues that I was sure we were not privy to. I was sure the briefings at Province Team level did not cover all the possible situations that we might face. We were basically on our own, with the only connection to our higher Headquarters by radio. Travel between our teams, re-supply, evacuation of wounded and sick, receiving replacements, and any other physical contact between the two levels of command was by air only. The Otter was scheduled to support us twice a week. Weekly or once every two weeks was more common and in one instance more than three weeks lapsed between routine visits. Critical supplies and replacements were ferried in by helicopter when available. Large caliber ammunition for the 4.2 inch mortar and 105 mm howitzer were air dropped by parachute. We were at the end of the line.

By this time, we had been able to work out a daily routine and of duties. Bailey, being an experienced medical NCO in addition to looking after our health, had the responsibility of managing our meager food supplies to ensure that we did not die of food poisoning. Sgt. Johnson got the job of keeping our Daily Log, encoding and decoding radio traffic and assisted the Deputy with any other administrative requirements. Sgt. Brown, in addition to his duties as the Team Sgt., looked after everything mechanical, which basically comprised the generator and some outboard boat motors that were cantankerous and hard to keep running.

We were trying to get along with each other. Being a small group and somewhat isolated from other U.S. soldiers, we had to deal with the problem of boredom and becoming just tired of seeing one another 24 hours a day, every day. We were too close. I had to find a way to get the men out, one at a time, to where they could relax and return to the team recharged. I was able to get them a couple of days at the Province Team, where there were 40 to 60 men, a club were they could have a few beers and not worry, a mess hall where they could get a much different meal from what they were eating back at Hai Yen, and the chance to catch up on the news, rumors, and what was going on was a treat. It worked. They were glad to get out and glad to get back and bring with them our mail, reading materials, and comfort or personal items such as soap, toothpaste, and razor blades.

Everyone had the mission when out of Hai Yen to scrounge some food. They were to bring anything at all and whatever they could beg or buy no matter what it was, if it was food. Examples included a case of frozen calve's liver, #10 cans of blackberries packed in water, powered cheese, cases of hot sauce, canned ham chunks, and powered eggs. It was then the job of Bailey and Bake to put it on the table; it was not always recognizable, but it was edible.

There were two non-U.S. members of the team. ARVN Sgt. Cao, our interpreter who spoke Chinese along with English and of course Vietnamese, was a rather cocky young soldier who had been working with the U.S. Forces for some time, perhaps too long. I caught him at times not interpreting my comments as I made them but as he thought what I should be advising. I finally had him replaced. The bodyguard had been wounded once and was married, but his family was not with him. He and Sgt. Cao had full run of the team house but did not sleep there.

During this settling-in process, the normal military activities went on as usual. These included patrols, ambushes, and visits to two of the outposts and the village of Cai Doi Ngon, which was the jumping-off point for offensive operations into the Quan Phu area. Over the next several months, we would get to know it well.

CHAPTER 11

ENEMY FORCES

When preparing an Operation Order, the first paragraph is always the SITUATION with Sub Paragraph a. being Enemy Forces and Sub Paragraph b. Friendly Forces. Because of the origin of the majority of the soldiers and the political influence that established this enclave of non-Vietnamese troops, I decided to reverse the normal order and discuss the enemy last. There were no NVA, the name usually used by the U.S. and friendly troops for the People's Army of North Vietnam (PAVN) units in the Hai Yen / Cai Nuoc area. There were rumors of some North Vietnamese officers being spotted but no concrete intelligence to support the claim. There may have been a liaison team from North Vietnam to coordinate trans-shipment of arms and supplies from offshore to supply depots located in the Nam Can jungle.

The VC, or the Viet Cong, were the military arm of the National Liberation Front. Their reach extended from the normal military organization to supplementing the political structure down at the lowest level of government, the hamlet. Viet Cong combat units were organized as Main Force or Local Force units. Main Force units comprised regiments, battalions, and companies composed of platoons, sections, and squads. They were recruited, trained, and deployed independently over wide areas. In later years, some regiments were organized into divisions.

Local Force units were recruited in a province and generally stayed in the area. They were usually battalions and independent companies. There were also guerilla platoons and squads at the village and hamlet levels, commanded by the VC political structure in the area. You must remember that there was a shadow government in place that was collecting taxes, conscripting recruits, teaching communist doctrine, and planning attacks on government institutions such as schools, medical facilities, government offices, roads, bridges, and transportation routes. Attacks on major government areas, district headquarters, or province cities were carried out by Main Force units, supported by the Local Forces who provided intelligence, guides, carrying parties, and facilities, however primitive.

Military forces around the world identify their units by numbers, letters, and (in some cases) by name only. Examples include Company A, 1st Battalion, 6th Infantry Regiment (U.S.), 43rd Ranger Battalion (ARVN), 3rd SAS Squadron (Australian), and the Capital Division (Korea). The majority of NVA units were numbered, as were VC Main Force units. Local Force units, mainly battalions, companies, and lower were quite often identified by the area from which they were recruited and operated. Two VC battalions operating in An Xuyen Province were the U Minh 2 and the U Minh 10 named for the U Minh Forest, which is a large mass of mangrove jungle located to the north of Ca Mau.

The Viet Cong units in the Hai Yen Area of Operations (AO) were known by their strongholds, Quan Phu and Cai Bot (or Cai Bot Lake). The area along the Song Bay Hop, the mangrove swamps bordering the Gulf of Thailand and the northern third of the AO, were basically dominated by the VC. Visits were conducted routinely to various hamlets to gather intelligence, rout the VC that might be there, provide whatever medical care possible, and assure the people that the government was their friend and had not forgotten them. Sometimes VC were in the hamlet being visited and fire was exchanged, usually without much effect as they withdrew. Sentries posted on the routes of approach, paths or canals, gave an early enough warning to allow the VC to exit the hamlet before we arrived. Only on one occasion when I was with a unit was the VC unaware of our approach and caught flat-footed.

The strongholds of Quan Phu and Cai Bat lie northeast and southeast of Hai Yen, respectively. They were approximately seven kilometers from Hai Yen and separated on a north-south line, about six or seven kilometers apart. They were centered on two of the largest plantations in the area, which had been overrun by the VC some years before They had been well sited on waterways to the open sea for shipment of their crops, which were mainly copra (dried coconut meat from which oil is extracted) and rice. Because of the need for workers, the two areas became reasonably sized population centers.

Most of the plantation's buildings had been destroyed. Those that remained were used by the local people as homes, with a number of families living together in the main houses of the owners. Some of the rice fields were planted, but the larger part was uncultivated. Coconut groves were not being tended, but the crop was gathered and used or sold.

Quan Phu lie between the outpost manned by 474 Company in the village center of Cai Doi Ngon and 471 Company Outpost located at the junction of Kinh Dong Cung and Rach Dong Cung. A stream, Lung Con Trang (a kinh is a manmade navigable canal - rach and lung are names used interchangeably for natural streams or water ways) meandered through five kilometers of the abandoned plantation and surrounding mangroves provided a dense jungle sanctuary for the VC. I was never able to determine the size of the enemy force located there. My best estimate was two companies to a battalion. They were in a perfect position to launch attacks on both outposts and the village of Cai Doi Ngon and frequently did.

Cai Bot Lake, or Cai Bot as we commonly referred to it, was a body of water into which 10 or 12 streams or canals fed into. Two of the waterways, one natural and one manmade, were links to the Song Bay Hop and the open sea. This area was a heavily protected VC stronghold and provided supplies, training, and a rest area for Main

81

Force units. The area had been contested for a number of years. In January 1961 a Hai Yen force of 90 men in the area was attacked by 400 VC which resulted in a three day battle of ambushes and counter ambushes costing the VC 172 dead. In 1967 it was still VC territory. My counterpart and his staff believed that 200-300 VC operated out of that area.

We had intelligence that a platoon was operating in the Tan Hung Tau area near the coast and the mouth of Rach Cai Doi. Village guerrilla squads of six to eight men were scattered throughout the area. An educated guess was that there were around 400 Viet Cong troops in the area, plus the VC political infrastructure. There appeared to have been little change in the enemy strength over the last few years.

In 1967, Viet Cong Local Force and Village Guerrilla Units were mainly armed with World War Two vintage weapons, carbines M1 and M2, Garrand M1 Rifles, some German Army Mausers, and a few old French Lebels. They had some Chinese small arms, but the AK-47 had not yet appeared. There were some BARs plus Chinese light machine guns, B40 rockets, rifles, and hand grenades of various country origins in use. Indirect supporting fire came from 60 and 82 mm mortars. The enemy used Chinese 82mm mortars, which conveniently could fire our 81 mm ammunition, but we could not fire the 82mm ammo in our mortars. There was an artillery unit with a U.S. 75 mm Pack Howitzer and two World War Two Japanese 70 mm artillery pieces. We were shelled both in Hai Yen and Cai Nuoc by them, but I don't know if the unit was permanently assigned to the area.

Modern artillery is normally towed by wheeled or tracked vehicles and needs a road network or solid ground for movement and firing. The Ca Mau peninsula provided little of either. The use of the howitzers by the VC in our AO had to be a major effort. Pack howitzers were designed for use in mountainous terrain and could be disassembled and transported by mules or horses. Moving them and the ammunition in our area could only be accomplished by sampans or larger boats or by being man-packed over land. The ability to "shoot and scoot" to avoid counter fire was an almost impossible task.

Last but not least was the VC's use of mines and booby traps, which inflicted a steady toll of casualties on our troops. The VC were very ingenious in converting unexploded bombs and munitions into effective anti-personnel casualty-producing devices. The first U.S .soldier to lose his life while with my team was a captain who had been assigned to us to conduct some training of our PF platoons. He was killed by a device fashioned from a USAF cluster bomblet. Pungi stakes, sharpened slivers of bamboo or fire-hardened wooden stakes, were frequently found in concealed pits, on canal banks, and in fortification walls. They were not lethal but caused serious infections and temporary loss of any soldier wounded by one. Trip-wired grenade traps were common and used on the trails and paths along canal banks. They were most effective in areas where movement was restricted by dense jungle foliage.

All things considered, however, firepower was pretty well balanced except for the south Vietnamese government side's ability to call for close air support during an engagement or bombing predetermined targets.

CHAPTER 12

OPERATIONS

For the purpose of this discussion, the term *operations* is defined as any movement or maneuver designed to close with and engage the enemy in combat.

As discussed previously, patrols, day and night ambushes, and one-day company or platoon operations were the larger part of our pursuit of the enemy. Multi-unit operations of three or more days in duration were less frequent. Stripping Hai Yen Camp and outposts of more than 50 percent of their troops for extended periods of time was a risk that no one wanted to take. For one thing, remember that the families of the troops in most cases were living with them, sharing the hardships of the area and the day-to-day possibility of losing their husbands and fathers of their children. There were also instances in the past when the VC targeted the dependents to break the morale of the soldiers. One example happened several years earlier but was very fresh in the minds of the Chinese: The VC crucified an 11-year-old boy and left with the warning that "it can happen to all your children." There were other incidents in the province where children were targeted by the VC in order to undermine the men's willingness to fight.

I convinced my counterpart that the advisors needed to visit all villages and hamlets in the Hai Yen Sub Sector to be able to complete a reporting requirement that had been placed on us by higher headquarters. (This ridiculous report, required to be submitted by all District Senior Advisors in the country, will be discussed in some depth later.) Many of these visits were actually offensive operations into areas not controlled by friendly forces, and frequently we exchanged fire with village guerrilla units. It was, however, our opportunity to meet the village and hamlet chiefs, listen to their concerns, and report them

84

through advisor channels to the province. Unfortunately, except in a few cases, this was the extent of my ability to conduct any civil or nation-building activities.

Over time, the Hai Yen commander, his staff, and subordinate leaders had become accustomed to having us accompanying the troops on operations. Team members also began to be more comfortable with the soldiers as they recognized their role and its limitations. Advice many times was given, acknowledged by the counterpart with a smile, and then completely ignored. This was frustrating and non-productive in the eyes of the advisor.

The first several operations that we participated in were confusing, consisting of trying to find out what was going on when contact was made with the VC. Soldiers were scurrying around, orders were being shouted, and the radio was crackling with traffic in Vietnamese and Chinese. The commander of the operation did not at first take the time to tell us what the situation was and what action he was taking. The advisor had to resort to asking the interpreter "what's going on"; by the time he found out, it was normally too late to present any thoughts or comments to one's counterpart. This pattern did greatly improve, however, as my counterpart and I established a respect for one another.

Combat operations became pretty routine except for attacks on Quan Phu, the VC base area.

CHAPTER 13

RAID BY SEA

I had accompanied Lt. Matalic and his men on two operations conducted by the SF A Team just prior to their departure from Hai Yen. The first was a mission to secure a hamlet so that people could vote. It was not a national election--just a local one. We were out two days and one night, only a couple of shots were fired by the VC, and the villagers were able to come and go without harassment from the Viet Cong.

The second was sort of an adventure, a raid into Viet Cong territory to kill or capture a VC commissar who was collecting taxes. Lieutenant Matalic asked me if I wanted to go along on the raid. Two days before, Charlie the CRP Platoon Leader, came to Matalic with information concerning a Viet Cong tax collector operating in the area. Charlie was so named because he was a converted Viet Cong from the area. (For that matter, half of the CRP was ex-VC who found the paid mercenary role better than being a member of the Viet Cong.) The information was that a Province VC tax collector had worked the area over and was now located in the northeast quadrant of our AO near the coast. Charlie knew the area and was all for trying to make a hit on him.

He was about 18 kilometers northeast of us. It was almost impossible to work our way up there over land or by canal without being detected. We could, however, go by sea and come ashore after dark near the enemy camp and try to take it at night. Of course, we could notify higher headquarters and perhaps put in an air strike, but chances of getting any positive results were small. Besides, we wanted to plan the raid and make the hit ourselves. Matalic, his NCOs, and I discussed the possibilities and decided, "Lets' do it!" It was the A Team's operation and although the senior officer, I was not in

86

command. Sergeant Brown and I were going to observe and participate as needed. Charlie was tasked to pick 30 to 35 men and be prepared to move out the following mid-morning.

The plan was simple, a little daring, but workable. We would take a force of 30 to 40 in boats, go down the canal to the Gulf out far enough so that we would be out of sight of the shoreline and then travel north until we were off the location of the VC camp. This was the tricky part, determining where we were when at sea and out of sight of land. Charlie assured us that he would be able to find the right area. The VC tax collector was in a hamlet about two to three kilometers inland on a small canal branching off from a larger one. The plan was to locate the canal from the sea in daylight, wait until dark, and then move to shore. We would paddle up the larger canal to the junction with the smaller branch and leave our boats there with a rear guard and proceed along the canal bank on foot to the hamlet.

There were well-worn paths along almost all canals that bordered villages and hamlets, so movement would be easy except for encountering VC guard posts. We would approach the hamlet, try to grab someone, determine where the commissar was, make our hit, and high tail it back to the boats and out to sea. It seemed simple except for knowing where the commissar was and how many VC were with him. The VC civilian officials always traveled with military protection. There were other worries, such as the chance that a boat motor would not start, a storm might come up, we could get lost, and the most pressing danger that we might run into an enemy force that we would have difficulty disengaging from.

We loaded into five boats either old engineer assault boats, the kind used when building pontoon bridges, or Boston whalers. Each boat held from six to eight men with equipment, had a .30 caliber machine gun mounted in the bow, and was powered by a 40 horsepower outboard motor. My interpreter, my body guard, and I were in one boat; Lieutenant Matalic and SP5 Robinson were in another. There was no need to take the chance of losing us all at once. We eased out of camp at noon traveling in our normal manner, 40 to 50 meters apart staggered from one side of the canal to the other heading downstream toward the Gulf of Thailand. We were on our way!

The canal from Hai Yen to the Gulf of Thailand was a natural waterway ranging from three to ten feet in depth. It was tidal and, like all water in the delta, coffee with cream in color. There was an outpost about a kilometer from the Gulf for the purpose of interdicting any VC boat traffic. The outpost garrison held approximately 70 men, mostly Chinese with an 81 mm mortar as their largest weapon. A small hamlet was 600-800 meters upstream from the outpost. We cleared the canal from Hai Yen toward the Gulf and had the outpost send out a patrol to make sure the canal was clear of VC down to the mouth. Once out into the Gulf, we went out until we could barely see the shoreline and then turned up the Gulf toward Cambodia and Thailand, both far beyond our destination. The water was rather calm and warm, and our progress seemed terribly slow. I saw my first flying fish, leaping out of the water for 50 feet or more. We checked our radios and waited, hoping that Charlie could spot the landmarks he was looking for.

He had spotted the mouth of the canal! The radio operator looked up from the receiver and relayed the message. Charlie's boat was a quarter mile ahead and running 500 meters to our right closer to the shore. After a chatter of Vietnamese, the operator spoke with authority into the mike and then looked out at the other boats expectantly. All boats shut down their outboards. (I hoped they would start again when it was time.) We drifted around until dark, starting our motors occasionally to maintain our position in relationship to Charlie's landmark on the shore. After dark, we closed up and started to shore running at minimum speed. When 500 meters from the shore, we cut the outboards and paddled.

Charlie's boat went on while we waited. Finally, a muffled flash of light told us that the mouth of the canal had been found. We paddled with excitement to join the lead boat. You could smell the jungle and feel the heat as we left the breeze on the water. We proceeded up the canal, hugging the right bank and keeping close together. We at first tried to put men ashore to precede us as a point (lead man in a formation), but trying to move on strange ground was too slow. A compromise of putting three on the bank to reconnoiter what appeared to be open areas was adopted. Finally, the branch canal appeared. It was 2400 hours, midnight.

The stay-behind party had already been selected and included the men most experienced in starting the cantankerous outboard motors. Their job was to support the raiding party by holding a secure area to fall back on, to support us by fire if necessary, and to have the boats running when we returned, as we expected to be in a great hurry with possibly an unknown number of Viet Cong hot on our heels.

After a few hasty last-minute instructions, we started off along a path on the right side of the small canal. Charlie and two men led about 50 meters ahead, with one or two soldiers following in single file 15 to 20 meters apart, and then the main body of the raiding party, about 20 in all. It was quite dark, with the trees and foliage thick overhead, but the path was well-worn and smooth. We moved slowly, stopping periodically to listen for any sound of human origin. After 40 minutes or so, the column stopped and the word was passed back that we had reached the hamlet.

We planned to approach the hamlet and capture or silence any guards we might encounter, and then set up a base of fire while Charlie, Lt. Matalic, and two or three others attempted to find the VC tax collector. We were then going to snatch (capture) him, grab the money, along with whatever documents, papers, and maps were in sight, and try to quietly get out. Charlie and one of his men had been there sometime before when they were on the other side, so we were hoping that they could find him quickly. It was expected that he would be in the Hamlet Chief's house.

A line was to be set up on the edge of the hamlet astride the path to cover the assault group by fire as they fell back on us after making the attempt to grab the VC tax collector . If they were discovered before we made the hit, the plan was to overcome the area by firing at every house and suspected area. If we were discovered while the hit team was searching for the right house, we would fire down between the houses where we thought our team was not. We would also cover the hit team as they retreated back to our line. We would then send them back to the boats while we brought up the rear, leap-frogging back. The group at the boats was to start the outboard motors when they heard the firing--all we needed was one of the motors not to start. The soldiers were carrying mainly M2 .30 caliber carbines and a few AR-15s (the forerunner of the M16), grenades, and an assortment of pistols and knives. We had one BAR and several M79 40 mm grenade launchers.

The path widened and the overhead branches must have been thinner, as it seemed lighter from the star or moon light filtering through. There were two rows of huts with a path about 20 meters wide between them and not a sign of security, guards, or any one awake. They were so far from government-controlled areas that they felt perfectly safe. As we stood there on the edge of the clearing, you could hear small sounds like a dog and once a child whimpering, then just silence. A line was formed with the BAR in the center. The Hamlet Chief's house was on the left side, so Charlie and three other soldiers began easing down between the houses on that side (a change in plans). I took the left side of the line and Matalic the right. Robinson had remained with the boats. I was carrying a Swedish K 9 mm sub machine gun, a pistol, and my Randall knife and found myself worrying that the weapons might misfire when I needed them.

Suddenly there was a shout in Vietnamese and a flurry of shots, and I knew it was on!

From all over the hamlet, there were shouts as the enemy awoke. There was a burst of fire from the vicinity of the targeted house, and then our line opened fire, with the BAR's steady thump dominating the sound of the lighter weapons. A popping sound announcing the firing of M79s, was followed by explosions among the houses. Running through my mind was the thought: What if we bypassed a patrol on our way in and they now attacked from behind and cut us off from our boats? We had dropped off two men to cover our rear and to warn us if someone came down the path before the attack started.

The VC were firing now but scattered; they had not found out where we were. Out of the darkness Charlie and his three men appeared. They were carrying two rice sacks.

"Where is the commissar?" I shouted.

"Fini," they grinned, and made off toward the path and the boats.

The right side of the line started to move to the rear. Our drill was that the right would move out first and the BAR would stay with the left side, which would move last from the hamlet, passing through the right side's new position. Once clear of the hamlet and any close contact, the entire party would move to the boats at top speed, with the BAR team bring up the rear. Our plan was working like clockwork: as we pulled out, firing continued to come out of the hamlet, a couple of houses were burning from M79 rounds, and VC were running and yelling everywhere.

I started moving off to the rear with the rest of the left side. Soldiers were firing six to eight round bursts at a time, many not aiming, just firing back toward the hamlet. The BAR man would fire a magazine in two bursts of 10 rounds and then run a few meters, reload, and fire again. His assistant, who was carrying nothing but loaded magazines for the automatic rifle and a pistol, would run along with the gunner and exchange with him a loaded magazine for an empty one. As we got further away, we stopped firing and concentrated on getting to the boats as quickly as possible before the VC could get organized and began to pursue us. I could hear the throb of the outboard motors and prayed that they all had started and were running.

While padding down this jungle trail with the rest of the raiding party, I thought of old World War II movies of John Wayne or Errol Flynn in the jungle and I began to laugh. This was just like them, only not so heroic!

Arriving at the boats, I noted that most of the troops were already loaded and starting to move out. I jumped into a boat with Charlie and Sgt. Cao right behind me. We pulled away from the shore followed by the last two boats, opened the throttle, and roared out toward the open sea. I kept praying please don't hit a log or anything! After a few minutes we slowed down and proceeded at a sensible speed. It was then that I asked Charlie how we did.

He held up four fingers and grinned; "VC fini!" Four of the Viet Cong civilian leadership had been killed.

"What is in the bags?"

"Sung Trung, Dong (rifles, money)."

"How much?"

"Bu cu dong," Charlie replied, indicating a sizeable amount of money. I then resigned myself to waiting until we got back to camp to see just what we had.

We entered the Gulf before daylight and turned south for the monotonous leg of the trip back. As we approached the canal leading to camp, I attempted to raise the team house on the radio. Finally Sgt. Johnson came on the air. "We have a problem," he announced. "About 130 Viet Cong have moved in and blocked the canal so that you cannot get by." Great, just what we needed. Sgt. Johnson, with a company of the Chinese, was on his way down the canal to roust them out and assist our return. As we passed the word among the boats, you could see the troops stirring. There was no sign of nervousness; in spite of the age of some, they were indeed old hands.

Our entry into and passage up the canal to Hai Yen was anti-climatic. The 130-man VC force turned out to be a squad or two who were scared off by the relieving force. After arrival in camp, we carried the captured weapons and money to the team house and found we had six assorted rifles, all serviceable, 220,000 piaster (about $1880 at the legal rate of exchange), and some documents. Lieutenant Matalic, as the SF A Team leader, took control of the money, stating it would be used to buy intelligence, though I suspect some of it went to Charlie and members of the CRP. The weapons were divided up, and I was offered the first pick. I chose a nearly perfect German World War II issue Mauser. I then began trying to gain information from the papers seized so I could file a report to the Province, but had little success. This was a Special Forces operation, and the intelligence belonged to them. Sharing it with the Province MACV team was not high on their list.

So ended my first raid. The results? We made a rather deep penetration into VC territory, we killed some VC officials, we seized some documents that might provide some important intelligence, and

93

we captured some weapons. We failed, however, to capture the tax collector, who was undoubtedly a political commissar. . That would have been a feather in our cap. Other raids or ambushes attempted during the rest of the two years I would spend in Vietnam would not always be this successful.

CHAPTER 14

THE HAMLET EVALUATION SYSTEM

The time has come to discuss the Hamlet Evaluation Report, commonly referred to as the HES. The Hamlet Evaluation System was reportedly originated by the CIA but thought by many to be a brainchild of Secretary of Defense Robert McNamara. It was designed to measure the progress being made in pacification by estimating the level of security at the hamlet level.

There were 2,500 hamlets in South Vietnam. The report was a computer-generated printout listing all 2,500 hamlets by name and location (by grid coordinates) in the village and province concerned. The report was forwarded monthly to the DSA for completion and returned on a monthly basis. The hamlets were rated by each district's DSA and assigned a letter designation ranging from either A to E or V. The rating was determined by a matrix applied to a series of questions contained in the report. The questions were identical for all hamlets in the country and were crafted to be answered with a yes, no, or unknown. An A rating indicated that the hamlet was under complete government control with no VC activity in the hamlet during the month and with elected leadership residing in the hamlet. There would also be a local defense unit, a school, and a bustling marketplace present. Other questions might indicate government presence such as a health station, electrification, and a potable water supply. A V-rated hamlet was considered under VC control.

The first major flaw with the report was the assumption that the advisory team visited or could visit each and every hamlet in their district each month. In provinces like An Xuyen, where the VC controlled 80 percent of the area, there were no usable roads. In fact, not all districts had an Advisory Team assigned, so the ability to accurately report on each hamlet was not possible. For example Nam

Can District did not have a team or even any civil officials, only a military garrison, which was withdrawn in early 1968. I was the DSA for Cai Nuoc but did not get to the District HQs for the first eight months I was in the district but was at Hai Yen. Additionally, the hamlet names and locations in the report were often incorrect. Hamlets were often moved either due to VC pressure or because the government was trying to protect the residents--or to eliminate a source of supply or manpower to the enemy. In my year as a DSA, I was never able to visit all the hamlets or even the villages, most of which were under VC control.

For example, in a Report for April 1969, out of the 305 Hamlets listed for An Xuyen Province, 63 were rated A. B or C hamlets were grouped under B, 44 were rated D/E, and 195 rated V. There was some recognition at the office of Civil Operations and Development Support (CORDS) and MACV Headquarters of the many errors that were possible, but still the Report was useful to indicate trends. The statistics, however skewed they may have been, still indicated that An Xuyen Province was for all practical purposes under VC control.

CHAPTER 15

QUAN PHU

There appeared to be an increase in enemy activity throughout the province. District towns and major outposts were experiencing more contact on patrols and sweeps, and mortar and rocket attacks on government positions were becoming more frequent. This was also true in the Hai Yen area. Our patrols to VC controlled villages and hamlets more often involved exchanging fire with small groups of local guerillas, who broke contact as soon as possible. In addition, VC cadres had stepped up their night-time visits to the villages, collecting taxes, drafting recruits, and eliminating government officials. In a hamlet less than a kilometer from Hai Yen Camp, one morning a Hamlet Chief was shot in the chest at the front door of his house. He was armed with a pistol but was unable to shoot his attacker.[1]

One afternoon while in the Team House, Dai Uy Thinh came in and told me "we are going to Quan Phu." It turned out we were to go through Quan Phu: we were going to visit and re- supply the outpost at Nga Ba Dinh.

"When?" I asked.

"Tomorrow," Thinh replied.

"How many troops?"

"Three companies and a platoon from 474 Company at Cai Doi Ngon, maybe 300 men. I will send over a copy of order tonight. We muster at 0430, leave at 0500."

After Dai uy Thinh left, I called the team together.

"At last we are going to Quan Phu," I announced.

Everyone knew that I had been prodding my counterpart to conduct operations into that area, heretofore without any success. The re-supply and visit was critical. Major Nuoc had requested through channels helicopter support to exchange some soldiers and re-supply the outpost by air. Each time that Nuoc made the request, unknown to him I asked the PSA to deny the request. I felt that as long as they could get to Nga Ba Dinh outpost by air, they would never try to clear the Quan Phu base area. I had ascertained that Major Nuoc was not aggressively inclined and had reported that opinion to Province. I also suspected that Nuoc was collecting some "taxes" for his own use.

[1]I later visited him in our hospital—the shot had not hit any vital organs, just barely missing a lung. When I asked if there was anything I could do for him, he asked for some Salem cigarettes--the last thing he could have with a hole in his chest! I later sent him a couple of chocolate bars.

I discussed with the team our participation. Sergeant Brown and of course Phong and our interpreter Sgt. Cau would accompany me. Sergeants Johnson and Bailey would remain in camp. Johnson was to man the radio, a critical position. Once we were on the operation, we might not be able to reach higher headquarters for necessary support, and Johnson would have to relay to Province on our single side band radio any messages I might have for them. Bailey would stand by to spell Johnson if needed and to assist in treating any wounded evacuated back to Hai Yen. We notified Province of the operation, prepared our gear for the next day, ate, and sacked out. 0400 hours would come early.

Muster did come early and after coffee and something to eat, the four of us joined the assembling troops. The three companies were each minus a platoon, which was left back to assist the two PF platoons that were to provide camp security. The companies were formed up on time, which was somewhat of a surprise to me--one of many I would have before the day was through. In addition to each soldier's individual weapon, I noted a few M79 Grenade Launchers and two 60 mm mortars, as well as some BARs.

I was carrying my normal gear: carbine, pistol, knife, two grenades (one smoke and one fragmentation), canteen, first aid packet, map, grease pencil, a small notebook, ball point pen, and the emergency kit issued to all field advisors. The kit contained some medical supplies, energy bars, and some dextroamphetamine tablets for the occasion when being awake, alert, and able to function at 100 percent was critical for one's survival or completion of the mission at hand. Also included were fish hooks, needles, thread, and other sundry items that might be useful. Most advisors, myself included, sorted through the two cases and carried what they deemed might be handy in one case and as time went by also discarded it. Although issued to us, we never wore helmets or flak vests on operations. They were just too much weight in the heat and the type of terrain in which we operated.

We were a little late in moving out, leaving close to 0530; the supplies in sampans that were to be delivered to Nga Ba Dinh took some additional time to get under way. Counting the command group of seven and the advisors, there appeared to be about 200 troops plus 25 we would pick up at Cai Doi Ngon from 474 Company. I found the command structure I had expected: Dai-uy Thinh was to lead the operation and Major Nuoc would be in command by radio from Hai Yen.

The plan was to move north from Hai Yen to Cai Doi Ngon, pick up the platoon from 474 Company, and proceed east straddling the Con Trang Canal through the Quan Phu plantations until reaching the junction with the Quan Phu Canal. From there, continuing in a northeast direction, we would reach Nga Ba Dinh in about three kilometers. The order of movement was the platoon from 474 Company was to lead out on the left side of the canal, followed by 472 Company.

The 475 Company would lead off on the right, with the command group next and 473 Company following. One platoon from 473 was responsible for the sampans carrying the re-supply items for the outpost. Coordination for supporting fires from the single 105 mm howitzer in Hai Yen (there was only seven pieces of artillery in the whole province) was planned, but requests for fire had to be made through Major Nuoc, who would decide to okay the requests or not. I was concerned that this would slow the response for fire support.

We were running late; it was about 0730 when the lead elements moved out of Cai Doi Ngon along the canal. The first two kilometers were heavily populated along the canal banks, thinning out as we got further from the village center. It was a normal day for that time of year, clear, not a cloud in the sky, the temperature already in the upper 80s, and promising to be in the mid-90s by noon. We were almost three kilometers out when there were several shots heard up ahead on our side of the canal. It was followed by a flurry of small arms fire, and then nothing. Dai-uy Thinh was on the radio, and the men became very alert. A few more shots were heard.

Sergeant Cao listening to Thinh on the radio said, "Two men hit."

Thinh was now talking to Major Nuoc back at Hai Yen and looked angry. He finished his conversation, handed the mike to his radio operator with some curt commands, and walked away.

Sergeant Cao said, "Operation over. Major order all troops back."

"What," I yelled, "over?"

As I walked over to Thinh, who was standing with his back to us, I noted some soldiers turning around and starting back the way we came. Dai-uy Thinh stated that Major Nuoc gave the order to return to Hai Yen and he must obey.

I motioned to my radio operator and he handed me the mike. "Get me on the unit's frequency."

Sergeant Brown came over and changed the setting and I called Major Nuoc. He immediately answered. I asked why he was aborting the operation.

"It is not a good day," he replied. "They are prepared for us. We will try again soon."

He then went off the net. I was furious. The enemy will always know when we are coming! I asked Thinh if he thought that we should continue or quit.

He would not answer at first, and then said, "I have no choice."

I radioed Sgt. Johnson and asked him to call Province and tell them the operation was aborted. We then started back toward Cai Doi Ngon. I noticed one sampan with two wounded aboard. Neither appeared to be serious or life-threatening, thus ended my first major venture into Quan Phu.

Upon arrival back in camp, I radioed Province and requested a meeting with the PSA as soon as possible. The following day I was picked up by Shotgun 46 and flown to Ca Mau, where I met with the PSA and the Deputy. They were aware of the problem with Major Nuoc and believed that the Vietnamese planned to replace him shortly with Captain Thinh, who was to be promoted to major. I reiterated my belief that Nuoc was collecting "taxes" for his own pocket and my request that no re-supply to Nga Ba Dinh by air be approved no matter how many times a request was received from the Province Chief's staff. Only if the outpost was in danger of being overrun or the level of supplies on hand became critical should relief be provided by air. The PSA agreed, at least for the time being.

Before returning to Hai Yen I was told that I could expect some visitors. Training Teams designed to increase the effectiveness of the PF Platoons were being fielded throughout the country to work with the district advisors, and one was scheduled to spend two weeks in Hai Yen. I thought that since we only had four PF platoons, it would be easy to facilitate the Training Team's efforts. In addition, some Vietnamese government personnel concerned with refugees would be visiting to provide support to civilians who had recently expressed a desire to move from where they were to an area under government control. We would look after the Training Team ,and Major Nuoc's staff would provide support to the government officials.

CHAPTER 16

INTERNAL TEAM PROBLEMS

The team was adjusting to the continued hot, dry weather, but some problems were beginning to surface in our adjusting to one another. We were, after all a small group: two Officers and three NCOs living together 24 hours a day, 7 days a week, in a very confined atmosphere.

The three NCOs seemed to get along well with their counterparts and the troops in general. My relationship with Major Nuoc remained somewhat distant, but my interface with Captain Thinh became more cordial each day. On more than one occasion, we spent several hours discussing everything from tactics and strategy to Vietnamese and U.S. polices and politics. Our discussions, which included the day-to-day life of the Vietnamese, aided me tremendously in understanding what was taking place around us. However, personality quirks of others began to surface.

My deputy, Captain Bates, newly promoted after joining the team, was an eager, abrasive, go-by-the-book young officer. He did not get along well with the Hai Yen officers and was sharply critical of our own NCOs. It was evident that he was competent and aggressive, but he needed to be seasoned in a larger organization, probably a TO&E unit. Rumors said that the DSA for Dom Doi District had him reassigned back to Ca Mau because of personality problems. My team was his second chance. Our environment required we make some adjustments in our interactions with one another. We were too few and too close.

CHAPTER 17

NOVEMBER

November, our first full month on the job, provided us with a preview of the coming months. We conducted three multi-company operations, only one of which I considered to have accomplished the mission. Two Medical Civil Action Program (MEDCAP) visits, which signified missions concerning medical support and treatment operations or patrols, were conducted to nearby hamlets that had not been visited recently. The mission of these type of patrols was to "show the flag" in an effort to convince the residents that the government, and not the VC, was in charge. The Vietnamese officer leading the operation usually spent time with the Hamlet Chief and his staff discussing support, gathering information about VC activity in the hamlet, and (I suspected) collecting taxes. Medics were taken along and set up sick call to treat any civilians who came forward. On each of these operations I sent Captain Bates and one of the infantry NCOs along with Sgt. Bailey, our medic, to assist in the sick call and to report back to me anything they saw of interest that might pertain to enemy activity.

Company-size one-day operations were routine, with light or little contact. One that Sgt. Brown and I accompanied conducted by 475 Company was a normal sweep of the area about two kilometers north of the camp. The terrain was uncultivated swampland with mid-calf to knee-deep grass interspersed with clumps of brush three to five meters high.

There were about 50 soldiers with the Company Commander conducting the sweep. The troops were generally in a skirmish line perhaps a hundred meters wide. Brown and I were with the commander in the center, situated 20 meters or so behind the lead soldiers. Suddenly there was an explosion on the left side of the line and a soldier went down.

"Foot mine," someone yelled.

Almost at once a burst of small arms fire erupted on the left, followed by returning fire from our line which had all gone to ground. There was some more yelling back and forth.

Sergeant Cao said, "VC in bushes" and pointed to a clump at the left front. Fire was being concentrated on the area and the enemy fire slackened. The Commander stood up and waved the right side of the line to swing to the left and advance on the suspected VC position. I was stunned as they swung around like a gate, firing as they advanced. The Company Commander ran to get up front and lead. I was stunned again. I had not before seen a commander rush into the line of fire. I ran to keep up and fired my weapon like everyone else. Four VC broke out of the brush at a dead run. Two went down, and the others disappeared into a larger stand of brush and palm trees. The troops were now firing on that area but stopped moving forward, squatting or kneeling down. All at once I knew why. The small group of VC that initiated the action may have been a decoy to draw us into an ambush by a larger and more heavily armed force.

I approached the Company Commander and saw him on the radio. He turned to me and said that he was requesting artillery fire and instructions. In a couple of minutes we heard the 105 fire and then the rounds impacting several hundred yards to our left.

"We are not to pursue," he said.

A search of the thicket revealed one dead VC plus the two that were shot retreating. We had only the one wounded soldier who had stepped on the foot mine. It looked like he was going to lose the foot. He also had some shrapnel in his groin and thighs. Thus ended what I was to find out was a routine daily occurrence.

Even though intelligence reported a number of VC seen by the local residents, close-in enemy offensive activities had not increased. But some of the district towns in the Province were being targeted: Nam Can was attacked six times, Cai Nuoc three times, and Song Ong Doc twice--all within a week. Two of our outposts were also attacked, including Midway.

We had a number of visitors during the month, some to see the Vietnamese and others to see our team. The PSA and a colonel from Corps came down to see how we were settling in and to discuss the political side of the Chinese and Vietnamese relationship. It was obvious that there was interest from Saigon in support of the Chinese. Personnel from the United States Aid for International Development (USAID), both U.S. and Vietnamese, visited several times to bring in supplies and some equipment, mainly for the families that had recently moved from an area that was considered under VC control .We were always glad to see them because they normally had room to take a couple of passengers back to Ca Mau.

A Captain Robert Gallan from Saigon arrived and informed us that he was ordered to bring a training team to work with our PF Platoons to raise their combat effectiveness. The team consisted of himself and four NCOs. Their mission was to attach themselves to a PF Platoon for a period of 12 days and stay with them during the training, day and night. Their objective was to train a platoon and that platoon could train others in the command. We only had four PF Platoons. Gallan and I selected the unit at Midway because it was the easiest to get to and support during the training.

Gallan stayed a couple of days, meeting Major Nuoc and inspecting the Midway outpost. He left and said he would return on the17th with his team. True to his word, he returned in a DeHavilland Beaver (a single-engine, high-wing, propeller-driven, short runway aircraft—a real bush plane) on the 17th with three NCOS. We put them up for the night and they moved to Midway the next morning to hold an opening ceremony for the training, which Major Nuoc and I attended. Gallan's team began the training immediately after the ceremony.

On Wednesday morning the 22nd, I was informed by Captain Thinh that he would be leading an operation to re-supply Nga Ba Dinh. We would jump off from Hai Yen after dark, around 2100 hours and proceed north to the village of Cai Doi Ngon. There we would pick up some troops from 474 company and continue north about two kilometers. After that we would then head east to the Kinh Dong Cung, a distance of six kilometers across uncultivated rice paddies and swampland. We expected to arrive at the Dong Cung Canal at sunrise, about 1500 meters from the Nga Ba Dinh Outpost. The outpost garrison would meet up with us there. We would have a sampan loaded with supplies and a few soldiers who were to replace some that would return with us to Hai Yen. Well, I was getting my wish. We were going to Nga Ba Dinh, but around Quan Phu at night in an attempt to avoid contact with the VC.

I gathered the team and briefed them on what I knew. Sergeant Brown would go with me, Sgt. Bailey would stand by to help with any casualties, and Sgt. Johnson would man the radios, keeping contact with us and the TOC (Tactical Operating Center) at Province. We would have our evening meal and take something to eat with us, as I was not sure if we would return by the next night or not. I estimated we would travel 20 or 22 kilometers on the operation.

At 1930, Phong, Sgts. Cao and Brown, and I walked to where the troops were assembling. Captain Thinh had told me that we would

107

take one company from Hai Yen and 20 or 25 men from 474 Company at Cai Doi Ngon, which would be our departure point. The force would number only 80 or so soldiers. Thinh said he wanted to move out from there at 2200 hours. Some of the soldiers would be carrying rucksacks loaded with supplies for Nga Ba Dinh. In addition, a loaded sampan would be dragged along, as the route was expected to be wet with several inches of water. We were going to find out that in many places there was quite a bit more water than we expected, as we passed alternatively through uncultivated rice fields and swamps. Moon rise was around 0200 hours, so we would have some light as we approached our rendezvous point with the Nga Ba Dinh forces.

We left Hai Yen on time, arriving at the marketplace in Cai Doi Ngon where the soldiers from 474 Company were waiting. After a quick briefing by Dai-uy Thinh, we departed Cai Doi Ngon, heading north on the east side of Rach Cai Doi canal. The foot path along the canal was narrow and hard-packed from constant use. Houses lined the bank, with a ramshackle dock at almost each one. Sampans and fish nets were in abundance. We moved along in single file at a good pace, slowing only when we had to go across single log bridges (called "monkey bridges" by Americans) that traversed small streams that emptied into the canal. Several men fell off the slippery foot logs into the watery muck, much to the merriment of their fellow soldiers. After an hour we shuffled down to a halt and prepared to strike out across country.

The route we were to take was six to seven kilometers, ending on the Kinh Dong Cung about 1500 to 1800 meters northwest of the outpost. Except for about 500 meters of rice paddies at the beginning, we would be crossing through swampland that was covered with water of different depths and interspersed with thickets and palm trees. Grass in places was the height of a man, with red ants present that had a bite so bad that troops had been known to stop and change their direction of movement in order to avoid them.

In the stagnant water, leeches were also plentiful. Sometimes you could even see them in the grass, thin as needles. They would crawl into any opening in one's clothing, ending along the waist where a belt and web equipment would restrict their further movement. Here they would attach themselves and suck ones' blood until many times they burst. Removing the live ones was difficult. Putting salt on them or holding a lighted cigarette would cause them to release and be removed. The local troops frequently experienced infected bite areas.

Fortunately, our approach was not a normal route of movement for government forces, and foot mines and booby traps were not expected to be a problem. A squad moved out as point, with the main body following just out of sight in a loose column of twos. The night was clear, and there was enough starlight to allow us to keep on course. Once out of the rice paddies, the pace slowed as we entered the high grass and water. Off to our right a smudge was visible on the horizon. I realized this was the Quan Phu area we were avoiding. Movement was relatively quiet, with only the whining of mosquitoes, the sound of men sloshing through the water, and an occasional splash when someone stepped into a hole or stumbled.

The small command group of Captain Thinh, the operations officer, his radio operators, and my group of four were in the middle of the column. We stopped frequently as information concerning signs of enemy activity, including any barriers to our route, was passed back from the point. Moon rise enabled us to begin to see further, but our pace slowed again as we realized that we were more visible to enemy security and needed to move cautiously. There was a sound of thrashing around in water. We had stumbled into an area where the water level was over the heads of the troops. This interrupted movement and generated un-needed noise. Fortunately the area was only a few meters wide, but it was unexpected.

We were only about 1500 meters or so from our rendezvous point when a flurry of excitement came down the column from the point. They had captured two men—two Viet Cong. One was carrying an old Chi Com (Chinese Communist) rifle. They claimed that they were not VC, just villagers that had come to set some fish nets in the stream we had just crossed. At 0330-0400 in the morning? With no nets? One armed? They were a VC listening post! They probably heard our point crossing the stream and had come to investigate.

They had no radio. Our immediate concern was whether there were more than two of them and thus whether someone had gone to alert an enemy unit nearby. Was there a VC unit between us and where we were to meet the troops from Nha Ba Dinh? We knew by radio that the soldiers from the outpost were on their way to meet us. It was now a little after 0400 and we could see a little brightness in the east, a prelude to sunrise. After the initial questioning, the two VC were bound and left with two soldiers, who were to follow behind the main body.

The chance of making contact with an enemy unit was greatly increased, so the plan of movement was modified. Along with the point, we put out troops to secure the flanks of the main column, and 30-40 minutes later changed from a column formation to a line of skirmishers followed close behind by two squads, one on each side of our line to support their side of the line if contact was made. The Command Group with the remaining troops, some 20 in all, remained in the center for control and to reinforce either flank as necessary.

Soon after we changed our formation, we could see a dark line on the horizon to our front. It was the tree line along the canal. At our present rate we would arrive there at or very soon after sun rise. We had no idea where the Nha Ba Dinh troops were, and that was of concern—firing on each other was a real possibility. As we approached the canal and visibility increased, the forward pace decreased as troops searched the area for any movement or signs of life. Suddenly there

110

was a shout from our left side, then shots, then firing all along the skirmish line. We then heard rifle fire from our front and the cracking of rounds passing overhead. Our line of troops went to ground with some still firing. Captain Thinh ran forwarded yelling, "Mau, lien! Mau, lien!" (Go, up! Go, up)! Men started to come to their feet and continued firing. You could now see VC running around on the canal bank. Our whole line now started forward. Some of the VC went down. It appeared that they were falling back and crossing the canal.

"They have sampans," I yelled at Thinh.

He nodded in agreement. A few shots came from the canal bank. A grenade went off. As we approached the water's edge, some fire was received from across the canal, then nothing. They were across the canal and gone.

The troops begin foraging around to find whatever the VC left behind. There was little. Four bodies were found, no wounded. I suspected they got any wounded they had into the sampans and perhaps one or more bodies, but I don't think they really had time to retrieve any of their dead. We were on them too quick. It was a surprise to them I was sure. And the good news was we had just one man wounded and only slightly.

But where were the Nga Ba Dinh troops? We raised them on the radio. They heard the firing and estimated that they were 500-600 meters from us. They joined up with us about 30 or 40 minutes later. They numbered about 20 and were led by a lieutenant. They were a really scruffy looking group. Two of them had bandages on, and all of them looked hungry and unhealthy but appeared to be in good spirits. Three were going back with us to Hai Yen, and five of those who came with us were staying at the outpost. The few supplies we brought in rucksacks and in the sampan really looked pitiful--radio batteries, some medical items, and small arms ammunition. After Captain Thinh and I

111

talked with the Lieutenant, I decided that I had to quit stopping the re-supply by chopper to Nha Ba Dinh. They needed too much. We were not in any time in the near future going to be able to clear and move supplies through the Quan Phu Plantation area.

It had taken us about seven hours to move eight kilometers from Cai Doi Ngon to the Kinh Dong Cung. We thought that we could get back to Cai Doi Ngon in five and a half to six hours, then an hour back to Hai Yen. We were wrong. We did not take into consideration that we had been on the move for nine hours, and we had to travel through the same terrain, even though it would be daylight. We would need to be prepared for enemy contact. They knew we were out there and we should expect some harassment at the least. We could and did vary our route a little, but the terrain remained the same.

We moved out at 0800, headed west with the Quan Phu plantation base area now on our left. Keeping 200 to 400 meters out in the swamp area, we would have to travel three kilometers almost dead west before angling southwest across rice paddies, some cultivated and other abandoned, intersecting the Lung Con Tranh two kilometers west of Cai Doi Ngon village to reach our jumping-off point of the previous night.

Soon after starting on our return, we began to receive sporadic small arms fire from the edge of the Quan Phu plantation. It was long range and just a nuisance. We could at times see flocks of birds rise out of the tree tops along the wood line. That was a giveaway that someone, most likely VC, was passing through the area beneath them. This was one method to be warned of the enemy's proximity.

We had not stopped to eat since the previous evening and were by this time famished. Sergeant Brown and I were carrying individual rations designed for indigenous Asian troops. Each meal consisted of a packet of either dried mutton, squid, or fish; a plastic tube of rice to

112

which you just added water and let sit till it solidified; a vitamin pill; some red pepper; a bouillon cube; some black tea; and a square of peanut candy. I was carrying two of these in my shirt, and after throwing the mutton away (nobody would eat it), ate the rest and was still hungry.

Everyone was becoming worn out. The almost constant sloughing through ankle to waist deep water hour after hour cramped our feet and calves. When stopping for a few minutes for a break, you frequently had to sit in several inches of water. And of course there were the leeches.

By early afternoon, we had left the vicinity of Quan Phu and were traveling without the occasional VC sniping. We were now crossing through cultivated rice paddies, and farmers we met either turned away from us or removed their hats and smiled. It was hard to tell if they were glad to see us or not. Shotgun 46 came on our net to see if we needed anything. He was on the way to Hai Yen with a drop for us and was passing over. I asked him to make a quick recon to see if he spotted any unusual activity nearby. All appeared normal, and he continued on to Hai Yen, which was one of several drops he had to make.

Once when crossing a narrow strip between rice paddies, we saw a banana tree with a large bunch of bananas that appeared to be ripe. Being hungry ,a couple of soldiers attempted to climb up to get them but could not shinny up that far. Then several tried to cut the stalk holding the bananas by shooting at it. That too failed and we moved on. Remembering the fable of the fox and the grapes, I said that they probably were not ripe enough to eat anyway.

We reached the Con Trang Canal two kilometers west of Cai Doi Ngon village, and the troops from 474 Company separated from the main group and headed along the canal home to the outpost. The

113

Hai Yen troops began commandeering boats to transport them to the village or all the way back to Hai Yen. I watched as the formation just seemed to disintegrate.

Captain Thinh hailed a boat and directed it to the shore, and after a brisk conversation with the boatman the Command Group loaded up and set off for Hai Yen. I did notice Thinh pass some money to the man operating the boat. We arrived back at 1800 hours on the 23rd: Thanksgiving Day. The drop that the Shotgun pilot made was a sandbag containing a partly frozen turkey roast, a can of cranberry sauce, a can of mixed nuts, and the standard U.S. Army menu for the Thanksgiving meal. The long list of entrees was crossed off. There was a greeting from Lt. Col. Culpepper on the menu wishing us a happy Thanksgiving. I kept and still have the menu.

CHAPTER 18

K.I.A.

Captain Robert Gallan was on his third tour in Vietnam, and his last. He had been on a temporary duty assignment (TDY) from Okinawa while assigned with the Special Forces, and later spent a year with a U.S. Division. He was 36 and had a wife and two children living in Fayetteville outside of Fort Bragg, NC.

Gallan and his team were out with 41 PF Platoon only a few hundred meters from the platoon outpost. The area was considered generally secure, although there had been some recent VC activity believed to counter the training being conducted by Gallan's team. The outpost was itself only 1500 meters from Hai Yen. A few nights earlier, the VC had fired a couple of homemade rockets at the outpost from the area that the PF were training in this morning. Gallan and the Platoon were conducting some training in fire and maneuvering only 200-300 hundred meters west of the outpost.

Insurgents --aka guerillas--never have enough munitions or as high quality munitions as their opponents. So they need to capture them or make them or both. In the Middle East today they call them *improvised explosive devices*, or IEDS. But they have been around a long time. The American irregulars probably used them against the Redcoats back in Revolutionary times.

IEDs do not come with a warning label. That makes them especially dangerous. And the most dangerous are the ones that have been remanufactured from captured munitions.

According to one of Gallan's sergeants, Gallan saw a bomblet and called out, warning everyone. He recognized it as a U.S. Air Force munition. He must have realized it was probably not placed on the ground by the USAF. So far so good.

Best practice was to back everyone away from the munition to a safe distance and attempt to set it off by rifle fire. If that didn't work, mark its location and leave it. People all make mistakes. Capt. Gallan picked up the bomblet while in a crouch and examined it. It exploded in his hands, sending hundreds of pellets into his face and torso, killing him instantly.

Fortunately everyone else that was close by had hit the ground and escaped the blast. The remaining members of the training team were quite shaken up, and I had them return to Hai Yen and stay at the team house until we received instructions from their headquarters.

I recommended Gallan for the Bronze Star Medal and Major Nuoc stated that he would recommend that he be awarded the Vietnamese Cross of Gallantry.

CHAPTER 19

MUTINY

The Nam Can district town was attacked on the 24th of November with mortar, recoilless rifle, and small arms fire. On the 25th, Nam Can was attacked again. David 25 (USAF FAC assigned to Ca Mau) was shot down over Nam Can at 0800. The DPSA, Lt. Col. Culpepper, was with David 25. They managed to crash land close to the Nam Can District Headquarters and outpost and made it on foot to the outpost just ahead of some VC that were trying to capture them. Some USAF F4s came on station later and worked the area over. Lieutenant Colonel Culpepper and David 25 were picked up by chopper and returned to Ca Mau.

Ong Doc District town received a ground attack in the daylight the same day. Unusual! On the night of the 26th four district towns -- Ong Doc, Thoi Bien, Cha La, and Nam Can--were all attacked. (Three of them had Advisory Teams.) The heaviest attack was received by Nam Can. It was now pretty obvious that the enemy was set on driving the government out of the Nam Can district. There was no civil authority present, only the RF troops. Because of its location, support was difficult. It was actually the southern end of the country, with the South China Sea on the east and the Gulf of Thailand on the west. It consisted of a thousand square kilometers of forest and mangrove swamps crisscrossed with tidal waterways, no roads, and an extremely sparse population.

The VC had almost free rein of the area now. Loss of the one government enclave remaining in the district would boost the morale of the enemy and be perceived by both the government and civilians in the province as an increase of the power and influence of the Viet Cong. Previous VC attacks on the Cai Nuoc District Headquarters, my intended assignment, had already caused the Government to relocate it

117

to Dong Cung, ten kilometers to the south on the Song Bay Hap (river) and the Nam Can District's northern border. This placed it only 14 kilometers from the Nam Can town and thus was the most likely next target for increased VC attacks.

Meanwhile in Hai Yen, we received a shipment of badly needed medical supplies for the troops and an air drop of ammunition for our one 105 artillery piece. Ammunition for our 4.2 and 105 were normally dropped by either a C123 or C130, usually four or six pallets at a drop. This drop was a bad one. It landed in camp, destroying two houses and one bunker. Lt. Bordeax (the replacement for Captain Gallan) and his team departed, their training mission with the PF Platoon completed.

It was now the first of December, and a helicopter from Corps designated as the "Pay" chopper arrived. On board was a pay officer from our supporting finance company, someone from the postal unit, a medic and a PX representative. The objective of this group was to visit all advisory teams in the outlying areas monthly and first pay them— needless to say, this didn't always happen! It was their first visit to our location and they had no pay for me. I had not been paid for three months, but fortunately allotments were going home for Ann, and the DPO at Province kindly supplied me with funds until I could repay him. I had established a checking account, as advised, with the Bank of America in Saigon while in-processing. It was the only time that the "Pay" chopper ever visited my team during the year tour.

The next day, the second of December, two outposts were overrun in the Province, Cai Nuoc and Nam Can were attacked, and a firefight very close to camp occurred that night resulting in four friendly wounded and enemy casualties unknown. A pilot of a chopper transporting 4.2 inch mortar ammunition from Hai Yen to Nam Can was killed over Nam Can that day. I had met him the day before but didn't even remember his name. I received word that day that the Province Chief was ordering one company from Hai Yen to move to

Nam Can on 4 December! Major Nuoc came to me quite upset. He did not think that the troops would obey. They were still mostly Chinese and had no interest in fighting outside of the Hai Yen Special Sub Sector. I radioed his concerns back to the Province TOC. I was informed that 985 Company was ordered to prepare for movement to Nam Can. I thought, "We will see how this ends up!" Later that day I was able to make a Vertical Reconnaissance (VR) aerial with Shotgun 18 over Cai Bot Lake and adjusted some artillery fire on what appeared to be a fortified camp. Results were unknown.

There was a lot of activity: 985 Company refused to move to Nam Can! They assembled on the air strip in the morning, and then as a group informed Major Nuoc that they would not go to Nam Can, and if forced to they would shoot down the helicopters that came to move them. I radioed province and talked with Lt. Col. Culpepper. His first question to me was "Are you in danger?"

I told him I didn't think so at all. They considered us as part of the local troops and not the Vietnamese Command that wanted them to go to Nam Can. I told him I thought that they were serious and that they did not consider themselves part of the Vietnamese Armed Forces. He told me to hold on and be careful. He was going to the Province Chief and see if he could get this called off. Everyone was in the team house, and I directed that no one leave without my clearance. I had Brown and Johnson move a radio into our bunker in case we needed to move there. A group of helicopters was heard and then seen landing. They sat there a few minutes without shutting down, and then departed empty. The 985 Company returned to their billets. This almost mutiny precipitated two events of significance: a visit from Father Hoa and the somewhat later reassignment of Major Nuoc.

The crisis at Nam Can continued. The province did reinforce the garrison plus take our 4.2 In. mortar and ammunition. One chopper was lost during the operation. Meanwhile our 471 Company threatened to

119

abandon Nga Ba Dinh Outpost unless a substantial re-supply mission was conducted. The following day four choppers ferried in ten loads of supplies, both ammo and soldiers. They would be okay for awhile. Business seemed to be picking up. A day operation that Captain Bates and Sgt. Johnson went on in the Cai Doi Vam area had contact resulting in three friendly wounded. The same night, we had four wounded near Quan Phu. Also at Tan Hung Tay, the troops killed three VC, one being a Platoon Leader. Two days later, we ran an operation into our favorite area, Quan Phu. Results were one friendly wounded, three VC killed, and three wounded. A few weapons and mines were captured.

I had been ordered to Saigon to attend a class and briefing at the American Embassy on Vietnamese culture. It would be the first time back to Saigon since September and only the third time I had been out of the Province since my arrival. Two days later, I caught the Otter to Ca Mau. I had a chance to discuss with Lt. Col. Gilland the problem of the refusal of the troops to go to Nam Can and the possibility of moving our team to Cai Nuoc—our original destination. The ongoing situation at Nam Can and the desire to maintain advisory support in Hai Yen weighed heavily on any decision to move us to Cai Nuoc. If Nam Can was to fall to the VC or be abandoned by the government, then Cai Nuoc would then become the southernmost government center in the province, and the next primary objective for the enemy.

CHAPTER 20

SAIGON

It was now almost the middle of December 1967. I was due at the Embassy on Monday the 18th but wanted to run some errands, get paid, telephone Ann, shop for some presents to send home for Christmas, and get some food for the team. A lot to do while there, and I did not know how long the briefings would take or how many of them I could skip. I considered my personal agenda to be of a higher priority, however, than the briefing or class.

On 16 December, I left for Saigon. I caught a USAF C123 transport to Can Tho, where I waited several hours for a seat on something going to Saigon. Air fields at all the major cities and towns in Vietnam were hubs of chaotic activity. All types of aircraft were coming and going: U.S. Army, U.S. Air Force, VNAF (Vietnam Air Force), Air America, the CIA's air service. and the Vietnamese civilian airline Air Vietnam. Hordes of travelers, both military and civilian, were waiting for a flight out to somewhere or in many cases to anywhere. Troops, some with families (who had low or no priority) would camp out at airfields, awaiting transportation.

I finally got a seat on an Air America C47 and arrived at Tan Son Nhut at 1800 hours. Tan Son Nhut was, at the time, the busiest airport in the world in the amount of daily traffic. The Air America terminal, possibly because of its ownership (CIA), was located away from the heavily used runways. The aircraft was quickly shut down, and the crew departed in a station wagon. Passengers, myself included, loaded into a van which took us to the main areas of the Base. After inquiring how to get to downtown Saigon, I was dropped off on a corner where I could catch a bus into town.

The corner at which I was waiting was next to a base recreation area with a swimming pool and tennis courts. The area was neat and well-kept, with the grass cut and bushes trimmed--a far cry from what I had become accustomed to. At the corner was an Air Policeman, armed and wearing a camouflage-patterned uniform. The Army at the time wore a jungle uniform of plain olive drab. The airman's uniform seemed out of place in the surrounding well-manicured grounds and neat buildings. I asked him why the camouflage, commenting that he sure didn't blend in. His response was that "he was an air policeman and they all wore camouflage."

I was able to catch a bus that the Military Transport Command ran. It serviced the many military facilities scattered throughout the Saigon area. My destination was the Caravel Hotel in the center of the city, in which MACV had established a billeting office there to provide quarters for the mass of personnel visiting the city on official business. Upon arrival, I found there were no quarters available. I was told to go out to local civilian hotels for lodging. The officer in charge of billeting was a major who I knew slightly from the brigade staff at Fort Knox. He advised me to try the Majestic Hotel at the end of Tu Do Street near the river. I caught a taxi, a small beat-up French car of a make unknown to me. The hotel was actually rather close and if I did not have my B Four bag it would have been an easy walk.

The hotel was built and run by the French. There were two armed Vietnamese civilians guarding the entrance. The hotel guests appeared to be mostly French and German. There were no U.S. military in sight. I got a room on the third floor without any problem, but the rate was much higher than I expected. The room had dated European style furniture--a bed, desk, chairs, and a clothes cabinet, but no radio or TV. There was a large bathroom with a tub, toilet, basin, and bidet. There was also a separate shower room. I had had maybe two or three hot water showers in the past three months, so I took a wooden chair from the room and sat under the shower for some 20 minutes or so. It was great!

It was now past my normal supper time, so I went up to the hotel dining room on the top floor. All the hotels in Saigon had their dining rooms on the top floor--I suppose in order to catch whatever breeze there might be and to provide a view of the city. The menu was in French and provided a rather small selection of very ordinary entrees at exorbitant prices. I ordered a whiskey and some food, which turned out to be some sort of stew. While eating, I could look across the city and see flares and tracers from occasional bursts of .50 caliber machine gun fire.

Upon finishing my meal, I proceeded down to the street to the Rex Hotel, located on Dai Le Loi, to visit the Officer's Club situated on the roof. The Majestic was on the corner of Tu Do Street, which led to a square on the Dai Le Loi where Rex and the Brinks Hotels were located. Both of these hotels had been leased by the U.S. for quarters and military offices. The Caravel was diagonally across the square from the Rex and Brinks and was the hotel almost exclusively used by the media. Directly across the square was the Continental Hotel with its large veranda, which was prominent in several movies.

Each of the hotels that had been leased for quartering military personnel had established clubs and mess facilities, but the Rex and the Brinks seemed to be the gathering spots for those who for whatever reason came to Saigon. It was to become one of my first stops during the few times that I was in Saigon during my two years in country.

At that particular time, the uniform for Army personnel assigned in or visiting Saigon was the khaki short sleeve shirt and trousers. Jungle fatigues were not the duty uniform unless you were passing through and only there for the day or overnight. I had brought one set of khaki (somewhat wrinkled) and my low quarter shoes. I also

123

had my .45 caliber service pistol and my personal unauthorized .32 caliber Beretta with me. Unless required in performance of their assigned duties, personnel were not authorized to be armed in Saigon. That policy changed drastically about a month later, after the Tet Offensive. In that a .45 pistol is difficult to conceal, I stuffed it in one of my boots, covered it with a sock and left the boots under the bed. The smaller pistol I put in my waistband covered by my shirt, and off I went up Tu Do Street to Dai Le Loi and the Rex.

Tu Do Street was teeming with activity. Children and old people were selling everything imaginable from the sidewalk. Scantily dressed young women were enticing GIs into bars, massage parlors, and jewelry shops with all kinds of promises. I managed to get up the street to Dai Le Loi without buying anything or being lured into any place of business. Dodging traffic, I crossed the square and entered the Rex Hotel. An old creaky elevator took me to the top floor, where a Field Ration Mess and Officers Club were in operation.

The Club was packed. A band was playing but was drowned out by the loud laughter and noisy conversations. I got a drink. Forty cents! Wow, what a bargain! I saw a couple of officers from either my Civil Affairs class or language school. After chatting with them, I left for my hotel around 2230 to beat the 2300 hour curfew.

The following morning after some breakfast at the Rex, I caught a bus to the PX located in Cholon, the Chinese section of Saigon. I bought a ring for Ann and something for Jennifer as Christmas presents and was able to get the items in the mail from there. I also bought a small radio for myself. My next mission now was to get some food for the team. A Commissary established for the U.S. civilians and military in Saigon was located next to the PX. In there I bought some cans of pumpkin, cranberry sauce, mixed nuts, dried beef, and some spices. I then took the items back over to a concessionaire at the PX, had them packaged, wrapped, and mailed to the team. Hopefully they would arrive in Hai Yen by the time I returned. My final mission was to get paid. I had not been paid since I in-processed in September. When I arrived in-country I, as advised, had opened a checking account with the Bank of America in Saigon. Out of my monthly salary, I had one hundred dollars placed in the account, thirty dollars paid to me in cash, some money deposited in the Soldiers Savings Account, and the remaining sent to Ann. My allotments to the Bank, Ann, and Soldier's Savings Fund were all in place, but because of my location I had not been paid for three months.

The method, as I previously mentioned, for paying advisors that were assigned to remote locations was by helicopter. Each month a paymaster accompanied by a medic, a postal clerk, and a PX representative supposedly would make the rounds and visit the teams for the purpose of paying the troops. While doing so, the medic would give any required shots and dispense items such as foot power, vitamins, and other minor medical supplies. The postal clerk would deliver any mail he might have and accept outgoing mail plus sell money orders to those soldiers who wanted to mail money back home. The PX rep had aboard a number of items, e.g.., writing paper, pens, razor blades, soap, shampoo, film, tobacco items, and various snacks for sale-- items that were available to the troops at units and bases.

The Pay Master would also convert Military Payment Certificates (MPC) to piasters for the soldier's use in the local economy. MPCs were designed to limit the amount of U.S. currency in the country to fight inflation. It was against regulations to use MPCs in purchasing from or paying the Vietnamese. Americans in Vietnam could only use the Vietnamese currency. MPCs were used instead by the U.S. personnel, both military and civilian, instead of U.S. currency within the American community.

The problem in getting paid was that many times because of the location a single helicopter was not authorized to visit unless covered by gunships, which were not always available. The finance unit supporting MACV was located in Cholon in an old Chinese theater. After stating my problem I was paid up to date. I was flush with money! Now that my reasons for being in Cholon were satisfied, I caught a bus back to the center of Saigon and the Rex Hotel.

Back at the Rex, I went to the Club to get a drink and ran into some people I knew from the Civil Affairs School and the DLI (Defense Language Institute) Vietnamese language course. Some were in Saigon to attend the briefing, like myself, or to take a class on Vietnamese culture at the Embassy. I found out from one of them that we were to report to the JUSPAO (Joint United States Public Affairs Office) Headquarters in or near the Brinks Hotel. After some food and a couple of drinks, I made my way back to the Majestic for the night.

The next morning I reported for the briefing. There were approximately 30 advisors on hand. I knew several of them, including Wally Young, who was from my Province. He was DSA for Thoi Bien District, the northernmost district in An Xuyen. Wally and I had not met but we each knew who the other was and where in the province he was assigned.

Wally was an old hand and on his second tour in Vietnam. He had a year at the Defense Language Institute (DLI) studying Chinese and a previous tour of duty in Saigon plus six months with the Special Forces. He was staying in the Star Hotel on Tu Do Street and urged me to join him there. That evening I moved out of the Majestic and into the Star Hotel. In the week that I spent in Saigon, I learned a great deal from both Wally and the class about the city, the Vietnamese, and Vietnam in general.

The class was taught by a German. I don't recall his back ground but the briefings were worthwhile in my opinion. Attendance at the class was a little lax as it was recognized that most of the attendees had other business that they wanted take care of while in Saigon at various organizations or headquarters, both U.S. and Vietnamese. I took time to go to the USO and place a call to Ann. I had to wait an hour or more to get a line.

I also paid a visit to CORDS Headquarters and discussed some problems I was having working with the Chinese and the An Xuyen Province Chief and staff. I had to be very careful here, as I was outside my chain of command. I went with one of my fellow officers in the class who was assigned to CORDS Headquarters and had been in country for almost four years. He invited me over to CORDS to talk about the problems at Hai Yen and I agreed to go over with him. I thought we would be chatting with personnel of our own grade, but he introduced me to then Brigadier General Forsythe (later Lieutenant General) , Ambassador Komer, and a Colonel whose name I cannot recall (also later a General). I was on very slippery ground and was careful what I said. When I returned to Ca Mau, I immediately briefed Lt. Col. Gilland on the visit to CORDS Headquarters.

Class was over on Friday the 22nd of December, and we were all anxious to get back to our homes away from home before Christmas. I was able to catch an early morning flight and arrived back in Ca Mau by 0900 on the 23rd. After briefing Lt. Col. Gilland and Culpepper and catching up on the current situation, I was ferried down to Hai Yen by one of the FACs. I arrived at 1600 and found that during my absence, we had two friendly killed and six wounded and a significant surprise. Father Hoa had arrived from Cholon to spend Christmas with his old followers.

CHAPTER 21

CHRISTMAS AND THE ARRIVAL OF FATHER HOA

The team caught me up on the activities, particularly the arrival of Father Hoa. The priest, accompanied by two soldiers or aides in uniform, was flown in on the IV Corps Commander's personal helicopter. The team was taken by surprise, as no one in Hai Yen or the Province Headquarters had notified them of his pending visit. Any time in the past when I inquired about a possible visit by Father Hoa, I was simply told "Oh yes, he is coming soon."

Captain Bates and the NCOs had noticed some sprucing up, but thought that it was in preparation for Christmas, which was sure to be observed as all the Chinese were Catholic. He also noted that all the troops in camp were mustered out in full uniforms with equipment and inspected. While unusual, we did not know what ceremonies or activities were normally conducted at Christmas; we had already experienced some customs that seemed strange to us.

One development, however, might have caused us to expect Father Hoa's visit. Around the Headquarters building there were always several soldiers, usually six in number, unarmed and just lounging around seemingly doing nothing. When I once asked what their duties were, the response was they belonged to the Commander. We certainly didn't need guards on the Commander's office and quarters inside Hai Yen. As reported to me by the team members, on the morning of the priest's arrival there appeared to be an air of anticipation among the troops and their families that the team members could not put their finger on. One highly noticeable change from normal was the appearance of the several soldiers who habitually hung around the Headquarters. They were now in full uniform, armed and alert.

A few minutes before the helicopter bearing Father Hoa and party touched down, a message was received from the Province TOC informing us of his pending arrival. When Captain Bates and Sgt. Brown went to the air strip to meet the chopper, they found Major Nuoc, Captain Thinh, the now heavily armed six Headquarters loafers, and a group of older soldiers and family members there waiting. Evidently they were the ones who had made the long trek from China with Father Hoa. The status of the six soldiers was now clear. They were Father Hoa's personal body guards. Captain Bates introduced himself and Sgt. Brown to Father Hoa, explaining that I was in Saigon and due to return shortly. He assured Father Hoa that I would meet with him at the earliest time convenient to us both. I went to greet him the evening I returned but did not have an opportunity to sit and discuss the current situation at Hai Yen until a couple of days after Christmas.

Christmas Eve was on a Sunday, and the Chinese soldiers and families, being all Catholic, attended several masses during the day and evening which were conducted by Father Hoa. Bates, Brown, and I attended one service, although none of us was a practicing Catholic. A truce had been announced and went into effect at 1800 hours on the 24th until 1800 hours on Christmas Day. Camp security was maintained but patrols were cut back, almost eliminated. We put up three small Christmas trees that we had received from various sources: Ann had sent me one along with a package of goodies; one came from some support group in the states; and Sgt. Brown's wife sent him one. In the afternoon, Lt. Col. Gilland visited escorted by gunships and brought us some food including a turkey roast. The day ended up being rather sad and melancholy. Everyone, I suspect, was thinking of home and family.

Christmas Day was quiet although we heard that Dom Doi District Town was attacked during the night despite the truce. Bake prepared a holiday meal with the turkey and trimmings that Lt. Col. Gilland had brought and using the items that I had mailed from the commissary in Saigon. He baked a pumpkin pie but without sugar or spices. It was terrible! Truly inedible, though the rest of the dinner was fine.

It was a quiet day for the team except for observing the Chinese celebrating Christmas. Although Catholic, they conducted traditional Chinese holiday festivities to include the Chinese Dragon. Several soldiers dressed in the dragon costume paraded throughout the camp, accompanied by drums and cymbals and followed by all the children. We were given small red waxed envelopes, which we were told were for tribute for the dragon. As instructed, we placed a few piasters in each envelope and tied them with string to the eaves of the Team House. The dragon came along dancing and reared up snatching the envelopes in its mouth. We also were expected to hand out gifts and small amounts of money in red envelopes to the children. Later we were invited to have tea with Father Hoa, Major Nuoc, and the staff.

There was one celebration that was quite different from what appeared to be normal for observing the Christmas holiday. In middle of the afternoon, an assistant to Ming Wi, the maintenance NCO, appeared at the door of the Team House and announced that a party was being held in their shop and we were all invited. Sergeant Brown and I decided to make an appearance and represent the team. Upon entering the maintenance shop, we were greeted by Ming Wi who appeared glassy eyed and obviously quite drunk. Displayed on the work benches was an assortment of food that included rice cakes, dumplings, papayas, melons, and some sort of greens. Nearby on a metal stand over a fire was a third of a 55 gallon drum. After accepting a glass of Japanese whiskey, I walked over and peered into the drum to see what they were cooking. To my surprise and disgust I saw a chicken, a small pig, and a dog boiling away in a gray scum. One of the soldiers who worked for Ming Wi and was also inebriated, was stirring the ingredients vigorously. He pointed at the drum and said, "An com (eat)."

As I turned away, Ming Wi waved at the boiling drum and work benches and announced, "We eat."

Brown and I with glasses of whiskey in hand walked over to the food on the benches and began to pick up selected items.

I whispered to Brown, "We have got to get out of here."

He nodded in agreement. After munching on a rice cake and some melon slices I thanked Ming Wi and told him we must return to the Team house to receive an expected radio message. We then left him and his drunken helpers to enjoy their holiday party. Thus ended my first Christmas in Vietnam. The next one there would be quite different.

The period between Christmas and the first of January was quiet. Troop activity was mostly confined to work within the Camp, with only minimum patrolling being conducted. We did receive word that to the north of us three advisors were kidnapped and killed. I believe they were civilian advisors. On 28 December, 475 Company had contact resulting in three enemy KIA and the capture of some weapons. The Tae Tau outpost in Quan Long District near the Province Capital was overrun, resulting in 18 friendly KIA, 17 wounded, and 3 missing. Enough weapons were lost to equip two VC Platoons. A truce went in effect again at 0600 hours on New Year's Eve, ending at 0600 hours on 2 January. We had a company out during the truce but no contact, although there were two air strikes on suspected VC base areas. 473 Company had contact on the 3rd, resulting in a long running firefight.

On the 5th, Dong Cung was attacked at 1800, Cai Nuoc Outpost at 1830, Cha La District Town at 1800, and Nam Cam at 2000 hours. Dong Cung lost two platoon outposts. The Cai Nuoc District Headquarters was overrun and the VC spoke with the District Chief on his own radio frequency. The Cha La Advisory Team took a round right in the team house. All in all three outposts were lost. The next day, air traffic over the fallen outposts received heavy ground fire.

A briefing was held at 1530 concerning a re-supply operation to Nga Ba Dinh Outpost which would take us through the edge of the Quan Pho area. Three companies plus a PF Platoon were going on two routes. I planned to have two advisor teams, Bates and Brown with one column and Johnson and me with the other. Time of departure was set at 0230 hours the following morning.

We rose at 0100 and Bates was ill, so I aborted one team. Johnson, Phong, Sgt Cau, and I accompanied the larger column. The mission was successful. We made the re-supply with light enemy contact and only one friendly wounded. The Quan Pho VC units were caught unawares, or either some of their troops were elsewhere on a mission of their own. However, our interest was soon to be directed to another area to the southwest near the gulf of Thailand.

CHAPTER 22

AMBUSH

Even at 0100, the night was thick and warm, causing one to sweat at the slightest move. Thirty-one Chinese and two Americans passed quickly and carefully through the wire and mines, entering out onto a well-worn foot path that followed the canal bank. The canal was not a manmade waterway, but rather a slow-moving tidal stream 25 to 30 meters wide and meandering southwest to the Gulf of Thailand. The soldiers in single file moved off down the path toward their objective, the hamlet of Cai Doi Vam, about six kilometers away. There was an occasional grunt as a man adjusted his muffled equipment or changed the carrying position of his weapon. These were the only sounds as the column moved beyond the sight and hearing of the camp guard posts.

Three days previously, Dai-uy Thinh came into the team house with a civilian in tow and stated that he had some A1 intelligence, the highest rating given for quality of information. The civilian, an old villager from Cai Doi Vam, told us that a VC unit came into his hamlet three or four times a week to eat and rest. By his description, they appeared to be a village guerilla squad. The weapons and equipment were mostly U.S. They were not wearing main force uniforms nor carrying AK47 rifles. The old man said they came early in the morning, laid up all day, and left after dark. This was completely opposite to the normal pattern of VC activity. Usually they entered government-controlled villages and hamlets at night and left before first light.

"They stay in the hamlet all day?" I inquired, "They are only a few hundred meters from our Cai Doi Vam outpost!"

133

"Yes," said Dai-uy Thinh. "They think that we would never expect them in so close."

"Why wasn't this reported to Trung-uy Ty?" I queried. 1st Lt. Ty, Commander of 786 Company, the unit that garrisoned the Cai Doi Vam outpost, was considered one of the better Company Commanders.

"Old man was afraid VC in outpost and would see him. He and his family would die," explained Dai-uy Thinh.

"Well, do you think he is telling the truth?" I followed up.

"I believe him," the captain replied. "We plan operation, ambush."

"When?" I asked.

"Soon, this week, I will command it myself," he replied.

"OK," I said, "I'll go, too."

Two days later Captain Thinh announced, "We go tomorrow night."

"How many men?" I queried?

"Ba Moui. (30). We leave at midnight," Thinh continued, "and ambush VC when they come to hamlet."

"We need to set up some reserve and plan for artillery strikes outside the hamlet to catch any VC trying to escape our ambush," I advised.

"My staff will plan the operation," he said and left.

I gathered the team and briefed them on the mission. Sergeant Brown would accompany me. Captain Bates would stay in camp with the rest of the team and monitor the operation by radio. I decided not to inform Province of the proposed ambush until it was over. At this early stage in my assignment, I had concerns regarding the security of radio transmissions, even though messages were encrypted, though later my concerns proved to be valid. Phong, my bodyguard, would also go along as usual, and a soldier would be assigned to carry our radio. We were good to go.

A bit after 0100, the column picked up speed and was proceeding at a good pace, surprising me with the quietness of their movement. The path along the canal was clear and easy to follow in the starlight. We passed a number of thatched huts so close that one could hear a murmur of voices or a baby cry. Occasionally a dog would challenge us with a flurry of barking then slink into a hut when he failed to scare us away. Sergeant Brown, Phong, the radio man, and I had held back and left the camp at the tail of the column to ensure the troops had closed up and there were no stragglers. During the movement we worked our way slowly toward the head of the column.

After an hour and a half, we were almost to the front when the troops abruptly stopped, bumping into one another like an accordion. We joined Dai-uy and his command group, gathered in a small knot and whispered, "What's up?"

'"We go in canal," Thinh replied. "Path ends, too much noise, canal not deep we walk in water."

"It will slow us down," I countered.

"Not as much as bushes." Thinh grunted as he lowered himself into the water. There was a titter of subdued laughter back along the column as the troops slipped into the canal. Splashes revealed those who lost their footing and slid down the muddy bank into the tepid water. It was about waist deep and the bottom, as everywhere in the Delta, was soft gooey mud. And it stank of rotting vegetation, like every waterway in the Delta. Fortunately the tide was ebbing or we might have been up to our necks.

We kept close to the bank sloshing downstream, weapons held up and followed by a cloud of mosquitoes and nocturnal insects that thought they had found bug heaven. Between them and the heat and stench, we agreed with them.

A little after 0400, the column stopped. Another whispered huddle revealed that we were only a hundred meters or so from the hamlet. A small group left the main body to reconnoiter ahead. Brown and I climbed out of the canal with Captain Thinh. The sky was brightening in the east, reminding us that dawn would soon be upon us and we needed to get our troops in place. The returning reconnoitering party announced that all was quiet in the hamlet. More whispering, then two soldiers, NCOs, moved back along the bank giving instructions. Several men climbed out and followed a sergeant moving off to the south, away from the canal.

The hamlet consisted of a row of 10 or 12 thatched huts located 20 meters back from the canal. They were square, built of poles with the walls and roof constructed from nippa palm fronds. Most of the huts had only one door, centered front; a few had a rear entrance. The floors were smooth, hard-packed mud built up about a foot above the ground level to keep out the water during the rains. Alongside each hut was a rectangular pit three to four meters deep created by excavating the mud needed for the floor. This pit served as a reservoir for rain water and was used for washing and cooking. The ground in front was bare and hard packed.

Behind the line of huts, going back 400-500 meters to the edge of the jungle, was an uncultivated rice field with waist high grass. In front of the huts along the canal, sampans were tied up to stakes driven into the bank. A small dock in front of one of the huts had a large motorized sampan moored to it. At the end of the line of huts was the typical delta latrine built out over the canal for community use by the inhabitants of the hamlet.

The ambush plan was simple. The men would string out along the canal in front of the huts. The canal bank would provide some cover from enemy fire. The small party that had left the canal was upstream approximately 70-75 meters from the first dwelling. They had two Browning Automatic Rifles (BARs). Their mission was to lay down fire, cutting off any VC retreating across the open rice field from the rear of the hamlet after the ambush was sprung. They would also provide support, if needed, by firing down the long axis of the line of huts. It was expected that the enemy would approach from the tree line behind the huts. When they were about to enter the huts, Dai-uy Thinh would give the signal and the troops pressed up against the canal bank would pour their fire into the VC or the huts. With the troops below the canal bank, it would be difficult for the enemy to detect them until it was too late, and the enemy would be silhouetted against the sky, which was steadily getting brighter.

Dai uy Thinh, Phong, and I were abreast and slightly upstream of the first hut, so that we could see out across the open rice field without obstruction. I was uncomfortable about the plan, not being able to understand Chinese and only a little Vietnamese. I had to hope that I was being told all that was going on. I nudged Thinh; "Everything OK?"

137

"A-OK," he replied, a favorite saying of his. "When VC come, soldiers fire when I give signal. If VC see us, me shoot, I give others signal and BAR shoot. Shoot everyone on ground. We stay in canal."

"Shoot everyone in and around huts?" I asked, surprised.

"Yes, everyone." he replied.

"What about civilians that may be in the huts?" I countered.

"They VC supporters," Thinh stated and turned away.

Dawn grew closer and my eyes were burning from straining to see something, anything, across the open field. My feet were cramped from standing still in the mud so long. Mosquitoes buzzed and circled around my head. Thinh grabbed my elbow. "Look! VC, VC!"

I strained to see and all of a sudden there they were, in two open columns walking slowly toward the hamlet, toward us. I started to count them, as we expected a village guerilla squad of six to eight. Ten, eleven, twelve, thirteen. Hell, it's a platoon! Fourteen! They seemed to be angling toward the second and third huts from the upstream end, just off to my right , about 25 to 30 meters. They were now up close and masked by the huts. Several came from between the second and third huts, stood for a few moments in front of the second hut, then started going inside. Where were the rest? The third hut must have a back door. Why hasn't Thinh given the signal to fire? Damn! They have some plan they didn't tell me! The VC had now all disappeared into the huts. Thinh raised his arm and waved it slowly. Now what's this, I wondered?

Several men began to climb out of the canal. My God, I thought, the VC will hear us! Six soldiers, two groups of three, were moving slowly toward the two huts, water dripping from their clothes.

They hesitated at the doors, then opened fire through the doorways, holding their weapons steady and empting their magazines. People were screaming and the soldiers, still in the canal, began climbing out and firing randomly at the other huts. I heard several explosions, grenades, and M79s. Dai-uy Thinh started out of the canal. I was out first and gave him a hand up. Phong was out of the water standing with his back to me, sweeping the area with his eyes and the .45 caliber Thompson. He was the always-ready bodyguard, and I was thankful for it.

Firing fell off, then stopped. Soldiers were shouting and running about. There were some children crying. Dai-uy Thinh went to the second hut, looked in, and waved to me. I ran over and went in. There, amid some pots, pans, military packs, and weapons, were a number of bodies.

"How many?" I asked. Six, no, eight by my count. A soldier rushed in, spouting Chinese.

Thinh turned to me and said, "Seven in other hut and one woman, one woman and man in here."

I looked more closely and saw one of the bodies was indeed a woman. Soldiers began dragging the bodies outside and searching through their clothes. Weapons were gathered. A soldier brought me a .45 caliber pistol.

"Who had it," I asked. He pointed to one of the bodies.

"VC officer," stated Sgt. Hy, walking up. Hy was a Master Sgt. and the senior NCO on the mission.

"He have radio and money," Hy stated. I walked over to where Hy was pointing and picked up the radio, a Sony AM/FM commercial set. Turning it on I was surprised to hear Cpt. Bates speaking.

"This set has been rewired as a receiver and is set on our frequency!" I exclaimed. Dai-uy nodded and did not seem surprised.

"VC radio," he said, smiling.

The ambush was over. Fifteen men and two women lay dead in front of the huts where they were dragged. Fifteen rifles, one pistol, and a number of grenades were gathered. One soldier was going through a pile of papers collected from the bodies. Medical supplies were being sorted through. Some were kept and some were being handed to the villagers who had come out of their houses. A group of soldiers, led by Lt. Ty, arrived from the nearby outpost. Ty seemed both surprised and embarrassed— embarrassed, I suppose, because the ambush had been conducted so close to his headquarters. Troops from the ambush were straggling over to the outpost. "We eat then return," stated Dai-uy Thinh. "Number one operation," he grinned, holding up his right thumb in the A-OK gesture.

I had a lot of questions, but they would keep until we were back in camp. During the planning of the mission, my thoughts were focused on the destruction of the VC unit and not on the villagers themselves. Afterwards, I wondered if the villagers were really VC supporters as Thinh stated, or merely victims of the war.

CHAPTER 23

RENDEZVOUS AT SEA

One morning a few days after the ambush at Cai Doi Vam, I was approached by Dai-uy Thinh and invited to accompany him on a visit to one of the outposts.

I asked him which one. "474 Company," he replied.

"That's Cai Doi Vam!" I exclaimed.

"Yes, I go inspect soldiers and outpost. We go by boat, leave 0700 hours tomorrow. Return in afternoon. Commander not know I visit."

"OK, I will go. Sergeant Brown and Phong will go, too. Will you give me a soldier to carry my radio?"

"Yes, I will see you in morning," he said while walking away toward his Headquarters.

That night after supper, I briefed the team on the next morning's activities. I asked Brown to alert Phong and tell him to be ready to go by 0700. Captain Bates and Sgt. Johnson would remain in camp. It seemed to be a routine visit, but I wondered if it was brought on by the recent presence of the VC platoon we had ambushed. Was Dai-uy Thinh suspicious of the reliability of the troops in the outpost? I didn't think they were disloyal--after all they were mostly Father Hoa's Chinese. However, they may have become lazy and slack in their duties. An unannounced inspection visit could provide an answer. I had quickly agreed to go with Dai-uy Thinh for two reasons: first to assess the posture of the outpost and the commander, and secondly to meet with Free Serpent Charlie, a U.S. Navy Swift Boat.

141

In an effort to curtail enemy movement by the open sea and into the many rivers and waterways in the delta, the U.S. Navy had initiated Operation Market Time to patrol the coast lines bordering the South China Sea and the Gulf of Thailand. Navy patrol boats identified as PBFs (Patrol Boat Fast), and more commonly known as Swift Boats, carried out a large part of this mission. They were about 50 feet in length, had a crew of six--one officer and five enlisted men--with a top speed of 25 knots when loaded. Their armament consisted of three .50 caliber machine guns, an 81 mm mortar, and an assortment of small arms.

They operated out of several bases, with Phu Quoc Island being the home port for those patrolling in the Gulf of Thailand. The District Team at Ong Doc was frequently visited by the Swift Boats operating in their immediate area. Our team kept in contact with the boats that patrolled our coast lines. Information was exchanged, and on several occasions the Swift Boats provided fire support with their mortars to units operating close to the coast, although use of the mortars was rather chancy. Firing from an unstable platform such as a pitching deck greatly reduced the accuracy and could endanger the friendly troops that they were attempting to support. Interdiction of maritime coastal traffic, however, was the Swift Boats' primary mission. Later their mission would include the rivers, canals, and waterways deep into the Delta.

My team, as did the SF Team we replaced, kept a running dialogue by radio with the boats, thus providing intelligence on operations that may be in progress near the coast and news in which we were all interested. Voices over the radio became recognizable, and although we had never met, we knew each other by call signs. This visit to the Cai Doi Vam Outpost, which lay less than 1,200 meters from the mouth of the canal on the Gulf, could provide me an opportunity meet the captain and crew of one of the Swift Boats.

A request to Dai-uy Thinh to provide me one of the boats to motor out to the Gulf and rendezvous with a Swift Boat was granted. I, of course, invited Dai-uy Thinh, but he declined saying he had much he wanted to do at the outpost. A radio message to Free Serpent Charlie from Seaforth Island Oscar (radio call signs) suggesting the meeting was agreed to with enthusiasm. A tentative time of 1100 hours at the mouth of Rach Cai Doi was selected. It was expected that we would have only 30 minutes or so, but we could at least meet face to face and would in the future have a mental picture of who we were talking to on the radio.

The following morning, the small flotilla departed on time. Three Boston whalers, each with nine or ten passengers, exited Hai Yen out on the Rach Cai Doi headed downstream towards Cai Doi Vam Outpost and the Gulf of Thailand. The lead boat had a .30 caliber machine gun mounted in the bow on a homemade pedestal. We were traveling at a moderate speed, and I noted that the soldiers seemed relaxed and not alert with their weapons as they usually were. I guessed that enemy activity was not expected. A number of sampans, mainly occupied by women, were met on their way to the marketplace outside the walls at Hai Yen. Some youngsters were fishing with nets along the banks. Except for the boats loaded with armed men, the scene was quite pastoral.

Ninety minutes later we tied up at a landing too crude to be called a dock. The outpost was a typical triangular fortification sited about 300 meters from the canal. The terrain outside the outpost was mud flats with little or no vegetation. Several bands of barbed wire were present, and the flat level ground provided excellent fields of fire. The outpost was manned by 474 Company--mostly the old original Chinese Sea Swallows. Indirect fire weapons available were one 81mm and two 60 mm mortars. Browning Automatic Rifles and .30 caliber machine guns provided supporting direct fire. The outpost was within

143

range of the 105mm artillery piece located at Hai Yen. Approximately 80 soldiers, many with families, were assigned to 474 Company.

As we walked toward the outpost, one of the soldiers yelled and pointed to the open area between the rach and the outpost slightly downstream from where we had landed. Looking at where he was pointing I saw several figures running toward the outpost.

"VC?" I asked.

"No, soldiers returning to outpost maybe stay in hamlet last night," Da-uy Thinh responded angrily.

He then grabbed a carbine from one of the men near him and began firing in the direction of the running soldiers. I quickly noted that he was firing high over their heads. They disappeared around the other side of the outpost from which we were approaching. Dai-uy handed the carbine back and said to me, "Soldiers must stay in outpost at night, they out maybe to see women."

"Or VC," I commented.

"Maybe, maybe no."

We entered the outpost through a heavy metal gate in the wall and were met by the Commander, Trung-uy (1stLt.) Ty, who appeared to be quite nervous. After exchanging salutes and shaking hands, Dai-uy Thinh ordered Trung-uy Ty to assemble all his troops for inspection. While the assembly was taking place Sgt. Brown, with the radio handset to his ear called out, "Sir Free Serpent Charlie is on the horn."

I took the mike from and responded, "This is Oscar Six over."

"Oscar Six, this is Free Serpent Charlie, we are two zero minutes from the rendezvous point. What is your location, over?"

"I'm at the Cai Doi Vam Outpost. It will take me 25 to 30 minutes to get out there to you over."

"Roger, we will wait, out."

I turned to Dai-uy Thinh and told him the Swift Boat was arriving and I needed get out there to meet them. He nodded and waved two soldiers over to us and said, "They will take you out to the sea."

"Thanks, I will see you later," I replied and started back toward the boats.

A few minutes later, we were headed down the rach and out to sea. Sgt. Brown and I both were anxious and a little excited about boarding the Swift Boat and meeting the Captain and crew we had been talking to for several weeks. Phong was his normal stoic and noncommittal self and shook his head no when I asked him if he had ever been aboard a U.S. Navy vessel. We exited out into the Gulf and saw Free Serpent Charlie lying about 300 meters out from shore. As we approached, we could see two members of the crew manning one of the .50 caliber machine guns and keeping watch toward the shoreline. We identified ourselves with a short radio message and then eased up alongside the boat where a chain-linked ladder had been lowered. A line was dropped over the side and grabbed by one of the soldiers to tie to our boat. The plan was that Sgt. Brown, Phong, and I would board and the two soldiers would stay with our Boston whaler. I started up the ladder and was given a hand up onto the deck by a young sailor dressed in navy denims and a baseball style cap. I was quickly followed by Brown and Phong. The sailor stepped back and looking at us in dismay, hesitated, then saluted and said "Welcome aboard sir."

145

I returned his salute and said, "I'm Major Dagenais, and this is Sergeant Brown and Corporal Phong."

I then started toward the bow and the pilot house where I expected to meet the Captain when the sailor called out, "Wait, you can't go in there, you are all muddy."

I stopped and then realized what the young sailor saw, three men in non-descript uniforms muddied and wet up to the knees, carrying an assortment of weapons and the leader without any visible rank or insignia. Before I could address his concerns a tall Naval officer dressed in a navy short sleeve tan uniform emerged from the pilot house and announced, "I'm Lt. Browser, Free Serpent Charlie's Captain. Welcome aboard."

After shaking hands I introduced Sgt. Brown and identified Phong as my assigned bodyguard. As he heard the term, the Lieutenant raised his eyebrows and questioned, "Bodyguard?"

"Yes," I replied, "assigned to me by the Hai Yen Commander. Seems that the VC have a cash reward for killing or capturing an advisor."

Lieutenant Browser shook his head and then led us into the pilot house and introduced us to members of the crew that were present. Phong who had entered last suddenly disappeared down a companion way to a crew sleeping area below the pilot house. A moment later he returned and stood by the entrance to the pilot house from the other side of the deck with his .45 caliber Thompson sub-machine in the ready position.

"What's he doing?" asked one of the Petty Officers.

"Watching for VC," I answered.

146

"On our boat, a U.S. Navy vessel?"

"Well, he is very conscientious," I smiled.

"Would you like something to drink, a cold Coke, or something to eat?" offered one of the crew."A cold Coke would be great," replied Brown.

The sailor left the pilot house and returned a few minutes later with a half dozen cans of Coke, which he handed out to everyone. Lieutenant Browzer and I sat down and began discussing the enemy situation as it pertained to each of our missions. We both agreed that the Navy should be operating up into the rivers. I stated that I would like to see them in the Song Bay Hop. Browzer said that the current rumor was that it was soon to happen. Meanwhile, Sgt. Brown had gone off with the senior Petty Officer to see if there was anything we could scrounge from the Navy. A few 81mm mortar rounds and a couple of cans of diesel fuel were loaded in our Boston whaler. After a promise to continue our radio contact, we loaded into our boat and started back toward the mouth of Rach Cai Moi and Cai Doi Vam Outpost. A few minutes after we had cast off, Free Serpent Charlie's engines roared into life and the Swift Boat was soon a speck on the horizon heading north up the Gulf.

As we approached the landing near the outpost, we could see that some soldiers were in the other two boats. I could see Dai-uy Thinh with others coming from the outpost toward the boats. Once ashore I started to meet him, but he waved for me to stay at the landing. When he was in hearing distance I yelled, "Are you finished at the outpost?"

"Yes," he replied. "Now we return to Hai Yen but eat first."

The remaining troops climbed aboard and we motored up the rach for a couple of kilometers and then pulled in at a small dock with several houses nearby. There we unloaded and made our way to the front of one of houses, which appeared to be a small store. Some tables and chairs were gathered and a lunch of dried shrimp and peppers along with Japanese Santory whiskey was presented and consumed with gusto. During the meal I tried to discuss with Dai-uy Thinh the results of his visit to Cai Doi Vam Outpost, but he was non-committal so I decided to wait to another time to broach the subject. The return to Hai Yen after lunch was uneventful, and at 1500 hours I was back in the team house. I never saw or sailed upon the Gulf of Thailand again.

CHAPTER 24

THE CALM BEFORE THE STORM

It was now the middle of January, and the soldiers and their families were looking forward to Tet, the lunar New Year. This was considered the most important holiday of the year. It was a time when the Vietnamese traveled to family burial sites to honor their ancestors. Civilian movement throughout the country was expected, and we were informed that a 48-hour cease fire would go into effect during the Tet festivities. We also were looking forward to the holiday, as none of us had seen a Tet celebration.

Meanwhile, there were several events that kept us busy. 474 Company carried out a very successful ambush resulting in 15 VC killed, one mortar and seven rifles captured, and three sampans sunk without the loss of a single soldier. Father Hoa returned to Cholon (Saigon). Before his departure I spent a long evening with him discussing the war, the future of his people who had come out of China with him, and his concern and mistrust of the Vietnamese Government. The last thing he said to me as he boarded a helicopter to depart was, "If you are in danger and Hai Yen is to fall, go to my brother." His brother was the Commander of 472 Company and the default leader of the Chinese in absence of Father Hoa. despite the Vietnamese command structure of the Hai Yen forces.

We also had several visitors. A civilian doctor was sent to us for a couple of days to see for himself the health and medical conditions in the contested areas. I never knew if he really represented a medical organization back in the states or if he was just on his own. He seemed like a nice guy and helped out with the wounded and the daily sick call. He had one quirk, though: He wanted to meet the VC. Once he asked me to let someone take him to a place where he could be left to meet the enemy. Can you imagine what would have happened to me if I had let him get captured by the enemy? I was glad to see him go. A couple of the Province Team Staff Officers also paid us a visit to ascertain the status of refugees of which we had none. Sometimes I thought people came just to say they had been there.

To round out the visitors, Lieutenant Colonel Gilland flew in and awarded Sergeants Brown, Johnson, and me the Combat Infantryman's Badge (CIB), one of the most coveted awards in the Army's combat arms. The CIB is the U.S. Army combat recognition decoration awarded to Infantry or Special Forces soldiers, enlisted men and officers, who *personally* fought in active ground combat.

We had a serious incident that could have put the whole team in jeopardy. A Vietnamese lieutenant, the S5 (Civil Affairs officer), had attempted to enter the team house in the early morning hours to kill Captain Bates. He was stopped by the priest's bodyguards and Bake. It appeared that Bates had had a public verbal dispute with the lieutenant, which led the Vietnamese officer to believe he had lost face in front of his contemporaries. Reportedly, the lieutenant intended to throw a grenade into the sleeping area of the team house, which could have killed or wounded any or all of us. I immediately contacted Major Nuoc. He had already isolated the lieutenant, who was one of the officers that was assigned to Hai Yen with the Vietnamese Command Group when the Chinese were integrated into the Vietnam Territorial Forces.

I notified Lt. Col. Gilland (the PSA) at once and requested that Bates be at least temporarily transferred back to the Province until the incident was investigated and the reason it occurred was determined. A USID chopper working in the Province was diverted to Hai Yen, and I sent Bates out pending the outcome of my findings. It turned out that the lieutenant's attempted attack on Bates had resulted from a verbal exchange resulting from a disagreement about where the Vietnamese lieutenant could sit to watch a movie that we were showing outside on the wall of a building.

Two days later, after I had completed inquiries into the incident, I flew to Ca Mau to discuss the disposition of Bates with the PSA. It was then that I found out this was the second time Bates had been pulled out of a District because of his inability to get along with the team and/or the Vietnamese to whom they were advisors. Lieutenant Colonel Gilland decided to transfer him permanently back to the Province Team and assign him to the TOC. As noted before, Captain Bates did have a somewhat abrasive personality when dealing with subordinates and the local troops. He was a stickler for following regulations to the letter, an approach that was difficult to maintain in an environment in which rules at times were broken in order to accomplish the mission. Bates did well in his new assignment, distinguishing himself during a major attack on Ca Mau in April.

Enemy activity seemed to be intensifying throughout the delta, which was unexpected in that we were approaching the Tet holiday.

On 20 January, we conducted an operation into our favorite area, Quan Phu. We did not do well. We had three companies and made contact early in the morning; we fought most of the day, resulting in 2 friendly KIAs and 11 wounded. We lost one radio and six weapons. We were under fire constantly for about four hours. I injured my left hand when a spent tracer round from a VC automatic weapon grazed the back of my hand, leaving a burn. Wow! That was close! Sergeant Johnson rescued our radio man by dragging him from a fire swept area. I planned to recommend him for an award for valor. All in all, it was not a good day.

Four days later, 474 Company ambushed a VC unit, killed 15 and captured a 60mm mortar and seven small arms, a much better day. Cha La was attacked on the 25 January and had seven wounded. Cai

Nuoc was mortared the same night. Then as expected, VC activity fell off as Tet approached. We were informed that the 48-hour ceasefire would commence at 0100 hours, 30 January. Our normal patrols and intelligence sources reported little or no VC movement. Reported but not confirmed was that a VC platoon was in Midway, one was in Cai Doi Vam, and two were seen near Quan Phu, all in for Tet. Some Company Commanders said that VC units seemed to be gone. At the time we didn't know why. We would later.

CHAPTER 25

TET 1968

YEAR OF THE MONKEY

On 30 January 1968, at 0945, we received word that the cease fire was canceled. Saigon was being shelled, and major attacks were being reported throughout the country. We went on an alert status after we heard that Ca Mau came under a ground attack at 0500 hours and had lost the airfield. Reportedly, Can Tho and eight province capitals in the delta were attacked. In addition to Ca Mau, the VC attacked the District towns of Toi Binh, Dom Doi, Song Ong Doc, Quan Long, and the hamlets of Cai Keo and Tom Ton Bi. By the morning of 1 February, Ca Mau had evacuated 40 wounded and the airfield was still under enemy control.

District towns of Cai Nuoc and Nam Can, as well as Hai Yen, surprisingly had not had any enemy contact yet. Both Cai Nuoc and Nan Cam had recently been frequent VC targets. Our 471 Company made contact with a VC unit of unknown strength that was supported by artillery. Contact was broken by the enemy. It was thought that they had a mission elsewhere and could not become engaged with our units. Intelligence indicated that five VC company-size units from our area left to support the attack on the province capital. Ca Mau claimed to have killed over 200 VC by then.

Fragmented reports kept coming in from all over concerning the fighting. Thirty-six of the 44 province capitals, 5 of 6 of the autonomous cities, and 64 of the 242 district towns were attacked. Within the province, the VC launched ground attacks on 2 February against Song Ong Doc and Tom Ton Bi. By 3 February, Ca Mau had had three ground attacks in three days. Headquarters MACV claimed that 13,000 VC had been killed throughout the country. Five to seven hundred VC were still holding out in the Cho Lon area of Saigon. It was believed that the VC Tet Offensive had run out of steam.

Then on 5 February, 100 mortar and artillery rounds were fired into Ca Mau, and the towns of Dom Doi, Dong Cung, and Cai Nuoc were attacked. On the seventh, Ca Mau was still receiving some occasional mortar fire and Cai Nuoc was attacked, resulting in 4 KIA and 12 wounded. Cai Nuoc and Dom Doi were both attacked the next day. We believed that an attack on Hai Yen was imminent. Two days later, elements of 475 Company were trapped by a VC force with at least three BARS and several M79s. I accompanied the relief column and we were able to rout the VC, resulting in the wounding of two of our men. Six VC were killed and we believed eight wounded. We did capture one rifle and a sub-machine gun. Determining the number of enemy KIA was easy--just count the bodies–but enemy wounded was more difficult. An enemy may be seen going down in an exchange of fire, but then no body would be found. Sometimes a VC could be seen limping off, being carried or assisted, and blood stains or trails were often seen, verifying that there were wounded.

The district town of Cai Nuoc was attacked twice in the next two days, continuing the loss of men and the destruction of the town. The Province Chief finally took action to maintain a government presence in the area. Nam Can District, the southernmost one, was already reduced to a military outpost with no government functions being carried out. This left Cai Nuoc as the southernmost seat of government in the province and the country. The District Chief of Cai Nuoc was ordered to move his headquarters--military and civil, with all personnel and equipment--to the hamlet of Dong Cung on the north side of Song Bay Hop and to establish that site as the new Cai Nuoc District Headquarters. This was the second movement of the District Headquarters.

Dong Cung was nine kilometers directly south of the soon-to-be-old Cai Nuoc. It sat astride the long destroyed Provincial Road LTL 12. The population of the hamlet ranged somewhere between 400 and 450, with one PF Platoon assigned for local security. There was a single street along the river, with a row of buildings on each side. The south side backed up to the river's edge, and there was a dock for river boats and the fishermen. There was no electric power. A wood-planked iron bridge spanned the river and continued the road to Nam Can, which was mainly a foot path. The Song Bay Hop was the border between the districts.

The government forces in Nam Can were evacuated, and the existing structures and fortifications destroyed. The RF Companies were redeployed, with one assigned to Dong Cung. There were three companies at Cai Nuoc: two moved to Dong Cung and the remaining one stayed in Cai Nuoc, which was to be known as Cai Nuoc Outpost. Dong Cung was now the official Cai Nuoc District Headquarters.

Although not directly involved in the Province's reorganization of government control and troop dispositions, I was keenly interested in the changes. Even though I was the Senior Advisor for the Special Sub-Sector of Hai Yen, officially I was the District Senior Advisor to Cai Nuoc District. I had never been to the District Town and had seen it from the air only. I had not met the District Chief but was still expected to know the status of the District's military and civil endeavors. I had always thought that I would someday move the Team to the District Town, but now with the increased VC control in the Province that seemed very unlikely. There were six district towns in An Xyuen: one, Nam Can, had been abandoned; another, Cai Nuoc, was forced to relocate; and a third, Dom Doi, upstream on the Song Bay Hop from Dong Cung, was only holding on by their fingertips. The possibility of my team ever reaching our designated location appeared to be remote.

CHAPTER 26

AFTER THE STORM

Normal military tactics dictate that after a major attack or assault, the battle goes into a lull. Opposing forces consolidate their gains or losses and either reinforce and re-supply for continuation of the attack or strengthen their defenses as necessitated by their position on the battlefield. By the end of February, most of the areas, towns, and cities taken in the NVA/VC assault were regained by government forces. Battles continued throughout the country and our province, but the enemy offensive had run its course. What was initially thought to be a major victory for the enemy turned out to be a significant defeat. The expectation of a major civil uprising against the government did not happen.

However, the loss and destruction of government assets was tremendous. Many cities and towns suffered major damage. Attacks on airfields and road bridges hampered the re-supply and movement of troops. Priority went to those units and areas hardest hit. Shortages of various classes of ammunition were critical. Sufficient air support became a problem. Routine flight schedules were scrapped as U.S., Allied, and Vietnamese Air Forces scrambled to meet the immediate needs of the ground troops. The normally scheduled flights to and from Ca Mau and the province were disrupted. Combat air support continued at a normal level, but supply and administrative requirements were drastically reduced. In my small corner of the country, it was 26 days before we saw the Otter, though Ca Mau did send in critical items by chopper or the FAC in their 01 aircraft.

Despite the shortage of air transport, there were two arrivals of note. Father Hoa returned via a IV Corps Headquarters' chopper to be with the Chinese; and an Air Force Medical Technician was sent from the Province to our team for duty. The Air Force medic was classified as a Rural Medical Technician. His name was Moats, was 21 years old, and an Airman 1st Class. He had received some excellent training and was excited to be in the field. There was one drawback. I was instructed that I could not take him on operations and that he was limited to duties in camp only. He was assigned to the Air Force medical team that advised and supported the Province Hospital. Apparently they were overstaffed (hard to believe) and were offering him up to one of the District Teams. I don't know who decided that he was to be assigned to us, but I was glad to get him.

Because of heavy fighting, carbine ammunition came to be in short supply throughout the country, including in Hai Yen. The M1 Garand and the M2 carbine, both of WWII and Korea War vintages, were the rifles being issued to the Vietnamese and local troops. U.S. soldiers were armed in most cases with the new M16, though some units still had the M14 with which they had deployed from the U.S. The M2 carbine was the weapon of choice of most of the Vietnamese troops because of the light weight of the rifle and ammunition. The M1 Garand was heavy and awkward for the small Vietnamese soldier.

Just as I became concerned that the shortage of ammunition might affect our offensive operations, I was made aware once again that there was much that I did not know about in Hai Yen. When I broached the subject with my counterpart, I was told that the Chinese had 60 .45 caliber Thompson Sub-Machine Guns that were going to be issued to alleviate some of the need for carbine ammunition. They had a large stock of .45 caliber ammunition on hand. The sub-machines had originally been given to them by the CIA and had been stored away by Father Hoa. The Thompson Sub-machine gun and the ammo are very heavy. They were now issued to those soldiers who normally manned the walls, security points, and conducted ambushes that were mainly static. Their carbines were then reissued to the troops conducting operations in the rice paddies and jungle. This exchange of weapons actually increased the lethality of the camp defense, as the .45 caliber round was much more deadly than the light .30 caliber carbine round.

February was drawing to a close, and I was completing five months in-country. Throughout many parts of Vietnam, ARVN, U.S., and other Free World Forces were aggressively pursuing the shattered Viet Cong and North Vietnamese units that were withdrawing to reorganize after the significant losses they experienced during their Tet Offensive. In other areas like An Xuyen Province, which had only a small number of friendly forces, contact with the enemy reverted back to platoon- and company-sized meeting engagements, ambushes, raids, and enemy mortar/ artillery attacks on outposts and district towns.

Two significant events ended the month in Hai Yen. First, 475 company raided a VC camp south of Cai Doi Vam, killing 15 and capturing 10 weapons. The unit had one friendly killed. Second, 73 families moved out of the VC-controlled Cai Bot area to the hamlet of Kinh Moi, which was basically under government control. The planned move took two days and was secured by two companies of RF troops. I contacted the Refugee Control and Agriculture Advisors on the Province Team and asked them to get the refugees some support from the government. They were quite excited, as there had been little movement of civilians to government-controlled areas within the province. Within days, Vietnamese officials and U.S. Advisors arrived with building supplies, seeds for planting, tools, cooking oil, rice, and money. Hai Yen provided a platoon of PF soldiers for security, as we were sure that the VC would attempt to lure or force the civilians back to Cai Bot.

I made several trips to the hamlet to note the progress of settling in. I took Moats with me, as I did not consider it a combat operation but one of nation building. He was more than glad to get out into the countryside. This was the first movement of civil population from the Cai Bot area, and I took this as a sign of discontent and pressed my

158

counterpart to conduct operations into the Cai Bot area. On 1 March, the Otter arrived with a case of meat, some canned vegetables, and Cokes but no mail. Everyone was disappointed. In the next two days, we received reports of a new VC unit with mortars arriving in the Quan Phu area. It did not generate a great deal of concern, as reports of enemy unit movement in that area were frequent and not unusual. However the presence of additional mortars was of concern. The next night, the outpost at Nga Ba Dinh received 15 rounds of 60 mm mortar fire.

CHAPTER 27

CA MAU AGAIN

Ca Mau was attacked again at 0330 hours, 5 March. Approximately 500 rounds of mortar, rocket, and artillery fire were poured into the city. Fifty rounds hit in or near the MACV Compound. The U.S. Air Force Radar Installation, POL (Petroleum, Oil, Lubricants), and Ammo Dumps were destroyed. The Province Air Field and Hospital were captured. Two planes were destroyed on the ground and two helicopters were shot down. Two U.S. advisors were wounded, and ARVN and civilian casualties were heavy. An F100 jet fighter was shot down over Ca Mau after day light.

The VC attacked the city from three directions: One column astride the one road connecting Ca Mau with Bac Lieu Province to the east, one from the northwest through the Province RF Training Center, and the third from the west, attacking straight into the center of the city. There was no report of major attacks on other Province Capitals in IV Corps. It did not seem to be a general offensive as was the Tet Offensive. Perhaps it was a demonstration by the VC that they were capable of further attacks despite the heavy losses they sustained just a few weeks ago. Province RF units and the 31st Regiment, 21st ARVN Division, which was assigned to An Xyuen Province reacted aggressively, containing the enemy and denying them the majority of the city. Due to less enemy activity elsewhere in the Delta, support by both U.S. and ARVN air assets did everything the Province Advisors asked. In one instance, a flight of VNAF A1Es caught a VC formation attacking across open fields in the direction of the Province Operations Center and the MACV compound. The assaulting force was almost completely eliminated. Reportedly more than 100 bodies were found in the area of attack.

By day's end, the assault had stalled. Remnants of decimated units began withdrawing, with the exception of a small number of enemy who had taken up positions near the center of the city and were continuing the battle. The PRU (Province Reconnaissance Unit, made up of hired soldiers and led by CIA Advisors) were going house by house trying to eliminate or capture the entrenched enemy.

The only other enemy group continuing to hold out was the one that had captured the hospital early in the attack. The hospital was taken by the column entering Ca Mau from the east. It was later determined that VC medical personnel were among the attacking force and had the mission of removing all medical equipment, drugs, and supplies. The building was found to be stripped of anything connected to medical care. The removal must have taken longer than expected, as later in the day friendly troops were able to surround the hospital with the VC still inside. They would not surrender and were killed to the last man.

Mopping-up operations continued during the next few days as VC soldiers in ones and twos were captured or killed throughout the area. Some that proved difficult to find had reverted to or were instructed to hide out and act as snipers. Planes and helicopters taking off from our small air strip came under rifle fire for several days before the VC snipers were eliminated.

When assessing the aftermath of the battle, it was determined that the core of the attacking force was the U Minh 2 and U Minh 10 Main Force Battalions, supported by Local Force companies and village guerrilla squads. The initial attack seemed to have been well planned and executed. However, by mid-morning the enemy assaults had slowed, possibly because of friendly supporting fires. In addition, many of the VC Local Force troops may have never been exposed to the amount of fire support by air that was available. A constant stream of rocket, machine gun fire, and bombs would have been terrifying for

161

those who had not come under that level of fire from above before. Communications between the assaulting columns may have been lacking. Radios could have been in short supply. Reaction to government forces was slow, perhaps due to lack of critical on-the-spot orders. The VC supported the attack with artillery, mortar, and recoilless rifle fire. It appeared that their fires, however, were not as effective as they could have been. Capture by friendly forces found artillery and mortars on one side of the city and stocks of ammunition for them on the other side. This indicated that civilians pressed into service as porters carried ammunition for supporting weapons to the wrong locations! This certainly reduced their ability to support the attacking units.

The damage to the Ca Mau was extensive. The hospital was lost. A villa used as the Headquarters for the 31st Regiment was largely destroyed. Many of the Province government buildings were damaged. The MACV Team received several rounds inside the compound. The two U.S. soldiers who were wounded--the Mess Sergeant and the other the Mail Clerk--were both non-combatants but essential. The USAF Radar Installation was so badly damaged that the Air Force Radar Unit packed up and returned to the Philippines. Their mission of vectoring aircraft was subsequently performed by a Coast Guard Cutter lying out in the Gulf of Thailand.

Buildings were soon repaired, however, in a few days it was difficult to determine the damage from the attack. Intelligence indicated that the VC units from nearby Districts--mainly Quan Long and An Doc--were used in the attack. VC troops from the more distant Districts carried on their normal activities during the attack on Ca Mau but reportedly were directed to be ready to lend support if it was successful and Ca Mau was taken.

I had the opportunity to see firsthand the results of the battle a few days later. I had been summoned to the Province Team

Headquarters to report on Major Nuoc. I had about an hour discussion with Lt. Cols. Gilland and Culpepper. Major Nuoc had been under scrutiny by the Province Chief for some time. I told them that he was disliked by the Chinese, rarely went on military operations, and that I suspected he was collecting his own "taxes" from the villages. I was informed that Cpt. Thinh was to be promoted and assigned as Commander. When asked, I stated that I wholeheartedly supported the proposed change. Thinh was aggressive, it was easy to discuss problems and courses on action with him, and the troops seemed, although it is difficult to tell at times, to like him. Lieutenant Colonel Gilland said he would recommend the change to the Province Chief, who had asked him for his opinion. Apparently it was already a done deal. The Province Chief was just going through the formality of consulting his US Military Advisor! After a short discussion on other matters and a visit to some of the staff, I was returned to Hai Yen via a FAC the same day. I briefed the team on the impending change and warned them to keep it close hold until we were told by Major Nuoc.

A few days later, Major Nuoc stated that he was being reassigned and that Captain Thinh was to be promoted and take command. I expressed my "sorrow" to see him leave and thanked him for his cooperation and support of my team. A Change of Command Ceremony was conducted, with all the troops assigned in Hai Yen mustered in formation. It was the first time I had seen that many of the soldiers at one time since I arrived. They were mostly in full uniform and flew the RVN and Sea Swallow flags. Major Nuoc departed that same day on the Otter. I felt that a new era had begun.

CHAPTER 28

A NEW DAY DAWNING

I quickly arranged a meeting with Major Thinh to congratulate him on his promotion and assignment as the Commander of Hai Yen, and to discuss his plans and strategy for the destruction of the local VC. During previous talks, he had stated that he was unhappy with the lack of offensive operations into areas that were strongly contested by the enemy. He thought too many of company-size operations were "walks in the sun." I took this opportunity to push for an operation into the Cai Bot area. It appeared to be one of the two VC strongholds in our AO, the other being Quan Phu. We had conducted several multi-company operations and numerous company size reconnaissance and combat patrols on the latter.

There were also a number of small settlements and hamlets where government forces rarely visited. They were generally on the periphery or borders of our responsibility and under VC control. Occasionally we had civilians from these areas come to Hai Yen, mostly for medical reasons, the results of combat and disease. They were mainly women with children. They were treated by the RF and our two medics, Sgt. Bailey and Airman Moats. An added benefit for us was the information on VC activities we gleaned from the patients. Major Thinh agreed that we needed to show the flag in these seldom visited communities and to begin a series of operations into Cai Bot.

First order of business for Major Thinh as the new commander was to review the overall conduct of the military efforts of the troops, both those at Hai Yen and those in the outposts. In the time already spent as deputy, he had been able to assess the various strengths and weaknesses of the defensive conditions of HaiYen and the outposts, the leadership of the company commanders, and the ability of the troops. He quickly called a command and staff meeting, where he established

164

his immediate priorities. Number one, keep up patrolling and ambushes; two, repair camp and outpost defenses, i.e., rebuild walls, clean out ditches, reset mines, clear fields of fire, and reinforce bunkers; and three, to prepare for sustained operations. He gave the commanders two weeks to accomplish these tasks. He set dates when he would review the troops in all locations except Nga Ba Dinh, which was almost impossible to reach except by air.

Major Thinh was concerned about how many troops were actually available. He used the same four categories of availability as I had when I arrived--the number of troops authorized, the number assigned, the number present for duty, and the number available for operations. Soldiers that had been on patrols and /or night ambushes were generally not available for a following day operation. At times, however, they were part of the defending force left to guard the home camp. Normally, the PF platoons in Hai Yen were left as camp security and the platoons in the outposts were not deployed on operations. As a result, 300 soldiers were about the most that could be mustered for an operation longer than one day. I had doubts about the number of troops available when I first arrived but found that Major Thinh's count was about the same and fairly accurate.

During this shake down or reorientation of efforts Thinh and I conferred several times on an operation into Cai Bot. Thinh picked a date two weeks off to allow adequate preparation for a three-day attack on the Cai Bot VC stronghold. Time would also be spent on gathering intelligence by recon patrols, interrogating suspected VC captives, and talking to various civilians, including Village and Hamlet Chiefs and local Cal Dai and Buddhist priests. It was expected that the VC would know we were up to something other than normal. As for information, the whole area was like a sieve, with VC seemingly always knowing our movements. No Vietnamese were allowed in Hai Yen after dark unless they were a soldier, but Hai Yen, the outposts, and Village offices were always being watched. Any movement or event was

165

reported to VC military or political leadership. Another facet we had to consider was that the enemy might disperse and not become engaged, or might attack one of our positions e.g., Nga Ba Dinh, the village of Tan Hung Tay, or perhaps even Dong Cung, the new Cai Nuoc District Headquarters.

I informed Lt. Col. Gilland of our planned operation and asked for priority on VRs and air support during the operation. He promised all the support that he could muster when requested. Now, all we could do was wait.

CHAPTER 29

CAI BOT

In order to set the stage for this operation, I need to give a detailed description and recent history of Cai Bot since Father Hoa and his people established the settlement of Hai Yen. The area is identified on the map as Xom Cai Bot (Cai Bot Settlement) and generally referred to by U.S. advisors as Cai Bot Lake because of its proximity to a body of water approximately 2 kilometers long and 250 to 300 meters wide. Fourteen manmade or natural streams flow in or out of the lake in all directions. It lies about six kilometers southeast of Hai Yen and five kilometers north of the Song Bay Hop, which empties into the Gulf of Thailand. A stream, the Rach Trai Cheo, meanders from the southernmost end of the lake to the river, while from the eastern edge of the settlement a manmade canal flows directly south to the river, terminating less than a kilometer from the Rach Trai Cheo.

The settlement was the remnants of one or perhaps two copra plantations. Once operated by French or elite Vietnamese land owners, the plantations were seized by the VC in the late 1950s. Coconut groves, comprising an area of two to three square kilometers, bordered the minor streams on the east side of the lake. The coconuts were harvested and the dried copra shipped out to market via the canals, the Song Bay Hop, and out to the Gulf of Thailand. The majority of the civilian population lived on the east side of the lake and had worked on the plantations. Others were fishermen and rice farmers who lived along all the waterways, with most along the canal between Cai Bot and the river.

Plantation buildings had been generally destroyed with the VC, and some farmers were occupying the ones remaining. Recognizing the remoteness from government control and access to the open seas via the Song Bay Hop, the area developed into one of two VC base areas,

167

the other being Quan Phu six kilometers to the north. By 1963 the VC were well organized politically and militarily. Defended by approximately 400 guerrillas, they provided supplies, manpower, and safe havens for main force units.

Hai Yen forces had fought in the area on a number of occasions. The most notable victory was on the 3rd of January, 1961, when a combat patrol of 90 soldiers was ambushed by a force of 400 VC, kicking off a three-day battle resulting in 172 enemy killed and the loss of 27 Hai Yen Chinese. There were a number of squad, platoon, and company-sized skirmishes and meeting engagements subsequent to the January1961 battle, but never an assault on Cai Bot. Recon patrols on the west side of the lake continued, and a U.S. SF Team member was captured in the area in August 1966. The most recent activity consisted mainly of both daylight and night-time bombing based on intelligence received from patrols and civilians.

Thieu-ta (Major) Thinh and his staff were busy preparing the Operations Order (Ops order), following the normal sequence of Enemy Forces, Friendly Forces, Weather, Terrain, and Mission paragraphs.. Frequent contact and local developed intelligence indicated that the enemy could be as much as battalion sized-plus in strength. Friendly forces were what we could safely muster, considering the protection of Hai Yen, the outposts, and government controlled villages. We could expect no assistance from Province's forces for two reasons: first, Hai Yen was a Special Sub Sector and not under the operational control or responsibility of the Province Chief; second, there were so few troops in the Province that promising support that would also require air transportation was not an option. We were basically, as usual, on our own with the possibility of some Tac Air and medevac support through advisors' channels. Our supporting weapons consisted of light and medium mortars, machine guns, LAWs (Light Anti Tank Weapons) used for attacking bunkers, and support from our one and only artillery piece located in Hai Yen. We were entering into

168

the wet season, so we could expect higher water levels in the streams and canals. This would slow our movement and perhaps provide defensive barriers for the VC.

Our objective, to attack the VC stronghold, was affected by the terrain and the disposition and location of the enemy forces. The majority of the VC positions were expected to be centered on the long axis of the east side of Cai Bot Lake, which had been the settlement supporting the plantations. Houses were built with walls made of a mixture of mud and rice straw. The walls were three feet wide at the base, tapering to about 18 inches at the roof level. Many of the houses also had bunkers built inside for protection from bombing.

Instead of the normal line of houses bordering the water's edge, they were built in sets of three and spaced that any two could fire in defense of the third if under assault. The complete group of structures was enclosed by a semi-circular mud wall two meters high that started and ended at the water. A ditch excavated from building the wall resulted in a moat-like obstacle filled with coils of barbed wire, pungi (sharpened hardwood) stakes, and long slivers of split bamboo. The areas between houses and the edge of the lake or streams were bare, providing no cover or concealment. Strangely, the plantation buildings, which were sited further away from the lake toward and into the coconut groves, were not known to be fortified.

Across the lake on the west side--the direction that an attack was most likely to come from--was a line of houses with small piers. Although possibly not intended, this served as what was known in military language as a COPL (Combat Outpost Line). It was designed to engage an attacking force at long range, deny them observation of the defensive area, and cause them to deploy before they had intended. This line of houses was a double-edged sword for the VC, as it provided a first line of defense, but the lake and streams would impede the withdrawal of their troops to the main defensive positions. They

169

would need to cross by boat and could be under fire by the attacking force. Conversely, the lake presented a water barrier that could not be crossed by the attackers without some type of watercraft. The VC would surely remove all sampans from the west side. The houses, once abandoned by the VC, could provide some cover for the Hai Yen forces, but crossing the lake could be lethal.

Thinh was considering three options: attack east by southeast directly from Hai Yen to the center of Cai Bot Lake; move north and cross the streams feeding the lake and attack south along the lake; or move south then east, crossing the streams south of the lake and attack north with the left flank guiding on the lake. He and I studied the three avenues of approach closely. The middle route of advance passed through three to four kilometers of heavy swamp, impeding the rate of movement and ending up at the widest part of the lake. There were a number of small streams upon which we could switch back and forth, as we planned to use six Boston Whalers and some sampans to move the lead element and to evacuate our wounded if needed. (The remaining troops would be on foot as usual.) The southern route also ran through a deep swampy area and had less navigable streams. On the plus side, it appeared that we would need to cross only one stream flowing from the lake to circumvent the south end. Using the northern route, we could move two kilometers to the northeast, crossing over cultivated or once cultivated land to the Kinh Moi Canal, which ran from our Midway outpost on the Rach Cai Doi direct to the northern end of Cai Bot Lake. The canal was fully navigable and our boats could leave Hai Yen initially loaded with personnel and supplies and equipment, rendezvousing with the remaining troops at a point along the canal. The north side of the canal had some swamp areas but most of the south side bordered on rice paddies, permitting more rapid movement of the advancing soldiers.

Approximately three kilometers from the lake, the Kinh Moi canal was bisected by another, which then paralleled the Kinh Moi at a slight angle, terminating some 500 meters north of it at the lake. It appeared that the boats could proceed down the northern canal and cross the upper part of the lake, landing the troops on the east side. They would need to hold the area until the boats could return to the column, pick up a second lift, and reinforce the initial group. They then could be used to shuttle the remaining troops, who may by this time have arrived on foot to the western bank of the lake. Of course, this all depended on what resistance would be encountered in route.

The northern route appeared to be the best option. It got us to the objective the quickest, the troops would be less tired, the problem of crossing the lake and its tributaries was lessened, and we had a route of withdrawal and evacuation that we had a better chance of holding. Of course, there were many pitfalls that could shoot our plans down. The biggest concern was that attacking from this northern location would place the VC stronghold of Quan Pho five kilometers or less to the rear of our forces as we attacked south into the Cai Bot area. To offset the possibility of an attack on our rear, Thinh planned to order 474 Co. to send out a strong patrol from Cai Doi Ngon toward Quan Pho. This was designed to cause the enemy to consider that both areas may be under attack and therefore keep all their forces available to repel an attack on Quan Pho.

It was decided we would go the northern route with all the boats supplemented by some motorized sampans. An additional benefit from using the northern option was that troops often left Hai Yen in a northern direction to either visit Cai Doi Ngon or to move against the Quan Pho area. VC agents noting our movement of troops would not likely interpret our movement as an attack on Cai Bot until it was too late.

It may seem to the casual reader that a great deal of planning went into conducting what in the scheme of the whole war was a really minor event in a small corner of the country. But you must remember

171

what was stated earlier: there were no reinforcements, little ground-supporting fires, and no possibility of a reserve without placing Hai Yen, the outposts, and government-held settlements in jeopardy. First and foremost, the Command had to live to fight another day. After all, the troops were mostly exiles from Communist China trying to carve out a new home in a communist-dominated environment. In my future tour in RVN in 1971, this operation would be facilitated with helicopters for air assault.

The die was cast. Thieu-ta Thinh ordered that plans be prepared for the operation to jump off at first light three days hence. In that we had not yet received a replacement for Captain Bates, I planned to leave Brown to staff our Team HQs and radios, with Bailey and Moats assisting with the expected causalities arriving at the hospital. Johnson, Phong, Cao, and I would accompany the command group. The operation was to be three days in length. Thinh was concerned that any longer could give the VC an opportunity to gather some forces and attack one of our positions from where we had drawn troops for the operation. So it was to be a day to move to and attack, a day to consolidate our gains, and a day to destroy the enemy camp and withdraw.

Three days later at 0430 hours, the troops mustered. As usual, the team was up, having coffee, and making last minute checks of equipment prior to the mustering. Preparation for operations became routine, like anyone who prepares to go to work. The team could gage the intensity of the operation based on what arms the troops were carrying and the seriousness of their mood. We began moving out at 0500. Thinh and the command group accompanied the ground column. The Boston whalers were under the command of one of the staff officers and loaded with supplies, crew-served weapons, and ammunition that was not expected to be needed until we neared our objective. The whalers were to leave shortly after and join the column at the juncture of the two branches of the Kinh Moi canal. It was at this

172

point that some items would be off-loaded or transferred to sampans and soldiers loaded on the boats for the initial assault across the northern end of the lake. Two other actions were necessary. After the ground column reached the rendezvous point, they sent a platoon-sized unit toward the lake to secure the canal for uninterrupted use. At that point, the boat crews must be ready to ferry the follow-up troops and supplies to the far side of the lake and evacuate any wounded.

We reached the canal without incident and crossed the southern or right branch by a foot bridge (one log) located a few meters below the canal junction and near several houses. A quick search of the houses revealed only women and children, an indication that the male inhabitants were VC or civilians afraid of the VC. In either case, we could be sure the enemy would hear that government forces were up to something. We could hear faintly the throb of outboard motors, and shortly thereafter the first two of the Boston whalers came into view. These two boats each had a .30 caliber machine gun mounted on a makeshift tripod in the bow. They were followed by two more and four sampans. We were one boat short.

"Where is the other boat?"

"The motor would not start," replied the Trung-uy (1st Lieutenant), the officer in charge of our small flotilla.

I was afraid this would happen, as the outboards were known to be cantankerous and hard to start. Two of the sampans were large enough to carry six or seven soldiers each and now must be used to move the troops. The advance guard moved out on foot down the canal on the right bank. I suggested to Major Thinh that perhaps we should have a squad on each bank, but he smiled and shook his head no. The two mortars were off-loaded and set up so as to cover the advance guard if necessary. I radioed the Province TOC and requested a Shotgun for recon and observation over the area of operation. One

173

would be on site in an hour, I was promised. The troops for the initial wave, if you can call four whalers a wave, were either in the boats or sitting on the bank alongside them. We now waited to hear from the advance party on what they were finding.

The NCO in command of the advance party reported every few minutes on their progress. They were not meeting anyone; the houses they passed were empty except for old women and children. What appeared to be some adult males were seen running in the direction of the lake, but no resistance was encountered. Approximately 1,500 meters from the lake, the houses ended and on both sides of the canal the terrain turned from rice patties to swamp with heavy foliage.

From this point, the canal widened to a 100 or more meters and continued at that width until it reached the lake. On the north side, the canal branched off to the northwest. Troops moving down that side of the canal would have had to ford the branch, also about 100 meters wide, to reach the lake. Thinh had taken the chance of leaving the north side open rather than having troops face what would be a water barrier to cross before reaching the lake. A few shots were heard, and three or four men with weapons were seen running toward the lake. Then the Trung-si (Sergeant) commanding the advance party radioed that they had reached the edge of the lake and could see no activity on the other side. The order was given to load, and those men that were still on the canal bank scrambled into the boats.

Thinh had already decided to across with the first group even though I had recommended that he wait and cross with the second wave. It would mean a delay of only 20 or 30 minutes and give him the chance to react to any situation without being pinned down on the opposite bank.

He responded, "I must lead."

I said, "OK," and, followed by Phong, climbed aboard. Johnson, Cao, and the radio man stayed back and would follow in the next group. In case something went wrong in the first wave, there was no sense in having all our eggs in one basket.

We moved down the canal two by two, with the two boats that had machine guns mounted leading. As we approached the far bank of the lake, the machine gunners swept it with fire. We slammed into it at a greater speed than I expected and I was almost jolted over the side but slid into the water and climbed out on the bank. Everyone was out of the boats in a matter of seconds. The boats were backing off from the bank and turning back toward the canal. We moved a few meters away from the bank and went to ground in a semi-circle. Including Phong and myself there were 25 of us. Now to wait for the second round of boats to bring us to about 50 more before we started moving to our right down the lake.

We were ashore in a grove of coconut trees, which appeared to reach 100 to 150 meters to the east away from the lake, ending at what appeared to be uncultivated rice paddies. The coconut trees also stretched for over a kilometer south along the lake, the direction that we intended to move. They were cut by four or more canals flowing into the lake. There were some structures and houses expected along these streams. In almost the center of the groves and 800 meters to a kilometer from the lake were the remnants of the plantation house and complimenting buildings. It was believed that the core of the VC fortifications as described previously lay along the largest one of the canals. That was our objective.

We had not received any fire nor seen anyone, so Major Thinh ordered a few men to scout ahead for a hundred meters or so into the coconut groves. The trees had been planted many years ago in rows and had not been tended since the landowners had been driven out. There were irrigation ditches between every other row that were now filled

175

with growth and debris. Under the trees, dead limbs and undergrowth limited visibility and made movement difficult. Mud bridges had been built to cross the ditches along paths that appeared to be in frequent use. Normally such routes of movement could be expected to be mined, booby-trapped, or used as firing tunnels.

The second contingent of troops had joined us, and the remaining would soon follow. In that no difficulty was experienced in crossing the lake, the sampans were pressed into service, and we could expect to have 125 to 130 soldiers on the east side of the lake within the hour. The order was given to move out in three columns separated by 50 meters each. The right-hand column would guide on the lake's bank; the left one put out a few men to the left to secure our movement from that flank. Johnson, the radio operator, and Cao had arrived on the east bank. I left Johnson there with Cao to hold the crossing site. We had an extra radio in one of the boats that he could use, so I took the radio man with me and joined Major Thinh near the head of the center column. We had moved only about 200 meters when we heard an explosion then several shots followed by a burst of small arms fire, then nothing. The radio crackled and the operator announced that a soldier on point in the center column had tripped a booby trap and was fired on by a single VC, who then ran. Fire was returned with unknown results. Forward movement now slowed down to a crawl as the leading troops became more cautious.

My radio came alive with a voice saying, "This is Shotgun One Five do you read me?"

"This is Oscar Six over," I replied.

"I think I am zero five from your area, can you hear or see me?"

"Yes, I can hear you."

"I see some troops and boats at the upper end of the lake."

"Yeah, that's where we crossed. Look down the lake in the coconut trees, we're in three columns."

"I have you, where is your lead element? I can't see it."

"I'll have the point pop smoke."

"Roger."

I relayed to Major Thinh my conversation with the Shotgun pilot and asked him to have the leading soldier to mark their position with a smoke grenade. A few moments later, Thinh said a red smoke grenade had been thrown.

"Shotgun One Five, smoke popped."

"OK, I see cherry smoke."

"Roger, red smoke."

"There is a canal running away from the lake, some of your guys have crossed, it is at the edge of the coconut groves."

"Yeah, I see it. We are coming up on it now," I replied.

"The overhead is pretty thick, I can't see much, there is a couple of hooches on the bank of the lake and several in a row along another canal three or four hundred meters ahead of you. Across that canal are more hooches, they look substantial."

"Roger, can you tell me if there are troops from our crossing site moving toward us?"

"Wait one, yes, about 30 or 40 are behind you and another bunch is following them, let me swing around back up front and see what's going on."

"Roger."

I turned to Major Thinh and told him what the pilot had reported. Thinh nodded and said that the second and third groups had now caught up with us and that the remaining soldiers were now all across on the east side of the lake. We now had 150 or 160 in the movement to contact mode .The boat operators, mortar crews, and a small reserve remained at the crossing site along with Johnson and Cao, who would accompany them if or when they were ordered to move.

"Oscar Six, Shotgun One Five, I see five or six bad guys I guess, running toward that first line of hooches."

"Roger, can you see anything else around the huts?"

"Yeah, the trees are pretty thick, but I think your guys are almost up on the second canal. The one with the first hooches, you are already across that small one without any structures."

"OK, One Five, how long can you stay with us?"

"About 30 or 35 minutes. I have four HE (high explosive) rockets on board that I would like to use before I have to leave."

"Roger. Maybe we can use them on the second line of huts if we don't have a problem with the first ones."

" That line or group of hooches seems to have a wall and a ditch."

"OK, we expected that. See any movement around them?"

"No, it's thick. I can't see the ground, only close to the hooches."

"Roger."

As I turned to brief Major Thinh on my conversation with the Shotgun pilot, there was a burst of gunfire and a couple of explosions to our front.

"M79s," stated Thinh.

Before he could say anything else, there were two louder explosions closer to us-- mortars, 60mm.

"Shotgun, we just got a couple of mortar rounds, can you see where they may be coming from?"

"Negative, I don't see any movement or what might be mortar positions."

The firing seemed to be increasing across the front, and one could distinguish an AK47 now and then, which was unusual. All three columns appeared to be taking fire and were deploying to a skirmish lime. Tieu-ta Thinh with his radioman squatting beside him was standing by a tree with the handset pressed to his ear and speaking rapidly, too fast, for me to understand what he was saying. I looked for Sgt. Cao and then remembered that I had left him with Johnson. I told my radio operator to have Johnson and Cao join me. Thinh had moved forward and I hurried to catch up with him; he turned to me and said that VC small arms fire all seemed to be coming from the first line of houses, and we had two more men hit. I noticed troops passing me from the rear and moving forward; evidently Thinh had ordered the second group to join the leading elements.

He continued toward the firing, and Phong and I followed. The underbrush between the coconut trees began to thin out, allowing us to see the line of houses to our front. The leading soldiers had gone to ground, and a steady but not heavy fire punctuated by the sound of M79 rounds was being directed toward the houses. I first thought they were well trained in fire discipline, but then realized that they were old experienced troops who were more worried about running out of ammo than fire discipline.

Thinh had moved to the forward edge of the line formed by the center column and was in a squat talking to two of his men, who then moved off to the right and left. He turned to me and said that as more men joined the ones engaged, he would increase the fire and have our mortars first fire on the houses and then behind and beyond them in the area bordering the next canal, where we expected the main VC force to be. When he moved the mortar fire, he would then order the assault on the houses. A few more soldiers could be seen running up from tree to tree and joining the ones already firing. Someone tapped me on the shoulder and I turned to see Sgts. Johnson and Cao right behind me. I briefed them as to the situation and told Cao to listen closely to the conversations between Major Thinh and his radio operator and to keep me up on what was said. Thinh would be very busy shortly and he would not have time to discuss with me what orders he had given or what reports he was receiving. I also told them to stick close to me when we moved out in the assault.

The VC fire seemed to be lessening. We were receiving some RPGs (Rocket Propelled Grenades) but little automatic weapons fire, and I had heard only one burst on our right. I wondered if they were pulling back across to the next canal to what we expected to be the main defensive position. The line of houses in front of us probably had

180

mud bunkers inside and other exits besides the front, which would allow them to fall back. We thought the canal between the first houses and the next could to be crossed by foot and not require boats.

I called Shotgun One Five. "Can you see any VC moving away from us across the canal, is there a foot bridge across it?"

"Oscar Six I am off to the flank keeping out of your mortar trajectory, let me look. No foot bridge that I can see or anybody moving. There are considerable trees there, though, and houses on the opposite side, too, then only two or three hundred meters to the next canal and hooches which look more substantial. I can fire my rockets on that first line of hooches if you want."

"No, I want to save them for what we think is the main position. If you have to leave before we get that far you can dump on them."

"Roger, standing by." Then, "Oscar Six, I do see three or four crossing the canal, are they yours?"

"Negative, they must to be bad guys, watch them and let me know where they go."

"Will do."

Cao was pulling on my arm and pointing to Major Thinh who was standing, waving his arm in a forward motion and speaking loudly into his handset. "Lien, lien, mau lien (up, up, hurry up)!" The troops started moving toward the houses in a ragged line, firing as they went. Enemy fire slacked then stopped. The troops began running.

"Oscar Six, there are about a dozen guys running from those first hooches and splashing across the canal right behind them! Watch

181

out, there are three hooches right on the bank on that side. Looks like that's where they are headed."

"OK"

"Oscar I must leave in zero five, what do you want me to do with my rockets?"

"Can you put them in those three houses? Are we too close?"

"No you're OK I'll dump these in two runs and then leave your AO."

"Roger, Shotgun, thanks for the help."

"My pleasure!"

I called out, "Major Thinh, Shotgun is going to hit those first houses with his rockets." Thinh nodded and spoke rapidly into his radio mike, and then gave me a thumbs-up gesture. He had warned his men to not cross the canal until the plane had finished firing and left the area. The bird dog made a sweeping turn, lined up on the houses, and fired off two of his four rockets.

"Major," Sgt. Johnson called, "the rockets missed. One hit between the huts and the other landed in the canal."

"OK, Shotgun can see that and adjust this time."

I was right; one of the second pair of rockets hit the last hut, but the other overshot and landed in some trees.

"Oscar Six, I'm leaving your AO, good luck and good hunting!"

"Thanks again ,Shotgun, for your help. Out here."

Major Thinh was urging his troops forward across the canal. He waved at me to join him. I splashed into the tepid water almost up to my waist, followed by Sgt. Johnson and the radio man. Phong had already crossed and was in a crouch with his back to me. There was some light small arms fire coming in from the direction of the third canal where the main VC position appeared to be located. I trotted over to the front of the centermost house where a small circle of four or five officers and NCOs were squatting with Major Thinh.

Thinh turned and said to me, "I move all soldiers here and form line. I move boats closer, to first canal, mortars, too."

"Then besides firing on the VC positions the mortars can fire beyond the other side," I observed.

"Yes," Thinh replied, "it is standard supporting-fire procedures." He was correct; indirect supporting fires i.e., mortars and artillery, are always used to destroy a fleeing enemy force and to interdict any reserves attempting to reinforce the units under attack.

"How about the 105? It's in range," I asked, referring to our one artillery piece back at Hai Yen. Thinh frowned, hesitated, and then said, "I use the 105 to cover withdrawal." I knew why he was reluctant to order artillery that would be close to the troops. His recent arrival and assumption of command had not permitted him to judge the ability of the artillery gun crew to provide close-in fires and did not want to take that risk unless it became absolutely necessary to do so.

"When mortars in new position, they will fire on VC camp, then we assault, first on the left then follow on the right." Again Major Thinh was correct in his evaluation of the situation. I could see why the attack would start on the left. If necessary, the attacking force had the

183

option to slide further to the left and attack the flank of the enemy. The right side was restricted by the lake. In a classroom study of tactics, the left would have been called the main attack and been weighted by more troops and supporting fires. The right would have been designated as the supporting attack, designed to tie down defending forces and prevent them from being used to repulse the main attack. Thinh's attack plan was a microcosm of the normal attack on a linear position. At first I was surprised but then remembered he had received his military officer's training in France. However, I was afraid that the VC position was a perimeter, the normal defense posture in Vietnam—that is, outposts, firebases, and base camps. We knew there was a wall, and now it appeared there was also an outer ditch, a moat. A wall with a ditch was pretty standard because of the isolation of military and government installations. I heard Bac-si (doctor) mentioned by one of the NCOs.

"What are our casualties?" I asked.

One killed, five wounded, I was told.

"How bad are the wounded?"

"Three stretcher, two walking wounded," Johnson chimed in.

"OK. Sgt. Johnson, call Province and request a medevac for this location. Tell them three pacs."

"Yes sir," said Johnson, as he beckoned for the radio man to hand him the mike.

I had noticed that a number of soldiers had now crossed the canal and taken positions along the line of houses. "Is that everyone?" I asked Major Thinh. "Do we still have a reserve?"

He pointed at our small command group and laughed. "We are the reserve! We now wait for the mortars to fire."

I knew it would take some time to get the mortars moved and set up to fire. We had brought two tubes, and once they were in position they would fire some single rounds while the troops furthest to the front would try to spot the round fired and give instructions by radio for adjustment. I expected the rounds to be long (fall beyond the target area) at first for safety reasons, and then be adjusted into the VC position. When they had the correct range, each mortar tube would fire multi-rounds while the troops tried to assault the position. The mortar fire would be lifted or shifted beyond the area just before the troops reached the VC fortifications in order to keep them down and from firing.

I looked across the area we would have to cross from our present position in the line of houses. It looked to be less than a hundred meters and had a few banana trees and some small shrubs. There was one building on this side of the canal that appeared to be much larger than the normal sized houses. Although the VC fire had lessened, I thought we were receiving some from that area. The canal did not appear to be more than six or eight meters wide with two foot bridges across it. I pointed them out to Thinh.

"We cross in the water, VC cover bridges."

"I hope it's not deep!"

Thinh just shrugged his shoulders. It then dawned on me that the canal was actually the moat or ditch created when building the wall. There was not anything else between the canal and their defensive position. We knew that once over the wall we would come under heavy fire. The houses were aligned so they could cover one another. I noted two soldiers with LAWs (Light Anti-Tank Weapons) moving up to the

185

front in the center. LAWS were frequently used for blowing holes in walls and bunkers. I pointed at them.

"When we go, they fire on that," Major Thinh said indicting the large structure on our side of the canal. "I have more LAWS for wall."

The mortars appeared to have zeroed in on the VC position, and there was an increase in explosions in front of us. I could see Major Thinh on the radio and men getting up and moving forward. Leaders were motioning the men to move and keep firing. Major Thinh dropped the radio handset and started off at a trot toward the left side. Sergeant Johnson and I with the rest of the command group followed. I heard a loud grunt and a sound as if someone had been slapped. I looked back to my left and saw a soldier down clutching his chest. Small arms fire was ripping by, most of it high. We were on the canal and in the water almost before I knew it. The water was a little less than waist deep. A number of soldiers were trying to climb out on the other side. There was a soldier holding his left arm with his right. A piece of bone was protruding out through the skin. He was huddling up to the canal bank trying to stay out of the line of fire.

I could hear a machine gun firing on our right and the sound of M79 rounds exploding on the other side of the wall. I looked back and saw the building that had been fired on with the LAWs was burning. I could also see a number of men still back by the line of houses that was our jumping-off point. I wondered, why are they waiting? A carbine fired a burst close to my right .I turned and saw Johnson firing at a VC on top of the bank, toppling him into the canal. Most of the men that had crossed the canal were now up against the wall. The mortar fire had all but ended. Thinh and his leaders were urging the men over the wall. Soldiers were pitching grenades over the wall then crawling up far enough to spray the other side without exposing themselves. A Lieutenant climbed up on top and jumped down on the other side.

186

Major Thinh followed yelling, "Lien, lien! (up, up)" Sergeant Johnson, Phong, and I scrambled up and over, falling into a shallow ditch.

I looked around, "Where is Sgt. Cao?" I asked. No one said anything.

"He didn't get hit, did he?"

"No, he there," said Phong, pointing behind us with his chin.

"I guess he will catch up," said Johnson.

I'll worry about that later, I thought.

In a crouch, I ran over to where Thinh was staring at the VC houses that were positioned to fire on the wall. I then realized that little fire was being received from the structures; most of the noise was from our troops.

"What's going on?" I asked.

A small group of soldiers on the left were approaching one fortified house, firing on it as they ran. Reaching it they entered.

A moment later, one stuck his head out and called, "No VC, gone!"

Troops then started advancing on the rest of the first row of houses. The bunkered houses were not in a line. They were staggered so as to allow the enemy in two to fire in defense of the third. There appeared to be other houses further back. The soldiers that did not attack in the first group now began to join us in the VC fortifications. The VC had pulled out! Or maybe, plan to hit us with mortar or artillery when we enter their abandoned positions. Major Thinh was

187

sending a couple of squad-sized groups ahead to reconnoiter the houses and bunkers further ahead. Our attack seemed to be in a lull, as some soldiers were sitting around resting while others were searching the houses and area. There were three wounded being treated off to the right side and what appeared to be one dead. I turned to Sgt. Johnson. "Check on that medevac."

He nodded as he keyed and spoke into the mike.

A few moments later he called out, "Major, Province says no ETA on our request. The medevac folks are backed up with missions and also they need gunships to come here."

I walked off in search of Major Thinh and found him behind one of the fortified houses giving orders to his subordinates.

He looked at me and said, "VC, gone, will not fight."

"Anything from the squads you sent out?" I asked.

"Nothing yet," Thinh replied.

I walked over to where Sgt. Johnson, Cao, and Phong were standing in the shade of a tree. "It looks like the VC have broke and ran. They are not going to defend their base camp," I announced. "Maybe they are regrouping to counter-attack," Johnson ventured.

"I don't think so, at least not now. They may throw a few mortar rounds in. They certainly know our location, or might attack after dark."

"Major," Cao interrupted, "Major Thinh is bringing the boats up the lake close to us to load the wounded."

"Load the wounded?"

"Yes, sir, to return to Hai Yen. He thinks medevac will not come here."

"I'm afraid he is right. Sgt. Johnson, call Bailey and tell him some wounded are coming in to them. They may also have a medevac coming in their direction."

"Yes, sir."

I could hear the boats coming, "Come on, Phong, I'm going to where they are going to load the wounded."

I started over toward where the canal widened into the lake and saw a group of soldiers gathered there. As I approached the group, I could see the wounded being loaded into sampans. Major Thinh was standing there watching the loading.

"Why are you loading them in the sampans and not the boats?"

"Sanpans take wounded to Hai Yen and stay. They no come back. I keep boats to shuttle troops. Hold more and faster."

I looked around and counted. "Seven wounded?" I asked.

"No, we have nine wounded and two killed."

"Damn!"

A few shots sounded in the distance. "Patrol," announced Thinh, "perhaps see VC."

It was now 1530 hours and about three hours before dark.

189

"What are your plans now, dig in for the night?"

"We return to Hai Yen."

"But we were going to be on this operation for three days!"

"Enemy gone, scattered, cannot follow one, maybe two VC, must have unit as target."

He was right. We couldn't dissolve the force into small squads and fan out searching for the enemy in their own backyard. The possibility of multiple ambushes was certainly high. I knew it was over. Thinh would carry out the final stages of his plan, which was to carry off anything of value, destroy the base camp, buildings, boats, and anything that they didn't want or couldn't remove. The wounded and dead would be returned to Hai Yen. That had already begun. The remaining troops would be ferried back to the site on the Kinh Moi canal where they first loaded, and then return to Hai Yen on foot.

Destruction of the VC base had already started. Explosions could be heard as grenades and the LAWs were used to blow up bunkers. I saw a soldier dropping grenades down a well. The few small sampans found were tied to the Boston whalers to be towed back with the troops. No weapons were found, but an assortment of ammunition was loaded. I had no idea what the enemy losses might have been No bodies were found. Ladders and sheets of nylon attached to poles that were normally used to carry the dead and wounded were found in several houses. Blood trails and some bloody rags were evidence that there were wounded and perhaps some dead, but we would not know until later when civilians would tell what they had heard or knew.

The several squads sent out on patrol were now returning. One had a wounded soldier and one dead. They were hit by a burst of fire but never saw the VC that ambushed them. The priority of effort was

190

now departure. Troops crowded into the boats and the captured sampans. The turnaround time was much shorter than the movement to contact that morning. They were using the shorter southern branch of the canal from the lake to the juncture of Kinh Moi. Most of the soldiers were at the canal bank to load. A few were still in the VC base setting fire to the houses. They would be the last to board for the trip up the canal.

I beckoned Sgt. Johnson to join me. "Get on the horn and have them divert the medevac to Hai Yen. Tell them we are out of here. Then request a Sky Spot for tonight. I will send them the coordinates shortly."

"OK Major, I already diverted the medevac. I'll get on the Sky Spot."

"Thanks, Sergeant."

A Sky Spot was a night-bombing mission on an area where there was information indicating a concentration of enemy forces. When the intelligence was good, the bombing missions were very effective. It was my hope that the VC would return to the Cai Bot base that night. When I provided the coordinates of the base, I planned to request the strike for around 0400.

It was now about an hour before dark, and the last troops were loaded. Major Thinh, myself, and the command group climbed in the last two boats and started up the canal. If we went all the way by water and nothing unforeseen happened, we would arrive back in Hai Yen in an hour. If we were to disembark and go overland with those soldiers on foot, it would be approximately three hours. I breathed a sigh of relief when we continued on past the morning's rendezvous site. And so ended my much sought-after assault on the Cai Bot VC Base. Little damaged was inflicted on the enemy, and as I would find out the following day we had suffered 3 killed and 11 wounded, of which 5 were serious. In the big picture, these losses seemed minor. However, when you consider the difficulty in their replacement, especially the Chinese who came with Father Hoa, the loss becomes significant.

The Sky Spot I requested was approved, and at 0200 hours the following morning, six 500-lb. bombs were dropped on the Cai Bot VC Base. Damage would not be known until a daylight reconnaissance flight was flown over the area and reports filtered in from the local population.

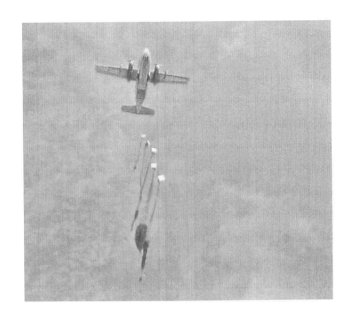

Above: Aerial drop of ammunition by a USAF C-123.

Below: The Team House during the wet season.

193

Above: Christmas Eve 1967, left to right: SGTs Johnson, Brown and Cao; in rear Bake and CPT Bates.

Below: Repairing bunker after VC mortar attack.

194

Above: A soldier's pet monkey killed by the author after it attacked a child.

Below: The author and his bodyguard Corporal First Class Phong.

195

Above: Crossing over one of the many "monkey bridges".

Below: Hai Yen troops assembled for operation into VC Quan Pho base area.

Above: Corporal Phong disarming a VC grenade trap on a path in Quan Pho.

Below: The author and the Operations Officer resting during a lull in an operation into the Quan Pho VC base area.

Above: Medics treating wounded for evacuation from Quan Pho to
Hai Yen by sampan.

Below: MEDIVAC chopper arriving to pick up wounded at Hai Yen.
Hospital in background.

PART II

CHAPTER 30

MOVEMENT TO CAI NUOC

While preparing an After Action Report to submit to the Province Team, I tried to evaluate the operation and decide if it was a failure or a success. Our objective was to attack and destroy the Cai Bot VC Base and eliminate the enemy forces occupying the area. So how did we do, I wondered? The planning was well done, and the initial execution went according to the plan. The reconnaissance, movement to contact, crossing the lake, and reinforcing the lead elements were conducted without incident. The troops performed well under fire and were generally responsive to orders. The enemy positions were as we expected, but the VC declined to defend the base. They retreated by what I am sure were preplanned routes laced with mines, booby traps, and multiple prepared ambush sites. Major Thinh decided not to pursue the scattered VC and declined to use his mortars because of the limited amounts of ammo on hand.

I advised him to use the 105 howitzer at Hai Yen to fire on possible areas the VC may have rallied to, but he did not feel he had enough information to do so. Some military supplies were captured and the camp was destroyed, but we did not eliminate the enemy force. Nevertheless, because it was the first operation into the Cai Bot area in many months and under a new commander, I considered it a plus for our side.

It was now nearing the end of April, and on the 27th I was ordered to Ca Mau to meet with Lt. Col. Gilland. An Army FAC picked me up in the morning, and upon arrival in Ca Mau I was greeted by Lt.

199

Col. Culpepper (the DPSA), with the announcement that there were two surprises awaiting me. One was that there was a replacement for my vacant deputy slot. The second and more important one was the decision to install an advisory team in Cai Nuoc.

Lieutenant Colonels Gilland and Culpepper and myself were to meet in the afternoon with the Province Chief to discuss the support and cooperation required to establish a U.S. team at the District Headquarters. It was now located at the hamlet of Dong Cung on the northern side of the Song Bay Hop, the dividing line between Cai Nuoc and Nam Can Districts. The recent abandonment of Nam Can left the District Headquarters of Cai Nuoc the southernmost government center in the province and the country. It was under VC attack almost daily, and the loss of it would result in two of the province's six districts being under almost complete enemy control. Hai Yen in the western half of the district would be the only area in Cai Nuoc with any government presence at all.

The meeting with the Province Chief went as we expected. He fully supported placing a team in Dong Cung but warned us that he could not spare any additional troops for Cai Nuoc. Presently assigned there were three RF companies (one was the remnants of a company originally from Hai Yen), a PF platoon, and a detachment of National Police.

The District Chief was an ARVN captain who had been there for two years. He had a small civil and military staff but had little control or influence over the district. The only means of reaching the District Headquarters was by air. Even though civilian boats traveled the river, they were stopped and taxed by the VC, who basically controlled the waterway. The Province Chief promised full cooperation from his staff and the District Chief and urged Lt. Col. Gilland to install the team as soon as possible.

We returned to the team compound to begin planning. We had to get our ducks in a row and present a plan to the Corps Senior Advisor to get his approval and support to place a team in Dong Cung, Cai Nuoc District. I wondered what had already had been discussed or decided. As Cai Nuoc was my original assignment when I arrived, I thought I should be involved in any efforts to place a team there. I had a number of questions and they were soon answered.

Lieutenant Colonel Culpepper, the S3 (Operations Officer), the S4 (Logistics Officer), and I joined Lt. Col. Gilland in his office and I asked my most pressing question: Who was going to Cai Nuoc? Was I going to move my team from Hai Yen to Cai Nuoc, or were they going to send in a new team?

"Neither." I was told. They wanted me to split my team and go into Cai Nuoc as soon as possible, and the Province Team would supply additional personnel later."

"Later, how much later?" I asked. "I'm short one officer now, my deputy."

"I know," Lt. Col. Gilland replied. "We have two officers and some NCOs due in. Matter of fact, your new deputy is here now and you can take back with you or we can keep him a couple of days so he can get oriented with the Province Team."

"Is he a captain?"

"No, he is a First Lieutenant, last assignment was Alaska. You can meet him before you leave today, but right now we must get on with this move. I would like you to split your team, take one or two with you at first, then if all goes well we will flesh you out. There is a captain due in a few days; he is in-processing in Saigon now. He will

201

be your replacement at Hai Yen."

"What about support? They are attacked almost daily."

"That's why you and I are going to go to the Corps this week to brief General Eckhart, the Corps Senior Advisor, and get his approval and assurance that we can get chopper and Tac Air support."

"That's a two slick with gunships area," I said. This meant the two unarmed helicopters would require gunships for protection in this area.

"I know that, Major, and that's why I want to brief the General personally, so his staff knows that he has blessed this move."

"Yes sir. When are we going?"

"If I can get on his calendar sometime this week, I want you to get with the S4 and work out what you think you will need to get set up."

"Yes sir," I replied as I started out of the office with the S4.

"One moment," called out Lt. Col. Gilland. "Introduce yourself to your new deputy before you leave. His name is Jim Harris. He will report down to you in a few days after he gets briefed here. I'll have someone to get you back to Hai Yen today."

"OK sir, will do."

On our way to the S4's office, we stopped by the mess hall for a cup of coffee where I noticed three civilians that I did not recognize.

"Who are those guys?" I asked the S4.

"Some news reporters, correspondents, or whatever you call them. One is Chinese. Want to meet them?"

"Yeah, why not, my troops are Chinese."

We walked over to the table where they were sitting and I greeted them. "Hi, I'm Major Dagenais, the Senior Advisor at Hai Yen," offering my hand.

"Hello, I am Carl Schoettler with the *Baltimore Evening Sun.* This is Mike Morrow, for *Black Star,* and Tekang Kai Yi with the *New China News* in Taipei, Taiwan."

"Hey, I'm from Maryland, Kent County, over on the shore! What are you three doing way down here in the Delta?"

"Well, we are kind of traveling together," Schoettler responded. "Yi wants to visit Father Hoa and his Chinese soldiers. I'm doing a column for the *Baltimore Evening Sun* and Mike is a freelance photographer."

"So I guess you want to visit Hai Yen," I said, addressing Yi. "You know you can only reach there by military air, don't you?"

"Yes, we found that out after we arrived this morning."

"Well, tell you what.There is a regular Otter flight down to Hai

Yen once or twice a week. If you can get yourselves on it, I will put you up for a couple of days or till the next available transport out. You need to remember, though, you are low priority. Mr. Schoettler, are you interested in interviewing me for your paper?" I queried.

"Please, call me Carl, and yes, I am indeed interested. I'm on a 120-day assignment reporting on Marylanders in Vietnam and would like to talk with you on your experiences as an advisor in Hai Yen."

Turning back to the reporter Yi, I informed him, "You know Father Hoa is not here, don't you? He is in Cho Lon."

"Yes," Yi replied. "I tried to see him there but he was traveling."

"Well, you are welcome to visit my team if you can get down to us, but you need to contact the Chinese troops to be sure you would be welcome."

"I have spoken with Mr. Niep, Father Hoa's brother," Yi responded, "and he has extended me a welcome."

"Good, then perhaps I will see you in Hai Yen," I said as I shook hands all around and continued with the S4 to his office.

As there would only be two or three of us at Cai Nuoc initially, I listed a few items that I knew we would need to survive. These included rations, a stove and fuel for it, cots, a gas lantern, radio batteries, toilet paper, and insect repellant. I planned on taking a PRC 25 radio from Hai Yen with me, and asked the S4 to replace it. We would take our individual weapons and ammunition. The Province

204

A&L (Administration and Logistics) Company supported the District with military needs, but at this time I did not know if there were any problems or shortages of supplies or ammunition in Cai Nuoc. I would have to ascertain that once I was there. I needed to make a ground reconnaissance and meet with the District Chief and to do that as soon as possible.

I left the S4 Officer and sought the S3 Operations Officer who managed the air assets within the province to arrange a flight in and out of Cai Nuoc. I was told that Lt. Col. Gilland had already directed him to schedule a flight to pick me up at Hai Yen and drop me off in Cai Nuoc for about two hours, and that he was working on it. I then asked if my new deputy was around and was told he was out with another officer visiting the Quan Long District Team, the only team accessible by ground. Oh well, I thought, I will see him when he arrives in Hai Yen.

I returned to Hai Yen by a FAC in the afternoon and briefed the team on what was going to happen. I selected Sgt. Johnson to accompany me to Cai Nuoc. Sergeant Brown would be in charge until an officer was assigned. I expected Lt. Harris to be present before the move to Cai Nuoc, but Brown would have to manage the team until Harris got acclimated to his new responsibilities.

My next tasks were to meet with Major Thinh and brief him on my move to Cai Nuoc, prepare to brief Major General Eckhart, visit Cai Nuoc and meet the District Chief, check out where we would physically need to set up the team, and look at the defensive posture of the hamlet. Dong Cung, or Cai Nuoc[1] as it is now known, had been attacked more than 40 times since Tet, mostly with mortar or artillery

205

fire and a few small night ground attacks. It appeared obvious that after the abandonment of Nam Can, the VC were intent on driving the government forces out of Cai Nuoc District.

The following morning I met with Major Thinh and informed him of the move to Dong Cung. He did not seem surprised, and I suspected that he had already heard of the intended move from the Province Headquarters. I told him that I planned to take only Sgt. Johnson with me and that I would leave Phong, my body guard, and Sgt. Cao with the team at Hai Yen. Corps would provide me an interpreter to replace Sgt. Cao. I also told Major Thinh that a replacement for my Deputy was at Ca Mau and soon would be arriving in Hai Yen. We discussed the logistics of the move and he promised to provide assistance in moving the equipment and supplies to the air strip. He was concerned about my replacement, and I told him of the captain in the pipeline who would be on site in a few weeks. Until then, Lt. Harris, with the help of Sgt. Brown, would be running the team in

1 - The Headquarters for Cai Nuoc District, which had been recently relocated to Dong Cung, was normally called Cai Nuoc by the U.S. Team whereas the Vietnamese called the location of the District Goverment Dong Cung referring to the hamlet. This caused problems for those unfamiliar with the current situation especially when maps of the area located the District Town and Headquarters approximately twelve kilometers north of Dong Cung.

Hai Yen. Sgt. Brown appeared and interrupted our discussion with the announcement that we had received a radio message from Province saying a chopper would pick me up that afternoon and that Lt. Col. Gilland and I were to brief General Eckhart at 1100 hours two days from now. Major Thinh and I ended our conversation, shook hands and I returned to the team house to prepare for my trip to Ca Mau and then on to Can Tho and the Corps Headquarters to brief the Corps Senior Advisor. Upon arrival at the Province Team Headquarters, I again ran into the three newsmen, who informed me that they had acquired seats on the otter flight to Hai Yen for the next day. I congratulated then on getting transport and said I would see them in a couple of days when I returned. Lieutenant Colonel Gilland was off somewhere, so I spent the rest of the day visiting various staff personnel and being updated on the current situation in the province and country in general. The small teams out in the districts suffered for the lack of news and information, and hearing the rumors and gossip at the higher headquarters was always a treat.

The next morning I met with Lt. Col. Gilland and the S3 and S4 staff officers to prepare for our briefing with the Corps Senior Advisor. Maps, overlays, and a list of requirements needed from the Corps were produced. We were allocated one hour for the briefing and hoped to return the next day with a favorable nod from General Eckhart. Twenty minutes prior to the appointed hour, Lt. Col. Gilland and myself were escorted to the General's private dining room by his aide to prepare for the briefing and were told we could expect to be invited to lunch with the General after the briefing. At 1100 sharp, General Eckhart, his aide, and two of his staff officers strode into the room. After brief introductions, the General settled down in a large arm chair, lit a long thin cigar, and announced "Proceed, gentlemen." We had planned for

Lt. Col. Gilland to conduct the briefing with me standing by to answer any questions that the General may have of the officer charged with going in on the ground. General Eckhart was a tall man of indeterminable age (reputed to be the oldest Major General on active duty) with a lean face, bushy eyebrows, and eyes so narrow that it was difficult to tell if he was awake or dozing off during the presentation. At the completion of Lt. Col. Gilland's comments, General Eckhart turned to me and said, "Do you think we should put you and a team in Cai Nuoc?"

"Yes, sir."

"Why?"

"Well, installing an American team in Cai Nuoc would encourage the Vietnamese to hang on. They have already abandoned Nam Can; if Cai Nuoc was given up, that would leave Dom Doi District as the only district in the southern half of the province with government presence. It would also place heavier enemy pressure on Hai Yen."

"Have you been in Cai Nuoc?"

"No, sir. I have reconned by air and talked with the District Chief on the radio. I plan to do a ground reconnaissance in the next few days."

"If I approve this move, what do you need from Corps?"

"I need supply and medevac support, plus Tac Air. The area is below the zero-zero line. That means we need two ships plus guns on every mission."

"I know what the zero-zero line is, Major. Colonel, when would you make this move?"

"Within two weeks, sir," replied Lt. Col. Gilland.

"And the Vietnamese here are aware and approve this move?" asked General Eckhart, turning to his staff.

"Yes, sir," replied the G3 (operations officer).

"OK, then it's a go, Major. You will get the support you need. You will have supply runs every two days," announced General Eckhart, looking at the staff officers present.

"Anything else?" he asked as he rose from his chair. "Then I have other things to attend to. Good day to you, and good luck."

"Well," I said to Lt. Col Gilland on the way to the airfield to return to Ca Mau, "it looks like we are going to get what we need in the way of chopper support."

"We shall see. As you well know, all doesn't always work out as planned. You need to get back down to Hai Yen and prepare for the move. I want you to be in Cai Nuoc around the 15th or 16th of May. I will get your new deputy down in a day or two so you will have some time with him before the move to Cai Nuoc."

"I am concerned, there will only be two of us going in. How long do you think it will be before you can send me some more people?"

"We have a Captain on the way in and I plan to send him to Hai Yen as your replacement," Lt. Col Gilland replied. "As soon as he is on board, you can pull Harris out and over to Cai Nuoc. I'll send you a couple of NCOs as soon as I can."

"OK, sir. You know they are under attack almost every day, and with only two or three of us we won't get much sleep."

"No, you won't, but I hope with your team there on the ground you can get more air support than ever before and that should cut down the number of VC attacks."

We arrived at Ca Mau in time for me to be transported to Hai Yen via a FAC before dark. Now I had to get ready; the game was on!

CHAPTER 31

CAI NUOC

The follow morning after breakfast, I gathered the NCOs and gave them a blow-by-blow account of the past two days' events. I talked to Sgt. Johnson, and he appeared to be OK with going to Cai Nuoc. He knew it was going to be more dangerous and certainly more primitive living conditions. I told Sgt. Brown that I was depending on him to help Lt. Harris when he arrived. Coming from stateside with his last two years spent in Alaska, he was in for a real shock and would need advice from someone who had been here for a period of time.

Later that morning, I met with Major Thinh and brought him up to date on the planning. He was pretty well aware of what was decided at the Corps and Province levels. The Vietnamese chain of command seemed to be keeping him apprised of what the Americans were planning. Sergeant Brown gave me an update on enemy and friendly activities during my time away. The report was not encouraging: It appeared that the VC had come out ahead. The outpost at Nga Ba Dinh had been attacked twice, receiving a total of thirty 60 mm. mortar rounds, resulting in one wounded. Cai Nuoc had had two killed and five wounded in a firefight outside their wire. Enemy snipers had killed two members of 475 Company while on patrol. The following day, 475 Company killed seven VC but had one man killed and two wounded, including the Company Commander. Outside our area of operations but within the province the VC ambushed elements of the 31st Regiment of the 21st ARVN Division inflicting 72 caualties. Also one of our U.S. Army light aircraft, call sign Shotgun 43, was shot down over the Ong Doc District, killing the pilot. He had been in country two months and

211

married only three. And lastly, information was received that civilians were being forced by the VC to install pungi stakes at five locations. We could not place any indirect fire (mortar or artillery) or call in air strikes on the areas for fear of killing innocent civilians. The validity of the information would have to be verified by a patrol and then a decision made to what action totake, if any. Enemy activity certainly had not declined.

The three newsmen that had arrived on the Otter had settled in nicely. They had been given a tour of the camp, met with Mr. Niep (Father Hoa's brother), the commander of 475 Company, and were interviewing with and taking photographs of the Chinese soldiers and their families. They asked if they could accompany a unit on a mission or operation and I denied their request. We did take them to the village of Tan Hung Tay, which was generally safe during daylight for even small groups. There they were able to talk to the Village Chief and visit the marketplace and a company outpost. We went to the village on foot and returned by sampan, a new experience for them.

The reporter from the paper in Taiwan spent several hours with the old Chinese who had been with Father Hoa from the beginning. Carl Schoettler and I held several conversations. He assured me that his interview with me would appear in the *Baltimore Sun Evening* paper and that the paper would contact my wife. I found all three of these newsmen inquisitive but undemanding and cooperative when given reasons for denial of any their requests.

The days were ticking by and the scheduled move to Cai Nuoc was approaching. I had not yet been able to get there to look over the situation and meet Captain Hy, who was the District Chief. The news reporters left on the next Otter flight, which also brought in my new deputy. First Lieutenant William L. Harris, a Californian, last assignment Alaska, was a tall, red-headed young man with less than three years' service. I asked Sgt. Brown to get him settled and introduced around. I would sit down with him that night and brief him up on the current situation. Little did he know that he would very soon be the senior American at Hai Yen.

The briefing with Lt. Harris went well. He appeared to be excited and eager to learn. I told him to feel free to ask questions of myself and the NCOs but warned him to be careful on what he discussed with the troops and local civilians. Our methods and goals in conducting operations against the enemy did not always coincide with those of our counterparts. He was advised to be friendly and listen to everyone. I assured him that he would soon be a valued member of the team. To get him familiar with the area and the Hai Yen officers and NCOs he would be working with, I scheduled a number of visits to the local hamlets, outposts, and the village of Tan Hung Tay. They were minimum risk; forays into more contested areas would follow in due time.

On May the tenth, Province notified me that a chopper would pick me up the following morning for a visit to Dong Cung. I would only have a couple of hours on the ground to meet the District Chief and walk the area. I notified Sgt. Johnson to be ready to go with me, and the helicopter, accompanied by two Cobra gunships, arrived mid-morning. They had ammunition and some supply items on board for Dong Cung that they were to drop off along with Sgt. Johnson and me. They were then to continue on to the District Headquarters of Dom Doi. There they were to pick up one of the advisors, leave him at Ca

Mau, refuel, and pick us up for return to Hai Yen. I would have no more than two and one-half hours on the ground at Dong Cung. As we approached Dong Cung I asked the pilot to circle the hamlet once so I could see the perimeter of the settlement.

"Roger, Major, I can do that."

"Tomahawk Six, I'm going to do a 360 so the Major can see the area before we go in."

"OK, we got you covered," responded the gunship leader.

We were approaching from the west, and the pilot held north of the hamlet proceeding east until we passed over then swung to the south over the river, turning westward then to the north and completing the circle, enabling me to get a birds-eye view of the settlement. I had seen Dong Cung from the air once before, but this time I paid close attention for obvious reasons: I was going to live there! The hamlet was spread for about 300 meters along the north side of the river. There appeared to be two rows of shed-like buildings, with one row backing up to the river. A street, perhaps 20 to 25 meters wide, separated these structures from a similar row on the northern side. Several separate buildings that looked like dwellings sat back behind the row and were reached by paths from the street passing through narrow gaps in the line of buildings facing the street. The western end of the street appeared to have a mud wall between it and the river. From that point stretching around the north side, a wall continued crossing the old road bed and ending a few meters further at a small canal which was the eastern terminus of the northern side of the fortifications for the hamlet. Barbed wire and some obstacles appeared to be in place outside of the wall.

The abandoned national road, which connected the districts with the province and its parallel canal, ran south from Cai Nuoc Outpost (Old Cai Nuoc) through Dong Cung across the Song Bay Hop, terminating at the Nam Can District town. It formed the eastern flank of the hamlet's defenses. The road bed rose in elevation as it neared the bridge, an iron arch high above the water. The bridge structure was intact, but the deck had been removed leaving only planking wide enough for foot passage. I could see a Republic of South Vietnam flag flying on a pole in front of a masonry building, which I thought must be the District Headquarters.

OK, I thought, that is about all I can determine from the air. I motioned the pilot to take us in. The landing pad was on the north side between the buildings and the wall. I could see a small group waiting to greet us and unload the cargo that was on board. As Sgt. Johnson and I jumped off the chopper, Captain Hy the District Chief approached, saluted, and gestured for me to follow him away from the landing pad. When we were far enough away from the noise of the helicopter, we exchanged introductions and continued into the hamlet.

We passed several small bunker-like houses and went through a narrow walkway leading through the long buildings I had noted from the air and that entered out into the street. The walkway was approximately 20 meters wide, dirt, and paved with small stones. The shed-like buildings on either side were sectioned off with what appeared to be store fronts extending to the right for perhaps 300 meters to the end of the street. We turned to our left, where the street ended a short distance away at the abandoned road and bridge. As we neared the road bed, I saw that a passageway had been dug through the embankment to the other side. The District Chief entered the passageway and beckoned me to follow.

Much to my surprise, it was not just a tunnel; halfway through there were two excavated doorways opposite each other and providing entrance into two rooms. The one facing toward the river was the larger of the two, probably four by five meters. It contained a table, several chairs, a lamp, and a wooden cabinet. A small curtained-off alcove held a bed, a small table, and a clothes rack mounted on the wall. The wall of the main room facing the river had two narrow windows cut through to the edge of the embankment, providing a view of the river and firing apertures for small arms. There were several filled sandbags lying along the wall beneath the windows for blocking the openings when necessary.

"My headquarters and home," announced the District Chief.

The entrance way across the tunnel opened into a smaller room containing two radios and assorted communication gear on a low table. A young soldier wearing only shorts and sandals sitting in front of the radios looked up and smiled. On the other side of the room sat a young girl on a cot. I realized that this was the radio room and communications center for the district.

The underground excavations had been shored up with timbers and planks which had once been the deck of the bridge. They had almost two meters of solid roadbed overhead providing protection against any direct or indirect weaponry the VC was known to have in the area.

216

After seeing the District Chief's Command Center under the road bed, we continued on through the tunnel and exited on the east side into an open area where the building I had correctly assumed was the District Headquarters was located. The building was masonry with an aluminum roof and was heavily damaged by shell and mortar fire. Attached to the end of the building closest to the river was a shed-like addition of wood construction, with a single window facing the river and a door opening to the front. It was small--I would guess three by four meters. As we approached the Headquarters one of the civilians gathered there pointed to the shed and said, "Your headquarters."

Upon entering the District Headquarters building, I discovered it to be one large room with sparse furnishings. There were several tables that could be formed into one long one, an assortment of simple wooden chairs, and several cabinets along the wall. There was no desk, table, or area partitioned off that designated the District Chief's personal space. The District Chief turned to the group of individuals who had followed us into the headquarters and, placing his hand on my shoulder, introduced me in Vietnamese as his American Advisor. Smiling and applauding lightly, they each came forward and extend their hand to meet me.

First in line was Lieutenant Hong, the Deputy District Chief, closely followed by a young man in civilian dress who greeted me in reasonable English. He introduced himself as Mr. Cho, the Deputy for Administrative Affairs and informed me that he spoke both English and French. The remaining personnel included a Chinese civilian who was the primary merchant in Dong Cung and a rather tall individual who owned a rice mill and appeared to hold some status among those assembled. I thanked them for their courtesy and turning to Dai-uy Hy

217

reminded him that I had only a short time before the helicopter returned for me. He nodded and led me out back toward the main part of the hamlet. As we left the District Headquarters, I saw Sgt. Johnson with several Vietnamese NCOs standing near the addition of the building we were to occupy. He looked at me and just shook his head. I had asked Sgt. Johnson to connect up with might appear to be a counterpart for him when we moved in and to look at as much of the area as he could so we could compare notes later on our new surroundings. He appeared to be doing just that. I could see a small note book in his hand. I pointed at my watch and motioned toward the landing pad. He nodded, indicating he would meet there when the chopper came for us.

Dai-uy Hy and I, trailed by Mr.Cho and a couple of soldiers, passed back through the tunnel and out into the street, where he pointed out the various activities located along the street:, a midwife's office, a laundry, quarters for soldiers, the police station, a couple of small eating stalls, and the store owned by the Chinese merchant I had already met. The fronts of all the establishments were all open to the street and closed at night, I guessed. I was surprised to see a pool table in one of the open shops. I walked over to look at it. Several Vietnamese soldiers were playing; though the table had no felt left on the playing surface and the cue sticks were warped and the balls battered and out of round, but the soldiers appeared to be enjoying themselves immensely.

The buildings on the left side of the street backed up to the river, and I could see a sampan moored here and there. About two-thirds of the way down the street, a wharf jutted out into the river where the larger boats docked. Although the VC almost completely controlled the river, commercial crafts were allowed to pass but only after being

218

inspected and taxed. There were several unoccupied buildings near the end of the street, one of which was a school, though there was no school in operation for the children in Dong Cung. A thick wall of mud mixed with rice straw closed the end of the street. It was in good condition, with several covered fighting positions.

The wall continued around the landward side of the hamlet to the old abandoned road which I had seen from the air. About 200 meters out from the wall, the trees and vegetation had been cleared at one time, but waist-high grass and shrubs presently covered the area. Because of the rapid growth in the tropics, maintaining clear fields of fire was a never-ending chore. There was no evidence that chemical defoliants were ever used, though mines, barbed wire, and booby traps were. Along the wall were several machine gun emplacements and a couple of soldiers with BARs. The positions appeared to be well maintained, as were all the bunkers and shallow trenches I observed. Because of the frequency of enemy attacks, all the inhabitants of Dong Cung recognized that their lives depended on maintaining well-prepared defensive positions.

We had now returned to the landing pad, and as we waited for the chopper I questioned Dai-uy Hy concerning his troop strength. I knew what he was supposed to have, but I needed to know what he really had in manpower and weapons. I told him we expected to come to stay on the 15th or 16th of the month. He promised to have our quarters ready for us. As we lifted off, he saluted. I returned his salute wondering if he would still be there when we returned. The first thing I heard when we landed back at Hai Yen was that Dong Cung was under mortar attack.

Upon returning to the team house, I gathered everyone so that Sgt. Johnson and I could brief the rest of the team. The visit to Dong Cung changed our preparations for the move a little. We had prepared the items we were going to take from Hai Yen, and I determined to request some additional items from Province to include more ammunition, sandbags, and some maps. Sgt. Johnson had a list of some additional items he thought we would need.

"We can't eat forever with the locals," he exclaimed. "We need to be able to cook some for ourselves."

"You're right, Province is supposed to furnish us a propane stove and fridge with tanks," I replied. "You better rustle up some pots to cook in and something for us to eat out of."

Sergeant Johnson shook his head and grinned. "Are we going to draw straws to see who cooks?"

"Oh, I'm sure we can make a deal with the District Chief for personal support until we get ourselves situated. Anything else you can think of that we need?"

"Not at the moment, sir."

"OK, then, that's all for now guys, stay loose, we could get the word to move at any time."

"Or it could be days. You know how it is sir, hurry up and wait," commented Sgt. Brown.

I had also requested an interpreter to be sent in with us or to join us as soon as possible after we were in. Sgt. Cao because of his fluency in Chinese needed to stay in Hai Yen. The Cai Nuoc District Chief, his commanders and most all of his troops were Vietnamese, so an interpreter that spoke Chinese in addition to Vietnamese and English was not needed. Now all I could do was wait for word from the Province that the Vietnamese were ready to receive us and the date for when Corps could supply the choppers and gun ship escort needed for the move.

The 15th and 16th came and went without air support for the move. I had received word through Vietnamese channels that Dai-uy Hy was ready and anxious for us to arrive. Finally at 1400 hours on the 21st, we received word that choppers were on the way. That's late in the day to start the move! It should have been in the morning, early. The team, along with some of the soldiers, got our gear out to the landing strip. I thought there would be no problem in getting it all on the two choppers unless there was a lot of cargo already on board.

Hearing the distinctive whop, whop, whop sound of a helicopter, I glanced up and noted the increasing cloud cover. The rainy season had started and short periods of rain were being experienced, soon to be followed by daily downpours. Finally a helicopter appeared descending toward the landing strip and touched down close to the cargo waiting to be loaded. Two Hai Yen soldiers jumped off the chopper, saluted, and trotted off toward the camp. There were two more soldiers still on board plus a number of crates and sacks--supplies and replacements or hospital returnees for Dong Cung, I guessed. The pilot, a First Lieutenant, was shutting the aircraft down as I ran over and asked, "Where is the other ship?"

"I'm the only one, I'm the Sector Ship," he replied.

"There were supposed to be two slicks with guns to move my team from here to Dong Cung on the river," I yelled.

"I know where Dong Cung or whatever it's called is," the pilot stated. "I was making the normal province mail and supply run to the districts when I was pulled off for this mission. You need to get loaded; we will have to return for a second trip to move all your stuff and the weather is not looking good. We gotta hurry," he urged looking up at the gathering clouds.

"What about the gunships?"

"Don't worry," the Lieutenant said. "Two Cobras were refueling at Ca Mau and will meet us at Dong Cung."

Well, I didn't have time to get on the radio and complain to Province, so I motioned to Sgt. Johnson to load whatever the crew chief would allow. "Only two pacs (passengers)?" the crew chief asked.

"That's a roger," Johnson replied.

When it appeared that we would only have one chopper and a return trip would be necessary, I first decided that I would go on the initial lift and Sgt. Johnson would accompany the second load. Then I realized that, if for some reason the pilot did not want to make the second run, he would be more compelled to do so to get the team commander on the ground. Based on that assumption, I told Sgt. Johnson to go on the first lift and I would follow making sure that all our cargo was aboard. A bad decision based on a poor assumption. At

1550 hours, the loaded chopper lifted off, initiating the installation of the first District Advisory Team in Cai Nuoc District.

As they departed, I asked Sgt. Brown to notify the Province TOC what we were doing and then waited to hear from Sgt. Johnson that they were on the ground in Dong Cung. Forty minutes later, the pilot reported that he was on the ground and unloading and should be back in the air shortly. Brown calls out, "Major, Johnson is on the net and needs to talk to you."

"This is Oscar Six, over."

"Six this is Three, we have a problem."

"What's the matter, are you OK?"

"Yes, sir, we are unloaded and the pilot is ready to return but there are six wounded that the District Chief wants medevaced to Ca Mau. You need to talk to the lieutenant."

"How bad are the wounded" I asked Johnson.

"Two are pretty bad sir, one stomach wound and one with half his leg gone."

"OK, I'll talk to the pilot, you just stand by."

"Tango One Two, this is Oscar Six, we can't ignore the wounded, what are our options here?"

"This is Tango One Two, we need to finish the mission of

223

getting you and your gear in here. We can pick up the wounded and bring them to Hai Yen, unload them, and get you and the rest of your supplies over here, then back to Hai Yen, pick up the wounded, and return to Ca Mau. Or we can leave them here, complete the second lift, pick up the wounded and return to Ca Mau. Another option is to evac the wounded straight to Ca Mau now, re-fuel, return, and finish the move for you. The third option would get the wounded medical attention ASAP. We might lose two of them if we delay getting them to Ca Mau."

"Yeah, taking them direct to Ca Mau is the best thing to do. I will just have to hope you can get them there, then back here to finish the move. I have been watching the cloud cover and it looks like it may storm. Go ahead and take out the wounded and get back to me as soon as you can," I directed.

"Roger, Oscar Six, we are on our way, will see you later."

"Sgt. Johnson, did you monitor all that?" I asked.

"Oscar Six, this is Oscar Three, yes sir, it was the right thing to do, sir."

"You may be there alone. I might not make it today, looks like a storm coming in," I warned.

"No problem sir. Dai-uy Hy will look after me."

"I know," I said," but I should be there instead of you!"

At 1745 hours the Province TOC notified us that because of the
224

threatening storm and lateness of the day, the Sector Ship would not be returning to complete our move. I got on the net with the DPSA, Lt. Col. Culpepper, and got his assurance that there would be two choppers with escort in the morning. Later that night we received a message that the VC was mortaring Dong Cung. The next morning was anti-climatic. The helicopters arrived early and by 1000 hours I was on the ground in Dong Cung, the District Town of Cai Nuoc.

CHAPTER 32

SETTLING IN

Dai-uy Hy, carrying a cane and accompanied by his Deputies, Lt. Hong and Mr. Tho, met me on the landing pad. Several soldiers standing by immediately began unloading the cargo from the chopper. Nearby were Sgt. Johnson and a Vietnamese Master Sergeant. Johnson saluted and with a grin said, "Welcome to our new home."

"Damn, I am sorry about the screw up yesterday. Are you OK?" I asked.

"Yes, sir, no problem, but we did get shelled last night."

"I know. Was it mortar or artillery?"

"It was small stuff, 60 mortar, six rounds I think, no one hit that I know of," Johnson responded. "Also a few rounds of small arms fire about dark."

"Small arms, rifle fire? Are they in that close?" I questioned.

"Yes, sir, it appears so."

I turned back toward Dai-uy Hy and greeted the two deputies. Dai-uy Hy pointed to the soldiers with him and said, "My men will carry your gear to your quarters. Will you meet with me this afternoon?"

"Yes, of course. What time?"

"Fourteen hundred hours, I send soldier for you."

226

"Fine," I replied, "I will be ready."

"Good," he smiled, and walked away pointing to the perimeter wall with his cane and speaking rapidly to Lt. Hong, who nodded in what appeared to be acceptance of an immediate concern of the District Chief.

"Follow me, sir," beckoned Sgt. Johnson.

Instead of turning to our left toward the tunnel under the road, he cut to our immediate left onto a path leading up and over the old road bed, ending down in the yard to the left front of the District Headquarters building. "This is the way that the civilians and most of the soldiers reach the Headquarters from the hamlet. Only the officers, NCOs and civil officials are allowed to go through the tunnel," stated Johnson.

At the right end of the headquarters building, I noted a wall of sandbags had been built to protect the front and the end of our new home.

"Only the front and side," said Johnson. "The back is wide open."

"The back is not sandbagged?"

"No sir," Johnson replied. "I guess because we back up to the canal, they don't believe we will receive any fire from that direction."

"That's ridiculous!"

"Well sir, the main building is not sandbagged."

"I know, but it is masonary and will at least stop small arms fire and some shrapnel fragments. These wooden boards won't stop anything! I'll talk to Dai-uy about it."

"OK sir, now let me show you the inside of our new spacious District Advisor's Headquarters and Team House," said Sgt. Johnson grinning. I walked through the sandbagged entrance and stepped through the doorway. From there I surveyed the whole room with a single glance. Two cots, one on each side, butted up against the back wall. They were separated by a small table fashioned from an ammunition crate holding an oil lamp and our team radio. Sergeant Johnson's and my personal gear was stacked at the foot of each cot. To my immediate right beneath the window was a small propane gas stove. To my left was a table with the three folding chairs and a Coleman gas lantern. Some shelves along the wall held a few pots, pans, and dishes. Pieces of web gear and clothing were hanging on several pegs on the wall.

"There are some C rations and cans in that box," announced Johnson, pointing to another ammunition chest under the table.

"There were four cots on the chopper. Where are the other two?" I asked.

"Stored away somewhere., There's not any room for them here anyway, also the stove doesn't work," replied Johnson.

"What's wrong with it?"

"There isn't any copper tubing to hook it up to the tank and none here anywhere."

"Damn, where have you been eating?"

"With the Captain in his bunker. Just had fish, rice, and some kind of greens. I've had worse."

"Well, we will have Province send us some tubing and hook ups for the stove; supply choppers are due in tomorrow. Now I must get ready to meet with Dai-uy Hy. Anything else I should know right now?"

"Oh, I guess not. The Captain took good care of me, I was with him when the VC mortared us last night," Sgt Johnson stated.

"Where?"

"In his bunker."

"How many rounds?"

"'Bout six I think, 60 mm, no casualties."

"OK," I replied as a rap on the door frame announced a young soldier who saluted and said, "Tieu-ta" then backed out of the doorway pointing toward the tunnel saying, "Dai-uy."

"Lead on binh-si (soldier)."

Turning back to Sgt. Johnson I said, "See if you can get a count on how many machine guns they have, also how much ammo."

"Yes, sir, meet you back here?"

"Yeah, don't know what time though, may be a while."

"I'll be here."

Dai-uy was waiting at the entrance to the tunnel accompanied by his seemingly ever-present deputy Mr.Cho. I just have to get an interpreter here soon, I thought to myself.

"Chao Dai-uy! What are we going to do?" I asked.

"We look at defenses," he replied in English.

We started walking northward away from the bridge along the raised road bed, stopping after a short distance where a square block house defensive position was located. It was built of mud and rice straw walls, topped with sandbags and an overhead roof. It was about three meters high, providing a 180-degree unobstructed view from left (west) to right (east) and centered on the road bed to the north, thus serving a watchtower function. The old road bed--now a well-used foot path--plus the adjacent canal was the main entry and egress to Dong Cung from the north. The area to the left outside the wall was the marsh with scattered undergrowth. Across the canal to the right, the bank was covered with brush and small trees.

Further ahead where the mud wall on the left reached the road bed, I could see a defense position dug in the center of the road. It was a meter or more deep and sandbagged a meter high above ground level. Four corner posts supported a thatched roof. As we approached, I noted a semi-circle of several two-man fox holes 10 meters in front of the dug-in position. The intent, explained the District Chief, was to block the old road which was the main approach from the north side of the river. In addition to being the most advantageous avenue of attack, the old roadway was also a much traveled route used by the civilian population visiting Dong Cung. Ten to fifteen soldiers manned the position at night, with a lesser number during daylight hours. Half of the men were in the fox holes and the remaining in the covered dug-in emplacement. A machine gun mounted in the watchtower to the rear provided supporting fire, and mortar concentrations were plotted in front of the position. A similar strong point on the Nam Can District side of the river guarded the southern approach to the bridge.

My concerns of covering the west side of the small canal where it passed by the hamlet and emptied into the river were somewhat alleviated when I was told that a squad was deployed there during the hours of darkness. I made myself a mental note to look at that area more closely in the near future. We were finishing up our walk along the river bank when I heard the snap of a couple rounds of small arms fire passing overhead. I looked at Dai-uy Hy. "Is that normal?"

"VC want you to leave. They will fire much mortars tonight. Maybe artillery," he replied.

"Well, I guess I had to expect that they would try to drive the advisors out, but we are here to stay," I announced.

"You and Johnson eat with me tonight 1800," Dai-uy invited. "VC attack soon."

"All right," I thanked him, "we will join you."

As I walked back to meet Sgt. Johnson at our new abode, I noticed it was 1700 hours already. I needed to make some notes on this afternoon's observations, call Province, and chat with Johnson on whatever he had found out today.

CHAPTER 33

UNDER SEIGE

At 1800 hours sharp, Sgt. Johnson and I were met at the tunnel entrance by a guard who waved us in. Dai-uy was waiting for us at in his bunker. The table was set with three bowls, spoons, and pairs of chop sticks. A U.S. Army aluminum wash basin filled with rice along with a bowl of greens and one of some sort of meat chopped up into small bits sat in the center of the table.

"Please sit and eat," invited the Dai-uy in English.

After we were seated, he took my bowl and filled it with rice. Upon returning it to me, he gestured to Sgt. Johnson to help himself. A soldier in a clean and nearly new uniform entered the bunker with a pot of tea and cups. Ah, I thought, the captain's orderly. He proceeded to pour tea for each of us and then left. We had almost finished our meal when there was a flurry of gunshots. Dai-uy jumped up and called out. A moment later the soldier from the entrance guard post stuck his head in and announced "Mortars!"

"Mortars," Dai-uy repeated, as he exited the bunker, grabbing his helmet on the way out.

Suddenly there was an explosion close enough we could feel the blast even under ground. Several more rounds hit but farther away as Johnson and I joined Dai-uy Hy. He was talking to two of his NCOS and then turned to me and said, "Sixty mortar, land outside wire."

The incoming fire had stopped. It seemed to have been only six or seven rounds, one inside of the hamlet and the rest landed outside of our wall and wire.

"What was the rifle fire?" I asked.

"They were warning shots," explained Sgt. Johnson.

The soldiers on guard fire warning shots when they hear incoming fire, and the range of 60 mm mortars is short enough that many times one can even hear when the mortar is fired and warning shots give the defenders a few seconds to take cover. Not so with the 82 mm mortars or artillery.

Several more soldiers appeared, and Dai-uy Hy beckoned to a lieutenant to join us. After a quick exchange in Vietnamese, the Lieutenant saluted and trotted off, calling to the group of soldiers to follow him.

"Patrol go up old road, only hard ground there," Dai-uy informed me.

I knew what he meant; most of the surrounding area was so wet and soft that it would not support the impact of the firing of a mortar or an artillery piece. Positions for firing of indirect fire weapons normally would have to be built. The old road bed presented a solid base for firing mortars and, as I was soon to find out, light artillery.

"I fini an com (finish eating)," said Dai-uy Hy.

"Yes," I agreed. "I am going to report to Province Advisors the mortar attack and check on tomorrow's supply choppers"

He nodded and then started back toward his bunker. Johnson and I went over the road bed and down into the yard in front of the headquarters building and entered our quarters. I raised Province on the radio and reported the mortar attack to the TOC and queried them concerning the supply run scheduled for tomorrow. I was assured it was still on.

It was now almost dark, and I saw the patrol come back in.

"Anything?" I asked the Lieutenant as he made his way toward the tunnel and the District Chief's bunker.

"No VC," he replied.

As Sgt. Johnson and I settled for my first and his second night in our new abode, a couple of rifle shots sounded off. I looked at Johnson and said, "What do you suppose that is?"

"I don't know. It was the same last night," he replied. "A few shots were fired off and on throughout the night."

"I'll check with Dai-uy in the morning and see what it is. Get some sleep and spell me later on. I think that for a night or two one of us should be awake."

"OK, sir," said Johnson as he pulled off his boots and stretched out on his cot.

As I sat there among the whining mosquitoes (there was no screen on our one window and the door was open), I wrote an entry in my journal on the day's activities and notes on what to discuss with Dai-uy Hy the next day. There were so many things I needed to know, both military and civil. But paramount was what must be done now to insure the security of Dong Cung, which for all practical purposes was the District Capital or Town. I had made a list previously to which I now added.

Suddenly there was a bright flash and loud explosion, then another one and another. Johnson jumped up and grabbed his boots.

"Incoming, and that's not any 60s either," I yelled.

Small arms fire broke out and I could hear the stutter of a machine gun.

"Grab the radio and let's get over to the tunnel."

As I ran into the tunnel, I saw Dai-uy Hy coming in from the other end.

"VC other side of river," he said, pointing toward the west end of the hamlet.

Another round landed a few meters from the tunnel and bunker on the north side.

"Eighty-twos," I said.

"Yes," the Captain agreed, "Sixties there," he said, pointing to the north, "eighty-twos over river."

I then heard the thunk of a mortar being fired.

"We return fire cross river," the Captain announced.

I counted two or three more incoming rounds impacting close by and then nothing. The small arms fire also died off and our mortar quit firing.

"We go see wall, VC may come," said Dai-uy Hy.

235

"OK," I replied, realizing that he was concerned the VC may launch a ground attack.

Our 81 mm mortar started firing again.

"They fire there now," announced Dai-uy Hy pointing to the north outside of our wall and wire.

Arriving at the defensive wall, I walked along it with my counterpart who spoke to each soldier, giving orders to some and words of encouragement to others. He sent one off running to our rear.

"I stop mortar fire, VC not attack."

He called several soldiers to him, gave some instructions, and then waved them off. A few minutes later, two of the Company Commanders reported to Dai-uy, and a dialogue began that ended in salutes and the two officers making off and shouting out to the troops.

"Checking casualties and damage?" I asked.

"Da Tieu-ta, no casualties, some houses hit. I go now to my bunker and radio Province. We check line later."

"Right, Sgt. Johnson and I will be at our quarters. Send a soldier for me when you are ready."

"Da phai, I will meet you." said Dai-uy Hy as he walked toward the tunnel and his bunker.

Johnson and I climbed over the roadbed and back to our quarters. I then reported to the Province TOC the night attack and again confirmed that we were scheduled for a supply run the next day. I did not see the District Chief any more during the night, even when the VC fired two more rounds into the town around midnight and then again just before daylight.

After the early morning mortar attack, Sgt. Johnson went off and returned with two glasses of caphe-sura, a hot drink made with sweetened condensed milk in the bottom half and then filled with rich French-style black coffee. The result when stirred was the finest tasting coffee I can ever remember drinking. Caphe-sura could be found throughout South Vietnam and was one of the positive remnants of the French influence in the country. While drinking our coffee, Dai-uy's orderly showed up with bowls of noodle soup for Johnson and me. I was to find out that if we were not going on operations or outside of Dong Cung, coffee was our breakfast. The noodle soup was added if we were expecting to be engaged in a more physical demanding day's activities.

When our morning meal was over, I entered the Province radio net and contacted Hai Yen. Sergeant Brown answered and I asked to speak with Lieutenant Harris. They had monitored the radio traffic between Province and me the night before and were anxious to hear the particulars of the attack. There was nothing going on there except routine patrolling, night ambushes, and a couple of minor skirmishes. Sergeant Brown informed me that an interpreter name Sgt. Hai was at Ca Mau waiting for transport to Cai Nuoc. Well, I thought, he can get down on today's supply run. I signed off with Hai Yen, called the Province TOC, and received bad news. The supply run to us was canceled. The gun ships required for our area were pulled off for a mission of higher priority. Perhaps tomorrow, I was told.

"Does the PSA know?" I asked.

"That's affirmative," the TOC officer responded.

"We have some replacements and hospital returnees up there waiting for transport also."

"Yeah, and an ARVN interpreter," replied the TOC. "If something breaks loose we will try to get at least one lift to you."

"Tell the S4 I need some screening to cover the windows and door to keep the mosquitoes out. Also don't forget the hookup for the propane gas cylinder," I added.

"Roger, will do. Out here."

After signing off, I asked Sgt. Johnson to mind the radio, as I was going to go see Dai-uy Hy. As I started toward the tunnel and Dai-uy's bunker, I met him crossing the yard toward me. He said he wanted to show me the rest of the defensive positions that I had not seen and discuss troop strengths and supplies. I agreed at once and added to the discussion the topics of air support, medevacs, plus personal support for the team, which was only Johnson and me at present. He readily agreed.

He led off up on the road embankment and out onto the bridge, a single lane iron structure 300-350 meters long and supported by five groups of wooden piling. As previously noted, most of the wood decking had been removed from the four-meter wide roadway and carted off for use in building bunkers and defensive positions except for a narrow two plank wide walkway from one side of the river to the other. A two-meter high metal railing on both sides ran the length of the bridge; considering how long the road had been gone, the structure appeared to be in reasonably good condition At the south side of the bridge, a platoon-sized defensive position similar to the one on the north side had been built. A few houses lined the bank downstream from the bridge and road.

"Fishermen there," he announced, and pointing at the road disappearing to the south said, "Nam Can, fini."

Halfway back across the bridge Dai-uy stopped and again pointing, this time up river to the north side and said, "Outpost."

After a moment of squinting I spied it, "Platoon?" I asked.

"Da," he nodded.

"Cai Keo there," he said pointing again, this time upstream on the south side of the river.

I knew from studying my map that the hamlet of Cai Keo lay about four kilometers upstream from Dong Cung. I did not know of the platoon outpost. Looking at my map, I placed the outpost at the mouth of a fairly large canal emptying into the river approximately 1,500 meters from Dong Cung.

"Do you have any other outposts?" I asked.

"Only at Cai Nuoc, one company, the 516."

So now I had account of units, three companies, and a platoon at Dong Cung; one company at Cai Nuoc outpost and one platoon up river from us.

"Also platoon of PF in Cai Keo," announced Dai-uy.

The next order of business was to get an accurate head count of troops, weapons, and ammunition so I would have a better idea of how we stood. I had found out sometimes numbers differed greatly between the levels of command. Most of the time they were less than the higher headquarters stated. As we were approaching the end of the bridge, an

239

explosion sounded and we could see where an incoming mortar or artillery round had hit on the north side of the hamlet. It was immediately followed by a rash of small arms fire from our troops. Another round hit in the same vicinity just outside of our wall. It was a 60 mm mortar firing at maximum range and just barely reaching the hamlet.

"They fire from road, we fire back," announced Dai-uy Hy.

Our 81 mm fired four quick rounds, and a few seconds later I heard them detonate to our north along the old roadbed.

Sergeant Johnson was waiting for me as we descended from the bridge and said, "Province called, they are sending Shotgun 46 with a drop for us."

"What are they dropping?"

"Some copper tubing and fittings for the propane tank, screening, and mail," replied Johnson. "Also run a VR for us if you want," he added.

"Great," I grumbled, "better than nothing," as I thought of the canceled supply ships. It was not unusual for a light aircraft to drop small items to ground units in areas where it was not possible to land and helicopters were not available. "After he makes the drop I will have him do a recon of the north and west side; perhaps he can spot where the VC were firing from."

I turned to the District Chief who nodded that he had understood the exchange between Sgt. Johnson and me. He pointed toward the Headquarters building and said "I have work there to do," saluted, and left in that direction.

I wanted to update Sgt. Johnson on what I was able to see from the bridge and the troops that we had not yet visited. We walked down the hamlet street to what could be identified as a snack bar. It was a porch-like structure extending from a small building on the river side of the street. There were two tables, each equipped with a tall can of wooden chop sticks and a bowl containing several spoons. The owner, a disabled retired Vietnamese soldier, sold tea, coffee, noodle soup, and some dumpling-like pastries stuffed with meat of unknown origin. Beneath the table roosted some chickens accompanied by a couple of dogs that were waiting for any food scraps discarded by the patrons, a custom in the eating places throughout the countryside. One who was eating would select a pair of chop sticks or a spoon, wipe them off on their sleeve, and proceed to eat. When finished, one would again wipe the items off and return them for use by the next diner. Sanitation was not a big thing. I ordered coffee for Johnson and me, which we sipped while discussing the morning's events. Almost simultaneously with the sound of an aircraft approaching, our radio burst into life, "Oscar Six, this is Shotgun Four Six, over."

"Shotgun, this Oscar Six, I hear you but don't have you in sight yet."

"Roger Oscar Six, I am northeast of you. I have two packages for a drop. One is a sandbag and the other a mail sack. Both are weighted. I am going to make a low pass right over the village center from east to west and pitch them both out at the same time. Tell your guys to watch their heads."

"OK, Shotgun I have a visual on you now."

"Roger, here we go."

The plane at only about 300 feet flew right down over the center of the hamlet and tossed out the two bags then pulled up sharply

241

banking around to the north. The drop was right on target; the sandbag landed in the street while the mail sack landed on the roof of the main row of buildings.

"How's that,?" the pilot asked.

"Fine," I replied. "Can you do a VR for me?"

"Sure, I have a few minutes. What do you want me to look at?"

"North along the old road for a couple of clicks, we were mortared from somewhere in that area a little while ago. Take a look over to the west from there also."

"OK, Oscar Six, I will be over that area in a couple of minutes. I need to get a little more altitude first. No need to tempt Charlie."

"Be careful, they have automatic weapons."

"Roger, looks pretty quiet, there is a couple of small sampans on the canal by the old road. Wait! There is a group moving west of the old road toward the tree line at that large canal or stream."

"How many?"

"Looks like nine, maybe ten. They are going out of sight under the trees."

"Were they carrying anything?"

"Couldn't tell, but they were hurrying. They are only about two or three clicks from your location."

"Thanks Shotgun, anything else?"

"No," replied the pilot, "I don't see anything else. I'm leaving your AO now, good luck."

"Roger, much obliged, out here," I thanked the pilot.

I started off to find the District Chief to tell him what the pilot had seen when I saw one of the lieutenants with about 12 to 15 men heading out onto the old road. He waved to me and yelled, "We look for VC."

"Great!" I responded and gave him the thumbs up gesture. Dai-uy is already reacting to the last mortar fire, I thought, but I still need to tell him what Shotgun saw.

The next round of incoming fire started an hour before dark. It was a mix this time of both 60 and 82 mm mortars and lasted for 12 to 15 minutes. A number of rounds landed inside our wire, detonating among the houses. One round landed in the yard in front of our quarters. We had a civilian and two soldiers hit. Including the one that was hit earlier while searching for the VC mortar site, we now had four wounded that needed to be evacuated. The result of that action was tit for tat. One VC was killed and a rifle captured, and one friendly wounded. A medevac was requested and one was promised for the next morning at first light.

Around 0400 several more rounds of mortar were fired into the hamlet, and at day break there was a flurry of VC small arms fire on the northwest side. District troops returned fire with machine guns and BARs. Approximately at 0900, a medevac chopper arrived without escort and picked up our wounded. Now I had three less soldiers to defend the District Town.

I left Sgt. Johnson, who had recruited a couple of soldiers to help him, with the tasks of getting the windows and door covered with

243

the newly acquired screening and of hooking up the propane tank. I went off to join Dai-uy Hy. He was in the District Headquarters building at a table covered with papers and radio messages. He waved to me to join him and offered a cup of tea. I accepted the tea mostly out of courtesy and began continuing our discussion on the status of the defense posture of Dong Cung.

I knew that we had three RF companies, the 371, 472 (originally one of Father Hoa's Chinese companies), and the 517. There was one PF platoon and six national policemen also assigned and present. The total authorized strength was 396; however, present for duty was only 229. There were 82 in 371 company, and 49 and 90 in 472 and 519 companies, respectively. The PF platoon had 18 men out of their authorized 32. Other friendly troops in the district included one company (the 526 at Cai Nuoc Outpost) and two PF platoons, one at Cai Keo and the other at the mouth of Rach Cai Muoi, which was midway between Dong Cung and Cai Keo. It was immediately apparent that current troop strengths did not provide sufficient forces to conduct effective offensive operations. One-day sweeps, raids, and ambushes were about the only tactics possible, as the troops were needed to defend the government-held hamlets. There were, however, a number of replacements and hospital returnees at Ca Mau awaiting transport to Dong Cung.

How could I lessen the effects of this manpower shortage on offensive operations? Two ways: First, arrange for additional chopper support to fly the troops at province to Dong Cung, and second, greatly increase the requests for gunship and Tactical Air support. Vietnamese commanders without U.S. Advisors present who requested support from U.S aviation assets experienced a lower priority than an American advisor, especially if he was in direct contact with the enemy. The army responded with Huey C model and the new Cobra gunships. The U.S. Air Force could provide support with mainly F4 and F100 fighter bombers. Also available were old C47s mounting Gatling guns, which provided an immense rate of fire. My job was to convince higher headquarters that the VC was attempting to drive out the recently arrived advisors by elevating their attacks on the Cai Nuoc District forces, and that additional fire support was critical. This I was determined to do.

When I told Dai-uy Hy I saw this as my first priority, he enthusiastically agreed and then said that supply was the number two problem.

"What type of supplies is most critical?" I asked.

"Ammunition first, medical, then many others," he replied.

Our small arms ammunition was mostly .30 caliber for the M1s, BARs, and machine guns. The .30 caliber carbine used a lighter round, and .45 caliber was for Thompson sub-machine guns and pistols. "M79s, we have 10 but no ammo," pointed out Dai-uy Hy. The M79 was a 40 mm shoulder fired grenade launcher, a valuable asset to infantrymen.

"None at all?"

"Khong," (no) said Dai-uy, shaking his head emphatically.

"How about mortar ammo?"

"Have but always short. Would fire more if have, must save for ground attack."

Well, I had the District Chief's two most critical concerns, troops and ammo. There was a long list of items that I needed to discuss with him, but that would come in time. Disposition of the troops when under attack and in an offensive mode was my next subject of interest, along with how his orders are communicated.

Dai-uy ended our discussion stating that he must rest as he expected to be up most of the night. We parted, he toward his bunker and I to our quarters. Around 1800 hours, the VC obliged us with their customary evening mortar attack. Several rounds fell this time at the far west end of town with negative casualties. The rest of the night remained quiet.

CHAPTER 34

VC RECEIVE UNWELCOME SURPRISE

The follow morning I woke up to a light rain shower. The rainy season had begun, and we could expect periods of rain varying in intensity and duration on an almost daily basis. I met with Dai-uy Hy and brought up our living conditions. We had to work out eating arrangements; I supposed that he may not want us at his table every night and that hopefully there soon would be additional members on the team. Also we needed to have our laundry done. That was no problem, he said. One of the soldier's wives would do our laundry--for which we would pay, of course. Until we got some rations on hand and could prepare our own meals, however, we could continue to eat the evening meal with him. I insisted, against his wishes, that we would pay for meals and when we became more settled in and were receiving supplies on a regular schedule, we would contribute food in our behalf. Until then, lunch would usually be fruit or something out of our C rations.

As an aside, bathing and latrine facilities were also of concern to me. The locals bathed in the river or by scrubbing and pouring water over themselves. The District staff used a platform built of small logs that extended out from the river bank 10 or 12 feet; it was enclosed with a screen of woven palm fronds. Several square petrol cans with the tops cut out and wire handles added were filled with fresh or clean water. To bathe, one would go out on the platform, strip down, and ladle water over oneself, soap down, and then rinse off. This procedure would change in the future due to a Chinook-load of building material that was delivered to us by mistake.

The latrine facilities for the local population in many places throughout the delta outside of the cities were the canals and rivers. A community would build a structure in the shape of a T with the base of the stem of the T at the bank of canal or river extending out over the

247

water and forming the top of the T by extending to the right and left. The structure consisted normally of poles to walk out on, with a hand rail to maintain one's balance. The user proceeded to the right or left and there assumed a squatting position to perform the needed bodily functions. A screen of woven palm fronds a little less than a meter in height provide some modesty by preventing direct observation from the canal or river bank. Advisors using this facility did draw some interest from the locals and provided a story which will be told later at the proper time. Though these "facilities" were not optimal, there was no remedy, so I did not broach them with Dai-uy.)

Having addressed our problems of existing, I queried Dai-uy on the day's activities. Two platoon-sized units had gone out that morning. One had ventured to the outpost upriver between Dong Cung and Cai Keo, and the other went to the north on the old road to visit a small group of houses that were homes of rice farmers. Both patrols were expected back by mid-afternoon. My expectations of the already late supply run were dashed when we were informed that the re-supply mission for us was canceled. We would have a FAC for a VR in the afternoon. When I told the District Chief he merely shrugged, said "tomorrow," and walked off towards the District Headquarters building.

There was a brief period of rain early in the afternoon, which was soon to be a daily occurrence. The two platoons returned at about 1500 hours. The one that went up river had contact, killed one VC, and brought in a captured rifle. An hour later we received several mortar rounds in the town. There was a brief lull, and then a steady barrage of 82mm rounds began impacting in the hamlet and nearby. In response to a radio call to the Province TOC for help, we were told that the promised FAC for a VR mission was already in route to our location, followed by a pair of helicopter gunships that were expected to be on station in 20 minutes or so. When informed of the arriving air support Dai-uy Hy said, "West, VC in the west. Look there."

248

I relayed his comments to the FAC. "Shotgun 46 we believe the VC are firing from the west of us on the north side of the river. See if you can spot anything there."

"Roger, will do."

"Oscar Six, the guns are ten minutes out. I am going to have them hold while I have a look see."

"OK Shotgun, we are still receiving fire."

"Roger."

"Oscar Six, I have a visual on them. I can't believe it! They are right in the open and are not paying any attention to me. I don't think they have seen me yet. Looks like maybe 20 or so VC and a mortar tube, maybe two."

"Shotgun 46, where are the gun ships?"

"They are about zero five out. I have them on another freq."

"What are they?"

"Charlie model Hueys."

"What are they carrying?"

"High explosives (HE), nails, and their machine guns are 7.62. I am going to be off your frequency for a while I work with them."

"Roger, the VC are still firing on us."

I turned to Dai-uy Hy and repeated my conversation with the FAC.

He nodded and then questioned, "Nails?"

"Fleshets, needles."

"Ah," he nodded, understanding the word commonly used by the U.S. pilots for fleshet rockets, deadly when used on troops in the open. Each rocket contained thousands of tiny barbed and finned needles that shredded any unprotected flesh caught in the target area.

"VC will fall back to canal, much bush," Dai-uy announced.

"Rach Dong Cung," I asked?

"Da phai," he replied.

The Rach Dong Cung, a natural waterway whose confluence with the river was only approximately a 1,000 meters to our west, was flanked on both sides by a couple of hundred meters of heavy undergrowth which would provide concealment from aerial observation. This waterway or canal was large enough to accommodate small boats and followed a sinuous course northwest to join the Kinh Dong Cung, a large, straight, manmade canal that ended in the Ong Doc District. It provided the VC not only a conduit from the Ong Doc District through Cai Nuoc District to the open sea via the Song Bay Hap but also a way to control a large portion of the area serviced by the route. Recognized as such, the outpost at Nga Ba Dinh, occupied by Hai Yen Chinese forces, had been established to interdict VC traffic moving along the canals. The results of their efforts were marginal, and the outpost was a constant target for the VC.

"Oscar Six, the guns are making their run on the bad guys now. They are breaking down and running toward the tree line to the west," reported Shotgun 46.

"Roger, Four Six, that's a major route of movement for the VC."

"Yeah, I know. I drew fire from that area a little while ago. The guns are finishing up; looks like we waxed eight or nine of them before they got into the tree line."

"That's great! The incoming has stopped so that must have been the only site firing on us," I said.

"OK, we're pulling out of here, good luck and yell when you need help. I don't think they expected any response from the air, we caught them flat ass out in the open."

"I know, before we arrived, the District Chief's request for air support was really low priority and the VC knew that. Thanks and thank the guns for us. I'll buy you a drink the next time I'm in Ca Mau," I announced.

"No sweat, Oscar Six, glad to help, out here," said the pilot signing off.

Dai-uy Hy left his bunker and moved out into yard in front of the Headquarters building, followed by a soldier carrying a radio. While speaking rapidly into the handset, he was also beckoning to soldiers who were appearing from whatever protection they had sought during the mortar attack. In a few moments, one of the company commanders and several NCOs joined him. A brief exchange

251

consisting of rapid-fire questions by Dai-uy Hy was followed by short answers and nods from the group, who then trotted off in several different directions.

Hy turned to me and said, "Need medevac."

"How many wounded?" I asked.

"One dead, four wounded, one woman."

"Woman wounded?"

"Da, soldier's wife," he replied.

Sergeant Johnson, who was on the net with the Province TOC, nodded to me indicating he was already requesting the medevac. A moment later he gave me a thumb's up, indicating that our request was being granted.

"Province says 40 minutes or so," announced Johnson.

"Well, let's hope it gets here before dark," I replied.

The District Chief pointed in the direction of where the mortars were seen by the gun ships and said, "I send soldiers to VC mortar position."

"Good."

"How much damage?" I then asked him.

He shrugged his shoulders, indicating he didn't know and said, "I go look, you come?"

"Da phai," I replied and started out around the perimeter with him.

Damage to bunkers and houses was minimal considering the number of rounds that we received. Repair to the damage was already under way. As we finished our inspection, I heard the approach of a helicopter.

"Here comes our medevac. That was a quick response!" I exclaimed.

I could see Sgt. Johnson on the landing pad ready to guide the chopper in; the wounded were being carried out to the pad. Three wounded and the one dead soldier were going out; the other soldier's wound was minor and could be treated here. The evacuation was completed without incident, with no enemy fire during the loading of the wounded, which was not always the case. It was now dark, and we settled in for an anxious night which passed with only a spat of small arms fire on the west side of the perimeter at day break.

CHAPTER 35

A KEY ARRIVAL

Sergeant Johnson and I were having our morning coffee and noodle soup when Dai-uy Hy, accompanied by two NCOs joined us, and asked about the supply choppers that we were expecting. I began to tell him that we had not checked on them yet this morning when our radio came to life with "Seaforth Oscar, this is Iowa One Two, over."

Johnson grabbed the handset and responded,"Iowa One Two, this is Oscar, over."

"Roger, Oscar we are a flight of two about one five from your location, over."

I motioned to Johnson to pass me the handset, "Tthis is Oscar Six, do you have an escort?"

"Negative Oscar Six, we are alone. We have cargo and personnel on board and are scheduled to make two lifts for you."

"Oscar Six here, that's great. Approach from the east and depart to the south. We can only take one bird at a time on the pad."

"I understand, approach from the east and depart to the south."

"That's affirmative, Iowa One Two," I replied.

"Roger, swinging to the east now."

The District Chief listened intently as Sgt. Johnson relayed the conversation between the pilot and me and then barked out orders sharply to the two NCOs with him, who ran off toward the landing pad calling to other soldiers. "I send soldiers to unload and alert guards."

"Good," I replied, "Let's get over to the pad. Bring the radio, Sgt. Johnson."

As we neared the landing pad, I noted a group of soldiers standing by to unload the cargo and heard the approaching supply chopper. It came in rather high and dropped rapidly onto the landing pad. It sat there while the passengers threw off the boxes and crates that made up the cargo and then themselves leaped to the ground. In less than three minutes, the chopper was empty and lifting off. Recognizing that they were highly vulnerable on the ground, pilots were always anxious to unload and get airborne as soon as possible. As the second chopper was touching down, the crew chief and door gunner were kicking off the cargo. It was grabbed up and carried away from the proximity of the helicopter outside of the radius of the whirling blades. The second chopper was off the ground in less time than the first and followed the lead ship to the south.

"Oscar Six, that was a good dump, your guys were all ready," noted the lead pilot.

"Iowa One Two, this is Oscar Six, they know you don't want to hang around on the ground. Besides we don't either, you draw fire."

"Don't I know it," replied Iowa One Two. "See you in about two hours."

"Right, we'll be here, thanks see you then, out."

The District Chief had greeted the soldiers that had arrived and was inspecting the cargo that was received when one of the soldiers detached himself from the group and approached Sgt. Johnson and me.

255

Coming to a halt, he saluted and announced, "I am Sgt. Hai, your interpreter, sir."

He was about the average height of a Vietnamese male, slight in build, and appeared to be very young. He was carrying knapsack, a duffle-style canvas bag, and a carbine. Returning his salute, I introduced myself and Sgt. Johnson. I then asked him if he had reported to the District Chief. A nod of his head indicated that he had done so. I told him to get himself settled as to quarters and meals, to become familiar with the District Headquarters personnel and area, and then report back to me for a discussion of his duties. He nodded, saluted again, and started off toward the Headquarters building.

Sgt. Johnson said, "I'll go with him and see that he gets treated OK."

The choppers' second lift brought us badly needed ammunition, rations, medical supplies, batteries, and some mail for Johnson and me, the first we had received since arriving in Dong Cung. I was relieved that both lifts were completed without VC interference or weather problems. It started raining shortly after the second lift but not before the VC fired three 60 mm mortar rounds into the hamlet followed by some rifle fire. The District Chief's 81 MM mortar crew counter fired a few rounds aimed at a known site used by the VC. The VC small arms fire was not very effective as far as sniping at selected targets, but it kept everyone on edge. The enemy 60 mm mortar firing positions were probably only 1,000 meters or so from us, while the rifle fire was maybe 300 meters or less. In other words, they were right on top of us. Dai-uy Hy had patrols out every day, but the VC still basically controlled the area outside of our perimeter wire. I needed first to stop the close-in fire we were receiving, but how?

Frequent aggressive offensive operations conducted into known or suspected VC positions would be the most effective means of eliminating the almost daily attacks on our positions. However, the small number of troops available restricted operations to small patrols and one-day company-size operations. The majority of available troops were needed to defend the District Headquarters and hamlet both day and night, with night time being the most critical time. We needed more troops, that was obvious, and also larger weapons. The one 81 mm mortar was definitely insufficient to counter the VC indirect fire we had been receiving. We needed a 4.2 inch heavy mortar or artillery.

I was pretty sure artillery was out of the question. To the best of my knowledge, there were only eight artillery pieces in the entire province, but a 4.2 mortar might be available. While on the bridge the other day, I was impressed with the distance one could see from the top of the span--probably more than a thousand meters. A .50 caliber machine gun placed at the apex of the bridge could dominate a 1,500 meter circle, thereby placing fire on VC 60 mm mortar positions and eliminating enemy harassing small arms fire. If we could obtain those two weapons, we could certainly push the VC further out from us and make it safer within the perimeter of the hamlet and the Headquarters. I thought that the combination of those additions and the increase in tactical air support would allow us to conduct larger offensive operations, though still limited to one day in length. I decided to discuss it with Dai-uy Hy and if he agreed then go directly to Lt. Col. Gilland with a request for both weapons.

CHAPTER 36

A BUSY DAY

The District Chief enthusiastically agreed with my suggestion on acquiring both the mortar and the machine gun. We would have to build firing positions and train crews to fire and maintain the weapons. Dai-uy Hy said two of his mortar men had experience on the 4.2 but didn't think he had anyone who had fired the .50 caliber machine gun.

"That's OK," I assured him, "in the early days of my enlisted service I was a machine gunner. I can train them."

"Gioi lam (very good)," he replied.

I then left him and returned to our quarters and radioed the province TOC, requesting to speak to the PSA. I was told he was not available at the moment so I asked he be informed that I needed to talk with him as soon as possible. Then, while briefing Sgt. Johnson on my plan, our new interpreter, knocking on the door frame announced, "Sgt. Hai here, sir."

"Come in," I invited. "Are you all squared away on quarters and rations?"

"Yes sir," he replied. "What are my duties?"

I spent the next 20 minutes explaining what I expected of him. He spoke English very well and had worked at various Province level U.S. advisory teams in the delta. If we were to be in Dong Cung for the day, he was to report after breakfast and be available throughout the day unless dismissed. He would immediately report to me any time we were under fire day or night. If we were going out on an operation or visit to a hamlet or outpost, he would always plan to accompany me

258

unless I felt I didn't need him. He would always be available if needed whenever the District Chief and I were in conference. Any time that I didn't think he was needed, he was free and on his own. If he changed where he was living, he was to let Sgt. Johnson know so he could be readily located. The most important thing that I wanted him to understand was that when interpreting dialogue between the District Chief and me, he was to interpret exactly what was said. No additions, no personal ideas or thoughts, just what was said. I wanted to be sure he understood that. I didn't want the same problem I had had with Sgt Cao.

It had been raining off and on all day, with a hard downpour around noon. The VC had fired one mortar round before the heavy rain started but none after the tropical shower was over. It was now clear and hot. In the middle of the afternoon, the Province TOC came up on the radio net, "Seaforth Oscar this is Seaforth Alpha, over."

"Seaforth Alpha, this is Oscar, go ahead," Sgt. Johnson responded.

"Oscar, Shotgun 46 is in route to your location with a drop for you."

I motioned to Johnson to hand me the handset. "This is Oscar Six. What does he have for us, over."

"Seaforth Alpha, mail, some money, and new SOIs."

"Oscar Six, this is Shotgun 46. I'm about two five minutes out from your location."

"Shotgun, I understand two five out, over."

"That's a roger, Oscar Six."

259

"OK, Shotgun."

"Seaforth Alpha, thanks for the heads up."

"Anytime, Oscar Six, Seaforth Alpha out."

I sent Sgt. Hai off to inform Dai-uy Hy that an O1 would be making a drop for us in 20 or 30 minutes. Sgt. Johnson and I took the radio and a smoke grenade and walked to the center of the yard in front of the District Headquarters building to await the drop. A few minutes later I could hear the drone of an aircraft engine.

"Oscar Six, this is Shotgun 46 approaching your location, same drill for the drop?"

"Yeah, try to come as close to the District Headquarters as you can, over."

"Roger, Oscar Six, I am headed east on the downwind leg, will make a one eighty and make the drop from east to west."

"That's fine," I replied, watching the plane pass over to the east and then bank sharply, lining up on our position.

"You want smoke?" I asked.

"Negative, I can spot the Headquarters building."

"OK."

We watched the plane make the turn and cut back his speed, lining up for the drop. As he passed overhead, a sandbag with an attached white cloth fluttering in the breeze was tossed out and landed within 50 meters of our position.

"Great drop!" I exclaimed.

"Yeah, I'm getting good at this," Shotgun replied as he increased his power.

As the plane cleared the end of the street, ground fire broke out.

"I'm receiving fire," the pilot calmly announced as he banked into a climbing turn to the north.

"I can hear it, I think it's coming from across the river. After you get some altitude, can you swing around and look?" I asked.

"Roger, after I get up a little higher."

The sound of small arms fire increased and then I realized that it was at the west end of the street and was directed at the hamlet and not at the plane. I saw soldiers running down toward the west end of the hamlet. There was a mud wall in place along with two bunkers that were a part of our perimeter defense. The river curved slightly at that location, allowing a direct line of sight across the river and up the street of the hamlet. The mud wall had been built to prevent that. Rifle and machine gun fire was striking up and down the street and into some of the structures on the right side between the street and the river. I could see two persons, a soldier and a woman, down in the street.

"I can see them," announced Shotgun 46. "I can't see any mortars but there looks like about 20 or so of them. I don't have any ordnance on board. I used it on my way to make your drop. I can make a swoop at them' maybe they will break off the attack."

"No, no, negative, call Province and tell them what's going on," I replied.

"Sea Forth Oscar, this is Sea Forth Alpha. We are monitoring your problem, over."

"OK, can you get us some help?"

"This is Sea Forth Alpha, we are requesting as I speak."

"OK."

"Oscar Six, I don't have enough fuel to hang around. Good luck," said Shotgun 46 as he departed to the north.

I had seen Dai-uy Hy, followed by several soldiers, making his way down the left side of the street along the houses toward the far end of the hamlet and the perimeter wall where some troops were firing across the river. Turning to Sgt. Johnson, who was right behind me with the radio strapped on his back, I said, "Let's get down to the end and join Dai-uy Hy."

We had come over the top of the road bed from the District Headquarters building and were on the right side of the street facing west. We started down hugging close to the buildings. The street was almost like a firing lane with the sound of small arms rounds snapping by. The distance had to be close to maximum range for rifle fire, but there appeared to be at least one machine gun firing. The row of buildings ended on the right side before reaching the end or the perimeter wall, thereby leaving us fully exposed unless we crossed over the fire-swept street to the other side. The structures on that side continued to the end of the street and the wall and had been fortified as firing positions facing the river.

"We have to cross over. I'll go first," I called to Johnson.

He nodded and, as I prepared to sprint across one of several civilians, a woman crouching up against the buildings jumped up and started to run across to the other side. About half way across she went down. I saw the dust fly from her clothing as she was hit. A soldier ran out from the other side and dragged her over out of the line of fire. I took off next and collapsed on the other side and waved to Johnson to join me. He made it across and fell in a heap up against the building wall.

As we both lie there panting, a soldier pointed at Sgt. Johnson and was laughing. We didn't know what he thought was so funny until we noticed that the long antenna mounted on Sgt. Johnson's radio was dragging on the ground. An enemy round had clipped it while he was crossing the street. Wide eyed from the close call Johnson, unscrewed the broken antenna and replaced it with the short one which was strapped to the side of the radio. After catching our breath, we began edging our way down to the perimeter to where the District Chief was crouched, peering over the wall across the river. As I fell up against the wall next to him he glanced at Johnson and me and then turned back, continuing to look at the other side of the river.

There were perhaps 20 soldiers along the wall firing at the opposite shore. Sergeant Johnson and I both had our carbines and bellied up to the wall to add to the firepower. I gestured to Dai-uy Hy that I had requested gunships and he nodded that he understood. The noise level created by the rifle fire plus one machine gun required one to yell to be heard. I saw an explosion on the other side and realized that we were also firing our mortars. It was then that I noticed that the Dai-uy had a radio on the other side of him from me and had the mike in his hand. He was directing the mortar fire. As rounds were impacting, the VC fire began to lessen and finally stopped.

I felt something pulling on my sleeve and turned to see Sgt. Hai standing there. I had forgotten all about him. I had not gotten used to

263

him being with us. When I had sent him to inform the District Chief of the drop, he was with him when the VC ground fire began and went with him rather than trying to cross over to the other side to join Johnson and me. He started to apologize but I told him he did the right thing and not to worry about it.

Dai-uy Hy called to Sgt. Hai and beckoned him over. Sergeant Hai joined him, listened, nodded, and returned to me saying, "Dai-uy requests a medevac."

"What do we have?" I asked.

"Two soldiers dead, three wounded. Two civilians wounded," he replied.

I turned to Johnson, who said, "I'm on it."

The troops were moving about and civilians were coming out from cover and in the street when three 82 mm mortar rounds impacted between the wire and the road bed. Everyone went to ground. After a few minutes and a tropical downpour of rain, no further incoming fire was received and normal activities resumed. An hour later, an unescorted medevac chopper took out our wounded. I was now five more men short.

Later that night Dai-uy Hy joined Sgt. Johnson and me outside of our quarters and announced that he was going out in the morning to examine a site reported to him where the VC were building a base from which to mount a ground attack on Dong Cung. He said the enemy's objective was two-fold: to drive out the U.S. Advisors and to eliminate the District Headquarters. I told him that Johnson and I would accompany him so that we could report accurately the size and location of the VC base.

He nodded and said, "Go at six," as he walked away.

To cap off the day's activities there was a spat of small arms fire from the old road north of the strong point, which was responded to with a burst of machine gun fire and a couple of flares that failed to reveal anything.

CHAPTER 37

A VC ATTACK POSITION

After some morning coffee, Sgts. Johnson, and Hai and I joined Dai-uy Hy and were assigned a soldier to carry our radio. With a contingent of approximately 50 men, we crossed over the perimeter mud wall out into the wire a hundred meters or so west of the old road where I had expected to go. When installing the defensive wire, several narrow paths had been planned to enable the defenders to egress the defensive area through the wire and mines. Moving in single file through one of these paths, we encountered booby traps placed by the VC. The soldiers passed around the devices, careful not to disturb them. When I asked why we didn't remove them, I was told that if we did the VC would only place more and we might not detect them. As long as we knew where they were, they could be avoided and not produce causalities.

Once out of the wire, the troops assumed the usual movement posture, a few men 50 meters out in front as a point and several on each flank. We moved in an east-by-north direction towards the canal Rach Dong Cung, 1,500 to 1,800 meters away. The ground underfoot was mostly ankle- deep mud with occasional shallow pools of water. The vegetation was knee-high grass and small trees. We could see taller trees and dense foliage to our front; they marked the canal bank.

In less than 30 minutes, forward movement stopped as one of the point men approached us and began speaking to Dai-uy Hy. Sergeant Hai listening intently, relayed in English that the leading point man could see what looked like a VC camp.

Dai-uy Hy nodded, waved the soldier back toward the front, looked at me and said, "Tieu-ta hieu (Major understands)?"

266

"Da phai (yes),"

He then spread his arms out shoulder high and the troops began reforming into a skirmish line and moving slowly forward. We soon came upon an arc of approximately 50 shallow foxholes protected by pungi stakes. A few meters behind them were nearly 30 bunkers built of poles and mud. Further to the rear were three platforms constructed of larger sized logs lashed together with strips of canvas.

"Eighty-two mm mortars," stated Dai-uy Hy, pointing at the platforms.

"Firing positions," I agreed.

"Da," nodded the District Chief as he called Sgt. Hai over, spoke rapidly to him, and then pointed to me.

Sgt. Hai turned and said, "Dai-uy wants you to know he received intelligence about VC base yesterday from farmer. Farmer told him VC work here during day time last two days."

"Why didn't we find them here today?" I asked.

Sergeant Hai shrugged, "I don't know," and looked at the District Chief.

"Maybe they hear us come, maybe they know we come," said Dai-uy Hy.

"Know we come?" I asked.

"Maybe, maybe we have spy," Dai-uy replied.

"Well, I am going to request an air strike on the site."

267

"Da, VC come back, maybe tonight. I think they attack us soon."

"You mean ground attack?"

"Da, night maybe day."

Dai-uy then spoke to Sgt. Hai, who said to me, "Dai-uy said VC want to drive himself and American Advisors out of Dong Cung. Out of Cai Nuoc District."

"Yeah, I know, but we're not going."

Meanwhile the soldiers were searching the area looking for anything left behind by the VC.

"VC leave here two, maybe three hours ago," reported one of the NCOs to Dai-uy Hy.

"They will return," he said and then motioned the soldiers to assemble.

"We go back to Dong Cung now," relayed Sgt. Hai.

I saw several soldiers with grenades in their hands and asked, "What are they doing?"

"They leave booby traps, grenade traps," replied Sgt. Hai.

"Oh, OK, I see."

The return to Dong Cung went without incident and we were back in the hamlet before noon. The operation, actually a reconnaissance, took less than five hours. After shedding my gear, I got on the net with the Province TOC and requested an air strike the following morning in day light and added that my request was based on category A1 intelligence. I had been on the target site today and expected the VC to be there tomorrow; I felt that a ground attack from that location was eminent. I encoded the grid coordinates and requested a reply to my request as soon as possible. The afternoon passed with a rain shower and three VC 60 mm mortar rounds around 1800 hours.

Radio traffic on the Province frequency was heavy throughout the night reporting VC activity. Cai Nuoc Outpost, Nga Ba Dinh, Dom Doi District Headquarters, and Thoi Binh were all mortared. The most significant and unexpected attack was Hai Yen, which was with 20 or more artillery rounds. They were 75 mm and mostly landed in the eastern end of the camp. Intelligence units had for some time insisted that there was a VC artillery unit operating in the southern half of the province. There were supposed to be four pieces--two 75 mm U.S. Army pack howitzers and two 70 mm Japanese howitzers of World War II vintage. Hai Yen had not had an artillery attack in over two years. Radio contact with Lt. Harris and Sgt. Brown confirmed the attack and that little damage had been sustained--only a couple of rounds had landed near the middle of the compound. Dai-uy Hy told me that there were reports of old Japanese artillery pieces in the Cai Nuoc, Nam Can area but he had not seen them.

"Sir, Col. Gilland wants to speak to you," announced Sgt. Johnson, who was minding the radio during our morning coffee.

"OK, thanks," I said, as I took the handset from him.

"This is Oscar Six, over."

"Oscar Six, this Sea Forth Alpha Six. The S4 has located a .50 caliber machine gun for you. It will be a day or so before he gets his hands on it and then down to you. The 4.2 mortar is another story; they are in high demand all over but we will keep on it, over."

"That's great, we can surely put it to good use. We will need ammo, some spare parts, and an extra barrel for it."

"This is Alpha Six, that should come with it, if it is a new issue. I will remind the S4 to be sure that you get everything. Now, I believe you have an air mission pending this morning. Good luck with it, Alpha Six out."

As I started to hand the mike back to Sgt. Johnson a voice announced "Oscar Six, this is David Two Five over."

"David Two Five, this is Oscar Six over."

"Two Five here, I am about three zero out from your location. I will have some fast movers for you this morning."

"Oscar Six here, recommend you make your approach east of my location then go west down the river a couple of clicks past us. There is a canal entering the river from the north. The target area is on the east side of the canal 1,800 to 2,000 meters from the hamlet."

"Roger, Oscar Six, I have the target description and coordinates. See you shortly."

I sent Sgt. Hai to tell the District Chief that our requested air strike was on for this morning and the air craft would be here in a few minutes. I then set off, accompanied by Sgt. Johnson with the ever-present radio, to the higher old road embankment to have a better view of the pending air strike. We were soon joined by Dai-uy Hy and Sgt. Hai. It was cloudy and threatened rain, which came almost every day now. The rain did bring cooler temperatures but affected our air support. This morning the cloud cover was high and would not hamper today's mission. A few moments passed and then the buzz of a light air craft could be heard approaching from the east.

"Oscar Six, this is David Two Five. I am passing your location on the south side and am turning north to the target area."

"David Two Five, we have you in sight. What do you have this morning?"

"A flight of two F100s."

"What are they carrying?"

"Five hundred pound frags (fragmentation bombs) and their 20 mm cannons, of course. They will have only about twenty minutes on station .They will make a pass over the target then I will put them in one at a time on their bomb runs then strafe with the twenties."

"Roger Two Five, my counterpart plans on putting troops into the area when you are finished."

"My guys are here so I will be off your push for a while but I will monitor your net."

"OK, Two Five, we will be watching the strikes."

We could see the two jets circling high overhead with the FAC much lower and to the north of the VC target area. Suddenly the jets queued up and made a swooping pass over the VC positions from east to west and climbed rapidly in a northerly direction. They circled again momentarily then winged over into a dive one a few seconds behind the other. The lead jet leveled off and we could the bombs falling in a forward glide as the plane passed over the target. The second airplane

271

seemed to be right behind the lead. My God, I thought, he's going to run right into the blast of the first bomb! Not so, the second aircraft was flying on a parallel track. Then we heard the blasts. The four bombs explosions were so close together they sounded almost like one. The planes were now circling again when one broke into a shallow dive over the area .We could hear the stuttering sound of the 20 mm cannons as the pilot strafed the VC positions. Climbing to a higher altitude he circled while the second jet lined up for a strafing run. The pilot seemed to skim closer to the ground than the first and continued out further before turning to join his wing man. They then banked over our location, dipped their wings and departed off to the north.

"Oscar Six, I think we were right on target. Don't see any fires, pretty wet down there. Saw a few VC running about, didn't draw any fire. Wait a minute I'm being fired on now!"

"Yeah, Two Five, we can hear automatic weapons firing. Clear the area and we will throw in some mortar rounds."

"Roger, I'm gone. Good luck."

"Give our thanks to the fast movers and be careful, Oscar Six out."

I repeated my conversation with David Two Five to Dai-uy Hy.

Sergeant Hai added a few words in Vietnamese and said to me, "Dai-uy understands what you said. He is ordering some mortar fire then sending soldiers into the VC camp."

I nodded in agreement to Dai-uy Hy, and then told him that we were going to get the .50 caliber machine gun I had requested. He smiled broadly and said, "We must prepare a position on the bridge."

272

"Yes, we must do it soon," I replied.

I pulled out the small spiral bound notebook I carried and gestured to Dai-uy Hy to join me sitting on a nearby crate. I started to draw a sketch for mounting the tripod of the machine gun when he interrupted me saying his men knew how to secure the gun and tripod to a solid platform to compensate for the weapon's recoil. We then discussed training a crew, providing them some protection from enemy fire and a range card with aiming points or stakes. The last task would be mine. I would prepare the range and deflections for known target areas. VC mortar firing positions would be easy to determine as there were few locations where the ground was solid enough to bear the recoil of mortars or artillery. A circle of sandbags could be built around the gun position providing some protection for the crew and aiming points representing targets could be established on the inside or top of the wall upon which the crew could align upon. These aiming points would be determined by test firing in day and would greatly assist in placing accurate fire on enemy positions during darkness or periods of low visibility. Dai-uy Hy said that he and I would select the exact position on the bridge tomorrow I nodded in agreement.

CHAPTER 38

VC SUPPORTERS

A little after noon, the troops returned from the VC site that had been hit by the air strike. Their report was less than I had wished for. The bombs appeared to be right on target, destroying a number of the bunkers and the prepared mortar positions. There were no bodies, however, although several blood-stained areas indicated that there some enemy causalities. No equipment or ammunition was found.

An analysis of the air strike revealed both negatives and positives. On the negative side there were no KBA (killed by air), no wounded captured, no signs of destroyed weapons or equipment, and no intelligence material found. Bunkers and firing platforms that were destroyed could be restored rather quickly; after all, they were mainly built of mud and small logs. On the plus side, we could be sure there were some casualties as indicated by the blood trails, and the establishment of an enemy position close to our location was interrupted--one that was intended to provide close indirect fire to support a ground attack. And certainly there was a boost in the morale of the soldiers and civilians in Dong Cung. Close air support, although requested many times, was seldom received. Dai-uy Hy was convinced that the air strike had delayed the ground attack he was so sure was coming. The afternoon passed with a few rain showers and several mortar rounds just before dark.

The following morning, the District Chief and I selected a site on the bridge for the .50 caliber machine gun. He informed me that he had already put men to work building a firing platform and would have the position on the bridge ready when the machine gun arrived. He then invited me to accompany him the next day on a short trip north to a small group of houses occupied by farmers reportedly friendly to the government. I jumped at his invitation, as I had not been out of the environs of Dong Cung since my arrival.

There had been activity to our north the previous night and again that morning. The Cai Nuoc Outpost had been attacked, and a patrol from the outpost, while on a sweep to the south, made contact with an unknown VC force, resulting in two friendly wounded. That meant a total of four, counting two others hit during the night mortar attack. I radioed for a medevac. Day by day, our troop strength continued to dwindle. Our now normal afternoon rain shower was particularly heavy that day, limiting a VC mortar attack to a single round. The afternoon passed without any other enemy activity aimed at Dong Cung. However, the platoon outpost 1,500 meters up the river received small arms fire and two RPGs (Rocket Propelled Grenades).

The continual enemy activity caused me an additional concern. Our two-man advisory team--Johnson and me--was stretched painfully thin. We had to be operational 24/7 with little downtime. We were up most nights, particularly during the pre-dawn hours, which were the prime time for a VC ground attack. There was little opportunity to rest our minds or our bodies. I was afraid that Johnson or I, or both of us, would lose our focus and make a costly mistake. Because I had no other advisor at present, Johnson or I had to do it all no matter what it might be. Sgt. Johnson was a fine NCO, but I had to consider that he as well as I could tire from constant pressure. We needed a day off, but that was not possible until I receive additional Advisors for our team. I kept an eye on Johnson, but his performance of duty without complaining was all I could ask for.

That evening, Sgt. Johnson asked me if he could be transferred to another location. He stated that he had been with me over nine months and would like to finish his tour of duty in an area where there were more U.S. soldiers present and the living conditions were not so primitive. Johnson had proven to be a good and dependable NCO, cool under fire, and deliberate in the performance of his duties. I recognized that even at Hai Yen there were fellow NCOs and frequent visitors with whom he could, in some fashion, socialize with, but here I was the only American he came in contact with except for brief contacts with chopper pilots. In the personnel pipeline, replacements for September rotations were probably already being selected but that was some still weeks off. I told Johnson I fully understood his request and the reasons for it and that I would ask the PSA to send the next available NCO arriving in Cu Mau to Cai Nuoc. Sergeant Johnson could then be moved to some position on the Province Team until the end of his tour. He was quite happy with my plan and said that he had some reluctance in leaving Cai Nuoc but believed he had done his share. I agreed.

We received the normal VC evening mortar attack around 1800 hours. It appeared that the enemy was trying to interrupt our evening meal. Twenty to twenty-five rounds impacted on the north side, mostly in the wire outside of our wall. They were a mix of 60s and 82s this time, which meant they might have been firing from two different locations. I immediately requested close air support but was denied. Most of the mortar attacks seemed to be concentrated on our northwest side.

While walking the wall after the mortar attack with Dai-uy Hai, he told me we would leave at 0800 in the morning. He wanted to talk to the civilians that resided in the small cluster of houses only a short distance from Dong Cung. He had sent word for them to report to him, but they had not come to the District Headquarters. I assured him I would be ready. Sergeant Johnson would stay behind and Sgt. Hai would accompany me.

Of course it was raining the next morning as we passed north through our strong point on the old road and onto the footpath. A few meters to our right, the canal, created by excavating material to build the road, ran north to south, parallelling the road to the old district town

276

of Cai Nuoc now known as Cai Nuoc Outpost. It was navigable by sampans and small boats.

The footpath was worn and appeared to be well used. In that it was actually my first foray north along the old road, I was paying close attention to the area we were passing through. The bushes and heavy growth on the left side of the foot path thinned out, ending in what appeared to be untilled fields, though I could see some small areas that were cultivated. In the distance, a tree line could be seen which I knew was the Rach Dong Cung. To the right, trees and brush prevented a view beyond the opposite bank of the canal. Our party numbered approximately 30, with a squad of eight or nine ahead of the District Chief's small command group and the remaining troops to our rear. I noted there were no supporting weapons, machine gun,s or a mortar, only a couple of BARs in the column. The Dai-uy must be confident that the chance of meeting up with a VC unit was slim. I was not. But then advisors were never sure that they were made aware of all the pertinent enemy intelligence.   We moved slowly in single file. The VC frequently placed mines and/or booby traps along the path, and the soldiers were very careful in every step they took.

It was a little more than an hour later when we reached our destination. Four houses in a row were sited 25 meters or so from the canal. There were several small sampans tied to a dock constructed of small logs. In front of the houses stood several elderly men, who nodded their heads in greeting to the District Chief. One came forward, stretching out his hands to Dai-uy Hy, who clasped them firmly and spoke in a courteous manner to him. The remaining men, who all seem to be a bit younger, came forward and were introduced to the District Chief, who then turned and pointed to me. Sergeant Hai interpreting quickly told me that Dai-uy Hy identified me as an American officer who had come to help him defeat the VC and improve the life of the citizens. They all nodded in greeting which I smilingly nodded in return.

277

The civilian leader then led us to some benches in the shade of one of the houses and invited us to sit down with him. We were joined by the others and a woman who brought out a tray with a pot of tea and small cups. She placed the tray alongside of the elder civilian and returned inside the house. Dai-uy Hy waited until the tea was poured before starting the conversation. I motioned to Sgt. Hai not to interpret the on-going dialogue. I did not want to interrupt the flow between the elder and Dai-uy Hy. I would get a summary later. The exchange began in a polite and measured manner, with the District Chief asking questions that were answered by the elder civilian; some answers elicited nods of agreement from the other men. From my limited knowledge of Vietnamese, I determined that he was just inquiring about their crops and their general welfare. Dai-uy Hy's tone suddenly became strident, and his questions were spat out so rapidly that I could not catch even a word. The elder responded unevenly, in short one- or two-word answers. The other civilians became visibly agitated. Suddenly the District Chief stood up and pointed to the group with the wave of his hand and spoke in a commanding voice. They also stood up but kept their eyes diverted, not looking at Dai-uy Hy.

He turned to me and said, "We go to Headquarters now."

He spoke to one of his men standing by, who called out to the soldiers to prepare to move out. Upon arrival they had spread out around the houses in a rough circle and now began moving toward the footpath for the return to the hamlet. Sgt. Hai fell in alongside of me as we moved out.

I asked him, "What did Dai-uy say just before we left?"

"He say they must move to Dong Cung. If they do not, he come back and burn their houses down."

"Are they VC?" I queried.

278

Sergeant Hai shrugged his shoulders. "Maybe, maybe supporters."

Well, I thought, I will get the whole story when we get back and I can sit down and talk with Dai-uy Hy.

It was only a little after noon when we arrived back and were greeted by Sgt. Johnson.

"Good news, sir, we have two choppers on the way. They have some men on board. Don't know if they are replacements or hospital returnees. Also some ammo and other stuff, don't know what."

"Great," I responded, "How soon?"

"Forty, forty five minutes. They are just leaving Ca Mau."

"They have guns with them?" I asked.

"No, sir, they are alone. There are already troops on the pad to unload the stuff."

"Anything else happen while we were out in the country side?" I asked.

"Yes sir, a patrol up the river between here and the outpost at Rach Cai Muoi ran into an unknown-size group of VC. There was no contact; the bad guys skedaddled."

"Scared of us, huh," I commented.

"Yeah, right!" Johnson replied.

The choppers came and went without incident during a brief shower. One of the pilots gave us a large salami sausage and a bottle of brandy. The brandy we would save for an evening night cap. The sausage we cut up for our lunch. After we had finished eating and had stored away our remaining sausage, I asked Sgt. Johnson to go and find Sgt. Hai. I wanted to know what exactly what went on with the villagers this morning. Johnson was back in a few minutes with Sgt. Hai.

"Sergeant Hai, tell us what happened out there with the villagers this morning."

"Yes, sir. The captain thinks the farmers there help the VC. They visit Dong Cung and report to VC what they see. VC want to know about Americans. Villagers say no, not true. Dai-uy say why not they come when he send for them. He tell them they must move to Dong Cong. They say they do not want to. He say he will return in one week and burn down their houses. Perhaps kill men."

"Do you think he would?" I asked.

"Oh yes, sir."

Our conversation was cut short. Enemy rounds began to fall. Everyone was scattering for cover when I noticed that the incoming VC fire sounded different. Damn, I thought, it's artillery! The incoming was scattered, with some landing on the east side and a few, two or three, impacting near the center of town and several in the river. In a minute or two it was over, a total of ten, perhaps twelve rounds. Outside of hitting the ground, Sgts. Johnson, Hai and I did not have time to take cover. As we stood up, Dai-uy Hy approached and said, "Nipponese gun."

"Japanese howitzer?" I asked.

280

"Da phi, 70 mm, VC have two," he replied.

"From the pattern of the rounds it looks like they fired from the west or northwest," I commented.

"From the west, on north side of river, maybe four, five kilometers."

"I will request a bird dog to VR the area, west of us down the river ASAP," I told him.

As I turned to search for Sgt. Johnson, I heard him say, "I'm on it sir!"

"Good, be sure to tell them that it is the first artillery attack we have had."

Dai-uy Hy, nodding that he understood and said, "I go check on damage" and strode off toward his bunker. I waved to Sgt. Hai to go with him so he might report back to me on whatever the District Chief found.

In my mind, I was trying to put together what was happening. We had been receiving mortar fire daily, which was not unusual. We had found a VC base being built in close proximity to us and a VC unit of unknown size was seen to the east of Dong Cung yesterday. Additionally there was some sniper fire and contact with the enemy by some of our patrols. Was this an increase in enemy activity? The artillery fire was certainly an upgrade. I was expecting some effort by the VC to push the American team out. Perhaps this was the beginning. Sgt. Hai returned and reported several hooches (houses) were hit, with one soldier slightly wounded.

"Dai-uy worried, expects VC soon attack. More soldiers on guard tonight," Hai volunteered.

"You mean ground attack?" I asked.

"Yes, sir," he replied.

"OK, I'm going to find Dai-uy Hy and see what he is planning," I announced. "Let me know if we get the VR we asked for. Oh! I guess I will hear it if we get one."

I met the District Chief coming out of the passageway to his bunker. He motioned to me to join him as he walked off toward our defensive positions on the north side of the hamlet. He went directly to the strong points that were astride the old road, the two fortified bunkers which were sited between the bridge approach and the dugout with the fox holes. Each of the fortified positions had machine guns and firing ports and was constructed to withstand small arms and grenade attacks. They could also support by fire the troops manning the foxholes to their front. He checked on the amount of ammunition on hand and had the soldiers fire a burst from each machine gun to ensure they were operable. At the foxhole positions with their supporting dugout, he told the soldiers they must be alert and not sleep. He then checked the ammunition and the condition of the one BAR they had.

Next we walked the wall encircling the northwest side from the old road to the defensive positions at the end of the hamlet at the river's edge. At the end of our inspection, Dai-uy gave instructions to several NCOs to repair and reinforce several firing positions on the wall that he was not pleased with. We then returned to the main street of the hamlet to the stand that sold coffee, tea, noodle soup, and dumplings. We ordered tea and began discussing his concern of an imminent ground attack. I said that we needed some intelligence, information on any concentration of VC units and the location of the artillery that fired on us today. Dai-uy Hy replied that he had civilians talking to the local people, and the National Police contingent was questioning families of suspected VC supporters. While we spoke, a familiar throbbing sound announced the approach of a light aircraft. A few moments later ,Shotgun appeared to our north. As we watched, he swung to the west following the river downstream in the direction of the Gulf of Thailand. We were then joined by Sgt. Johnson carrying our radio.

"I have Shotgun 46 on the net," he said offering me the handset.

Keying the mike, I transmitted, "Shotgun 46, this Oscar six, over."

"Oscar Six, Four Six here, understand you had some incoming this afternoon over."

"Roger, Four Six, we believe it came from the west. It was short range we think, maybe only four to six clicks out. I know we will soon lose the light, but check out the canals on the north side. We know there are civilians living in that area and probably VC or VC supporters."

"OK, will do. I will be over that area in a minute or two."

We watched the plane fly downstream then make a slow turn to the north. Dusk was arriving rapidly and it would soon be dark. A few minutes later Shotgun 46 came back on the net.

"Oscar Six, this is Shotgun 46, over."

"Shotgun 46, this is Oscar Six. Did you spot anything?"

"Negative, only the houses along the canals, quite a few with sampans tied up in front. Sorry I couldn't see more. Perhaps you can request a Delta Hawk mission; they have that night-seeing radar. It's worth a try."

"Yeah, I'll give it a try. Thanks for your help."

"Any time, Oscar Six, out here."

We watched as the FAC disappeared into the growing darkness. It was nearing 1900 hours and past time for our evening meal of rice, fish, and greens accompanied by a couple rounds of enemy mortar fire. We were not disappointed. Several rounds were received, resulting in two casualties.

CHAPTER 39

DAYLIGHT GROUND ATTACK

The District Chief's concern did not seem to have been transmitted down through the ranks. I could not detect any increase in the level of alertness resulting from his prediction that the VC would soon launch a ground attack. The nightly defensive posture seemed to be routine, but when I checked a couple guard posts, I noted there were extra men in each one. Sergeant Johnson and I retreated to our quarters. Johnson tried to get an hour or two of sleep, while I wrote a report of the day's activities. I contacted the Province TOC and requested a night aerial recon of the area west and north of Dong Cung. I was told there was no chance for tonight, though perhaps one for tomorrow night; I would get an answer to my request in the morning. Then the Team S4, Captain Morse, came on the net and told me that he had my .50 caliber machine gun with spare parts and an additional barrel plus ammunition ready to ship down to us. He said they were new, still packed in the original crates. I had worried that we might get a hand-me-down.

"Great," I said., "Be sure you send a cleaning rod, patches, and some oil."

"I will get it all on the next lift down to you," replied Morse.

"Thanks, we will be looking for it."

Good news, I thought. I will tell Dai-uy in the morning so we can be prepared to assemble the weapon and get it mounted on the bridge. I then pulled off my boots and shirt and lay down on the other cot to catch a few winks before I made my normal 2300 to 2400 hour tour of the guard posts.

The recognizable "thump thump" sound of a BAR firing abruptly ended my attempt to sleep and brought me to my feet.

"What's going on?" I asked Johnson.

"Don't know, it sounds like it's up near the dugout on the road," he replied.

"Well, let's get up there and see what's going on," I said, as several rifle shots rang out.

As we exited our quarters, we could hear some shouting and then Sgt. Hai appeared out of the darkness and blurted out, "VC traitor."

"What?"

"One soldier VC, shot three others, run away with BAR," he replied.

Trailed by Sgts. Johnson and Hai, I started toward the noise when I met Lt. Hong coming toward us.

"VC shoot three soldiers, then run away. One soldier dead two wounded. Need medevac," he reported.

"OK, we will call in a request. Where is Dai-uy Hy?'

"There," Hong replied, pointing with his chin toward the north, "near wall."

"Sergeant Johnson, get a medevac request in. I think we have four now that need to get out. I'm going to find Dai-uy. Sgt. Hai, come with me," I ordered as I started off again toward the site of the

286

shooting. Arriving at the wire, I met Dai-uy Hy who, shaking his head, pointed to the dead soldier and the wounded who were being carried to our aid station and said, "VC agent, new soldier."

"A replacement?" I asked.

"Da phai. VC may attack. I put more soldiers on wall."

I could see small groups of three or four soldiers in each fanning out along the mud wall. I knew that the District Chief's concern about a ground attack had greatly increased in the past several days. Does he know something that I don't? Is there something he hasn't told me? Unfortunately, an advisor might think that the rapport between himself and his counterpart is great, but he must still realize that his counterpart may or will not completely confide in him. The rest of the night passed without any further excitement. In the morning we received good and bad news from the Province TOC. The medevac was on, but our scheduled supply run was canceled and promised for the following day.

The medevac chopper arrived around 0900 without an escort and took out our wounded. During a morning walk around the north side, I noted that the additional soldiers placed on the wall remained, which meant I could expect less men out on patrol today; we only had so many. We really needed to get the men we had waiting for transport in Ca Mau down to Dong Cung. The few that were able to get on our supply runs barely replaced the losses we were experiencing.

We had our daily dose of rain showers around noon. I had not seen Dai-uy Hy that day as he seemed to be busy with some civilian matters. It had become a daily routine that if we had not seen each other during the day, we would meet in the late afternoon. He would brief me on the day's activities, and we would discuss our plans and the problems we needed to address. Defense and security was still at the top of the list. I wanted to hear what his thoughts were on the VC turncoat and deserter of last night.

It was almost 1500 and I started to walk over to Dai-uy Hy's bunker to see if he was there when several mortar rounds began exploding within the perimeter. I hastened into the shelter of the tunnel entrance and was joined by Dai-uy Hy, who was entering from the other side. The intensity of the attack increased. I counted roughly 30 or more rounds, both 60s and 82s, before they began to taper off. The mortar barrage seemed to be over. Then I heard some small arms fire that sounded at a distance, followed by the crack of rounds passing overhead. I could now distinguish friendly fire. Our guys were firing at something. A soldier came rushing into the tunnel shouting "VC come, VC come!"

Dai-uy Hy looked at me and said, "We go!" He then put on a helmet handed to him by a soldier, picked up his cane, and with a pistol tucked in his belt strode out toward the north side perimeter wall.

I turned to Sgt. Johnson, who had joined me in the tunnel and directed, "Get on the net with Province and tell them we are under a ground attack and see if they can get us some air."

Johnson handed me his carbine as I ran out of the tunnel entrance to catch up with the District Chief. We made our way between the houses out to the perimeter wall. There I saw some troops crouched or sitting behind the wall, and others firing over the top in the general direction of the distant wood line. The incoming mortar fire had ceased and I could see a line of VC soldiers advancing in our direction. They had reached the outer edge of our barbed wire and were firing as they began picking their way through looking for the paths used by our troops to pass through the wire tangles.

288

Dai-uy Hy began shouting "Lien, lien! (up,up!), ban, ban! (shoot, shoot!), and climbed up on the wall waving his cane at his men. The enemy, perhaps 50 or 60,were about a third of the way through the wire and were firing erratically. A machine gun opened up on our side, soon followed by a BAR. More soldiers were standing now, leaning on the top of the wall and firing. A second BAR started firing. The VC line appeared to falter then stopped. The friendly fire increased. You could see enemy soldiers dropping. Suddenly they began to fall back. However there seemed to be an increase in the enemy fire. There must have been other VC covering by fire their advance and now their retreat.

I yelled at Dai-uy Hy. "Get down off the wall. You are going to get hit!"

"No," he shook his head. "I must not show fear."

The VC had now reached the far edge of the wire and the speed of their movement toward the tree line increased. I saw one VC go down and another turn back toward the down man and retrieve his weapon and continue his way to the rear. In a few moments they had disappeared from sight. The District troops continued to fire.

I called out to the Dai-uy, "Fire mortars on the tree line!"

He nodded in response.

"Major," said Sgt. Johnson coming up behind me, "I got hold of the TOC and requested air support. They are going to send something. Don't know what but whatever they can get. The attack will probably be over before they get here."

"Yeah, you're right about that. It's over now. But we can pound that tree line and canal bank. You know they used the canal to stage, and are using it now to withdraw."

The District Chief had jumped down off the wall and was walking along the line. I hurried to join him and found he was complimenting the troops and checking the wounded. We were really fortunate; no one was killed and only four were wounded. At least 17, perhaps as many as 20 of the enemy were killed in the attack, and causalities from our mortar fire may have added to that figure. I told the Dai-uy that we had some air support on the way. He nodded and said, "Maybe they catch VC resting, treating wounded."

About 20 minutes later, the drone of a FAC could be heard.

Then, "Oscar six, this is David Two Five over."

"David Two Five, this is Oscar Six over."

"Heard you had some trouble, sorry I couldn't be here to help but I got something different for you today."

"What's that?"

"A pair of Australian B 57 Canberas."

"Two engine bombers?" I asked.

"This is Two Five, that's a roger, loaded with 500 and 1,000 pound bombs."

"Well, that's great, because I have an area target for you. I want you to hit a section of a canal line on the northwest side of our location. The VC launched their attack from there and we believe they fell back to that area to rest, regroup, and later disperse. I will give you two coordinates along the canal and then that area is all yours in between."

"Roger, feed them to me, I think I know the area anyway."

"Two Five, here they are, six digit 018787 to 011800 that is the east side of the canal, look at both sides though."

"OK, Oscar, I'm off your net for a while."

"Roger, Two Five, Oscar Six out."

Almost simultaneously, the two bombers appeared to the northeast flying at a lower altitude than we normally saw large aircraft. They, apparently being guided by the FAC, circled over the target area then off to the north, banked 180 degrees and began their run over the target. We could easily hear the bombs exploding, some louder than others--the difference between the 500 and 1,000 pound ones, we guessed. Each plane made two runs north to south then climbed rapidly to the north and were quickly out of sight. We counted what we thought was eight bombs dropped. We could see David 25 circling the area and then turning and passing over us.

"Oscar Six, this is David Two Five, we have completed the mission. Nine bombs were dropped. The foliage is such that I can't do a decent BDA (bomb damage assessment). There were some hooches that were hit, only a couple."

"This is Oscar Six, that's OK, we will get some folks in there to see what happened."

"Roger, let us know what you find."

"Will do, thank the Aussies for us. Oscar Six out."

291

That night we received several mortar rounds fired from across the river, I guess to let us know they were still out there.

CHAPTER 40

NEW BLOOD

In the morning a Huey chopper brought our .50 caliber machine gun along with ammunition and other needed supplies, plus two soldiers who were hospital returnees. The crew that Dai-uy Hy had selected began unpacking and cleaning the weapon. The tripod was immediately carried up to the position on the bridge and the feet bolted down with iron straps to the wooden mounting platform. Cleaning the machine gun was quite a chore; it was in the original shipping crate and covered with cosmoline, a preservative that was difficult to remove.

I wanted to mount the machine gun and get it sighted in before dark. I knew that I would have to set the timing and head space and show the crew the immediate action drill needed to clear a stoppage or malfunction. Although he was not overly familiar with the weapon, Sgt. Johnson worked with the crew, pushing them along. As a result we had the gun mounted, sighted in, and ready to fire by 1600 hours.

A range card had been developed and aiming points placed on the sandbag parapet around the gun position. Placing the aiming points was easy, as the areas that mortars could be fired from and avenues of approach used by the VC were generally known. All we had to do now was to sight in on the targets, fire, and zero in. We could then adjust the stakes so that by sighting on the aiming point, in either daylight or darkness, the weapon would be aimed at the target.

The first rounds we fired were right over the center of the hamlet street. We had not thought about warning the people in the hamlet that the gun would be firing, in many cases over the community. The loud noise and the echo sent the residents scurrying for cover. They were used to small arms, mortar, and artillery fire, but the sound of a .50 caliber machine gun firing over them was something new. However, they soon got used to it.

The crew caught on quickly, and now we had a direct-fire weapon that could easily engage targets out to 800 or 900 meters. It made it possible to eliminate most 60 mortar and sniper fire; however, I was worried that the crew was not experienced enough to function when under attack. I planned that if I was present, I would join the crew until they gained the experience needed.

I met with Dai-uy Hai that evening, and over a glass of coffee we discussed the enemy activities over the past two days. He was sure that the ground attack was a result of information provided by the deserter. I didn't know if I agreed. The VC must have already known the number of troops and weapons we had. And the size of the VC force, which appeared to be less than a hundred, was not large enough unless the District forces were totally unprepared and poorly led. I told Dai-uy that I thought it was a probe mainly to see what the reaction would be now that there are American advisors here on the ground. After a few moments, he nodded in agreement.

"Maybe you are right," he said. "I need more troops. I need soldiers at Ca Mau." I knew he was referring to the replacements and hospital returnees awaiting transport to us. "Need more ammunition, more mortar ammunition, M 79 ammunition. I have none," he continued. The M 79, a shoulder-fired weapon resembling a single barreled shot gun, could fire a 40 mm round 250 to 300 meters and was relatively new to the Vietnamese troops. It gave the individual soldier the ability to project area-type munitions far beyond the hand grenade range.

"If I have more men, ammunition, weapons, I can attack VC. But now not enough, only can hold District Headquarters. Must hold

Dong Cung. Headquarters was in Cai Nuoc, move here, cannot move again."

"I know," I replied.

I had to break loose the log jam on the re-supply, I thought to myself. I was promised supply runs every other day and they were not happening. I had to talk to the PSA.

"Dai-uy, why are most of all our attacks coming from the north and northwest and none from Nam Can? The area has no government, and the VC control the whole district."

"Da," the District Chief replied, "but VC will not attack Dong Cung across river, will cross river to the west then attack on our side."

I had asked a stupid question. Of course the enemy would not attempt to attack across a water barrier. They could use artillery and mortar, indirect fire, to harass us or support a ground attack from the north side but would not attempt a direct assault across the river.

"When I have enough soldiers I attack VC areas," Dai-uy Hy stated, pointing in a northerly direction.

Later, I contacted the Province Team TOC and asked to talk to the PSA. I was told that Gilland had rotated back to the States and a Lt. Col. of Japanese descent had taken his place. His name was Nagota and was in processing at MACV Headquarters in Saigon. I then asked for Lt. Col. Wright, the DPO. Over the past several weeks, he had been the most helpful person at the Province Team level. He knew of the supply problem and said the Province Chief's staff was working on a plan to move all the Cai Nuoc troops down to us. He promised that he would do what he could to expedite their efforts. He then had a surprise for me: the replacement for Sgt. Johnson was in and would be on the next flight. His name was Blair and this was his second tour in Vietnam as an advisor, so I would not be getting a newbie. That was both good and bad news. I was getting an experienced NCO but I would miss Sgt. Johnson who had been competent and reliable.

The following morning arrived with the normal rain shower and a few VC mortar rounds. I had Sgt. Johnson notify Province, and I was off running to the machine gun position on the bridge. We had not yet had the opportunity to try and knock out the 60 mm mortar fire and I wanted to supervise this first attempt. As I jumped into the gun position, I saw that the Vietnamese NCO in charge had aligned the gun on an aiming stake we had positioned in hope that it corresponded to one of the areas we thought the VC used to fire from.

"Fire away," I yelled.

The gunner fired a burst of 10 to 15 rounds. They were passing diagonally over the center of the village street and the sound of the firing was deafening to the ears of the individuals that were under the passing rounds. I motioned to the gunner by waving my hand from side to side to traverse the gun while firing. I had previously tried to explain the cone of fire and the dispersion of the rounds at various distances. Abruptly the incoming mortar fire stopped. We waited for several minutes but there was no resumption of enemy fire. We had shut them down! I heard the sound of our mortars firing and guessed that Dai-uy Hy had ordered the counter mortar fire, hoping to catch the VC mortar crew before they could make a safe withdrawal.

As I descended off the bridge, I met the District Chief. He was grinning broadly and said, "VC 60 mortar attacks fini!"

I nodded, "I hope so."

"I send out squad to check VC mortar position," Dai-uy stated.

"Good," I replied. "I am going to call Province and tell them to be sure that our ammo shipments include .50 caliber."

Dai-uy saluted as he departed in the direction of the Headquarters building.

I was highly pleased with the results of the first use of the heavy machine gun. It appeared that the addition of just this one weapon was going to make a great difference in the close-in defense of the District Headquarters and Dong Cung. And at night, the .50 caliber tracer rounds were an impressive sight for those who might have not seen them before. They gave the appearance of large balls of fire arcing rapidly through the darkness. But I also recognized that the VC would make a concerted effort to eliminate the machine gun. It would be a hard target for small arms or indirect fire weapons but would be vulnerable to direct fire weapons such as RPGs or a Recoilless Rifle. It had been reported that Local Force VC units had a U.S. 57 mm Recoilless Rifle. Now if only I could get the 4.2 Mortar, we would be able to provide supporting fire for our troops out to six kilometers or more.

Over the next several days, the VC mortared us with their 60 and 82 mm mortars, then one night with the 82s only. One night we could hear the VC urging the defenders via a bull horn to "kill the Covans" (kill the Advisors). Although Sgt. Johnson and I trusted the troops, we were still a little apprehensive.

When our counterparts found out that Sgt. Johnson was leaving, the NCOs arranged a farewell party for him. He was well-liked by the troops and their families. Johnson asked me if he could stop in Hai Yen for a couple of days before reporting at the Province where he would complete his tour. I told him he could certainly do so. I would clear it with the Province Team. We kept in contact with the team at Hai Yen on a daily basis, and I knew that Johnson would like to visit

297

with them before he rotated home. Although it was not for a couple of months yet, it would be unlikely that he would have the opportunity to return there for a day or two. I planned to hold Johnson for a couple of days after his replacement arrived so he could help him get acquainted with the contacts he had developed among the NCOs and others during the time he had been in Dong Cung.

Enemy activity throughout the province appeared to be increasing in general. By monitoring the Province radio net, we were able to keep up upon the cadence of engagements, attacks on outposts, ambushes, and assassinations of civil officials. Hamlet and Village Chiefs seemed to be prime targets. Hai Yen forces were busy in the Quan Pho area, as usual, and along the Gulf of Thailand in the northwest quadrant of their AO. Closer to home, in addition to attacks on Dong Cung, Cai Nuoc Outpost was receiving an increase in enemy attacks, including some clashes with VC by their patrols. Additionally, the platoon outpost east of Dong Cung at the mouth of Rach Cai Keo was receiving mortar fire almost every day, and small groups thought to be VC were spotted in the vicinity of the outpost. Dai-uy Hy advised me if they came under ground attack at night, he would not go to their aid. Air support would be the only help they could expect. They were on the outmost range of the artillery at the district town of Cha La. Firing in support of the outpost would be very risky. I had not been to that outpost but was told that it had less than 30 soldiers, and two BARs were their heaviest weapons.

My concern over our strength had not been alleviated. We were losing two or three KIA and five or six wounded a week. However, a couple of hospital returnees or replacements were arriving on each supply lift that we received, which kept us at about 50 percent of our authorized strength. We needed the 90 plus troops waiting at Ca Mau badly, and the only response I could get from Province was they were working on it.

The sniper and 60 mortar fire had all but ceased and the District Chief began planning some offensive excursions into suspected VC encampments that lay between us and Cai Nuoc outpost to the north. The operations would be only raids or one-day sweeps, as Dai-uy Hy still felt that he could not risk the security of Dong Cung by not having all his troops there at night. The stock of ammunition was now sufficient, but we badly needed the men at the airfield in Ca Mau. The next supply run brought one soldier and Staff Sergeant John M. Blair, Johnson's replacement. As Blair stepped off the chopper he saluted and said, "Staff Sergeant Blair reporting for duty sir."

"Welcome to Cai Nuoc District. I'm Major Dagenais and this is Platoon Sergeant Johnson, the man you are replacing," I announced.

Johnson, grinning from ear to ear, stuck out his hand and said "Sgt. Blair, I'm sure glad to see you!"

After shaking hands, the two NCOs picked up Blair's gear and Johnson led the way to our quarters. I watched them walking away and felt a little sad. Sergeant Johnson had been a good soldier and companion. I would miss him. He would leave on the next supply run and return to the Province Advisory Team as agreed upon, where he would complete his tour before returning to the United States.

CHAPTER 41

SIEGE FINI

Great news: We were going to get the 4.2 inch mortar I had requested! I received a message from the DPO, Lt. Col. Wright, that the Province Chief had agreed to place a heavy mortar in Cai Nuoc District. It was supposed to go to the Nam Can District, but that had been abandoned. We were to get it in a week it would take a couple of lifts to move the mortar, ammunition, and maintenance items to our location.

Dai-uy Hy received the news through his channels at the same time as I did through mine and came to tell me that he had already ordered the preparation of a site for its installation. The 81 mm mortar would be moved and that location would be enlarged to accommodate the larger weapon. The site was on the old roadbed; this provided the firmest ground available, which was needed to withstand the considerable impact of firing the 4.2 mortar. This addition to our indirect fire weapons would greatly increase our defense and provide supporting fire for offensive operations that were under our control. Training a crew for it would be a problem, but our good luck continued. Newly arrived Sgt. Blair was a qualified mortar squad leader and could assist in transitioning our mortar crew from the 81 to the 4.2. When I had sat down to chat and become acquainted with Blair's experience and background, this qualification came as a welcome surprise.

The brief respite we were enjoying from the close-in VC fire was interrupted one afternoon. The enemy fired a half a dozen 60 mm mortar rounds from across the river into the western end of the hamlet. We responded with our own 60s and the heavy machine gun. There was no following-on enemy fire, and Dai-uy Hy sent about 20 troops across the river to the site, but the VC had left.

The VC use of the light mortar gave them the ability to conduct a quick unexpected attack with a minimum chance of incurring casualties. As an example, four or five VC could travel in one or two small sampans with a mortar tube and several rounds of ammunition. They could set up and fire five or six rounds before the first one landed in the area targeted. Several more rounds could be fired, the mortar disassembled and loaded in a sampan, and the enemy mortar crew on their way before the defending government forces could determine the source and respond. The key to being effective is the VC must know in advance the areas where the terrain is solid enough to support firing a mortar and to be able to fire a number of rounds rapidly at a target such as a hamlet, village, or outpost.

This type of "shoot and scoot" attack is only effective as a harassing type of fire and not usually effective against a point target. It serves to keep the defenders on edge, nervous, and wondering if the attack is a prelude to a more severe assault. To counter the effectiveness of these minor mortar attacks, the defenders need to know the most likely firing sites and be able to engage them quickly to suppress or end the VC fire. This we planned to do with the heavy machine gun, as we could return fire more quickly than countering with our own mortars.

After this particular attack, the troops returned and reported that there were two mortar positions prepared but it appeared that only one was used, indicating that they had only one mortar tube with them. They did not touch the sites except to place some grenade traps in the immediate area. Two nights later we heard some explosions from that direction. The following morning Dai-uy sent a squad across the river to investigate. They returned with three bodies which they threw upon the hamlet dock where the residents came to look at them to see if they were known. Needless to say, those grenade traps were successful.

301

After our evening meal, while Blair and I wandered through the hamlet, we noticed that the bodies were still on the dock and walked out to where they lay. They had been there since early morning and the heat of the day caused them to swell and smell. Flies were buzzing around them. While we were looking at them a soldier joined us and said smilingly, "VC fini" and made a gesture across his neck indicating slashing a throat. He then noticed a ring on the hand of one of the bodies partially hidden by the swelling. He stooped down and attempted to remove the ring, which refused to come off. The soldier then produced a knife and cut the finger off at the upper knuckle joint. Holding the finger by the nail end he now tried to pull the ring off from the knuckle end. It still did not come loose. Then the soldier popped the knuckle end of the finger into his mouth and with his teeth managed to pull the ring free. Holding the ring up admiringly, he threw the finger in the river and strolled back into the village. Blair and I looked at each other in stunned silence. Then Blair muttered, "What are we doing in this Godforsaken part of the world."

The following day the District Chief announced, "I have made operation plan." "What are we doing?" I asked. "We go," he said pointing to the north, "meet soldiers from Cai Nuoc Outpost and catch VC between us." He then explained that he had information that the VC were establishing a headquarters along the old road between Dong Cung and Cai Nuoc Outpost. He believed that they were planning an attack on either Cai Nuoc Outpost or us. Dai-uy felt that is why the VC activity had decreased--that they were preparing for a major effort.

The plan was that our 472 and 371 Companies would move north along the old road and that a platoon from 518 Company would advance parallel to them on the east side of the canal along the roadway. Two platoons from 526 Company (Cai Nuoc Outpost) would proceed south to meet 371 Company, with the third platoon on the east side of the road and canal. The order of march from Dong Cung would be 371 in the lead, with the command group and 472 Company following. The platoon across the canal would maintain a 200 meter flank from the main column. The platoon from Cai Nuoc outpost would stick to the old road, with the flanking platoon the same 200 meter distance as the platoon northbound. There would be sampans on the canal to return wounded to Dong Cung or for other use as needed.

I alerted the Province Team TOC to our operation and requested a bird dog for VR (air reconnaissance), as well as close air and medevac support. Our operation was planned to be a combination of warfare from decades ago--with foot soldiers, no artillery, and transporting wounded by sampan--and the modern concept of fire support by air—with rapid evacuation off the battlefield of the wounded and aerial re-supply. Hopefully all would be available if required. Aviation assets were a priority and we were at the bottom of the list.

Dai-uy Hy announced that we might go in the morning or maybe the next day. He would let me know during the night so I could keep Province notified. I knew he would wait until the last possible moment to initiate the operation in order to deny the VC any information of a move against them. At 0300 his orderly came to our quarters and told us that it was a go and 0700 was the jump-off time. At 0630 Blair and I joined the District Chief on the old roadbed just off the north end of the bridge. A light rain was falling as the leading element began to shuffle forward in a single file on the road past the strong point and through the wire.

The foot path was well defined from use, though not as much as one might expect. The local civilians used the adjacent canal for most of their traveling to the District Headquarters, the hamlet, and out onto the Song (river) Bay Hop. The VC frequently placed foot mines and booby traps along the path, however, causing it to be it a treacherous route of movement. The troops moved slowly, searching closely before each step forward. A 4- or 5-meter interval between

303

soldiers was maintained without constant reminding from the NCOs. A gap of 15 to 20 meters was maintained between the last squad of 371 Company and the Command Group, which consisted of Dai-uy Hy, two soldiers serving as security, his two radio operators, myself, my radio operator, Sgt. Hai my interpreter, Sgt. Blair, and a medic. The number increased or decreased as individuals from the units came and went as directed by the District Chief. I was anxious to see how Sgt. Blair would act under fire if we had contact. Blair seemed quiet and spoke softly and seldom. He had a previous tour as an advisor and I had a good feeling about him.

A map of the area indicated that the old road was almost completely lined with houses between the two locations, but VRs revealed that many houses no longer existed. They had been abandoned or destroyed by the VC or the government. The ones still left and occupied all faced the road and the canal where sampans were tied up to stakes or crude docks. Behind each house were small patches of vegetables with larger plots of rice further out. From the rice plots stretching west to a line of trees was a 300-400-meter expanse of uncultivated grass. The Command Group stopped in the front yard of one of the larger houses. A quick search found that it was empty, and the yard became our command post. Dai-uy Hy and I were studying the map when he stabbed a finger at a spot about four and one half kilometers north of Dong Cung where a short, straight, manmade canal that connected with other waterways to the east and west was crossed by the road.

"VC have storage bunkers there. Provide ammunition, supplies for units to attack Dong Cung or Cai Nuoc."

"Well, I can get some air strikes on the area and destroy whatever they have."

The Dai-uy shook his head, "Very strong bunkers, one concrete."

"Concrete, I can't believe that!" I exclaimed. Materials required to build concrete bunkers were not available. Bunkers were normally constructed of logs, dirt, mud and sometimes sand bags.

"Da phi (yes)," he replied, "it under road. One end closed with mud wall."

I looked at the map and realized what Dai-uy Hy was telling me. It was a concrete box culvert built to allow a stream to pass under the road. The VC had probably diverted the flow of water, built a mud wall at the upstream side of the road, and now had a concrete bunker with perhaps two or three meters of roadbed as overhead cover. Wow, a storage bunker impervious to all but a direct hit by a sizable bomb.

"Are there any others on the road?" I asked.

"No, all others smaller, only have drain pipes. I think much ammo there, VC will protect."

"Well, I guess we will find out soon." "Yes, soon I think," Dai-uy Hy replied.

Our answer came sooner than we thought. Only a few minutes after I found out about the concrete box culvert shots rang out at the head of the column on the road. A few at first were followed by a rise in volume for a moment or two and then fell off to a steady exchange of fire.

Dai-uy was on the radio with the 371 Company Commander. Sgt. Hai, standing by Dai-uy turned to me and said "Dai-uy Hy tell 371 Commander to hold, bring up his other soldiers, prepare mortars. He say he will have 472 Company send one platoon up to 371 Commander." The District Chief continued to issue orders and spoke to Sgt. Hai while pointing to me. "Dai-uy say to tell you he pulling platoons on the other side of canal close to canal in case need them on this side," Sgt. Hai relayed.

I nodded that I understood and then told Sgt. Blair to tell the Province TOC that we were in contact and to request a bird dog for a VR. He nodded, took the hand set from the soldier carrying our radio, and began transmitting. The light rain that was falling had ended earlier but now returned along with a thickening cloud cover. That's all we need, I mused, a heavy rain or storm which would prevent air support.

Troops from 472 Company began to appear from our rear. They were waved on forward except for the 60 mortar crew, which was held out and began setting up on the edge of the roadbed 50 meters or so south of our position in the yard. The rest of 472 Company now formed our reserve.

The firing at the front of 372 Company continued. I could hear an occasional explosion, which I assumed to be grenades, as we had no M79 ammunition. There was a lull followed by a sharp increase in the volume of fire. The District Chief was sitting in a squat and was now constantly on the radio. He looked up at me and said, "Commander 372 say VC try flank on left," pointing to the west. "He send 472 platoon to protect flank." Ah, I thought, that increase in fire I just heard was the 472 platoon.

"We have wounded," Dai-uy Hy announced. "How many?" I asked. The Dai-uy just shrugged his shoulders and was back on the radio barking out orders. I again turned to Sgt. Blair and said, "Tell the TOC we have wounded. Don't have a count yet." Blair nodded that he understood and went back on the net.

306

An NCO and several soldiers from 472 Company joined the Command Group, as added security, I suspected. The NCO, a Master Sergeant, was Chinese, one of the few old Sea Swallows that were left from when the unit was transferred from Hai Yen to Cai Nuoc. He approached me, saluted and said, "Toi la nguoi Tau" (I am Chinese)." "Toi biet (I know)", I replied. "I come with Father Hoa," he labored in English. "Gioi lam (very good)," I said.

He then smiled, saluted again, and walked back to soldiers that were with him. He looked to be about 50 years old and I wondered why he was not at Hai Yen with the rest of the original Sea Swallows. Surely he could be reassigned if he wanted. I supposed he had his own reasons.

I walked over to where Dai-uy Hy was now sitting on a low stool which had been taken from the house, sipping on a cup of tea. He held the handset to one of the radios and the other was lying in his lap. He was listening to both radios and seemed to alternate transmitting on each net. I suggested that perhaps we should join the 372 Company to see the situation for ourselves.

He shook his head. "No. the Commander is a good officer. He must fight that battle. I must be prepared to fight everywhere."

I knew this was a relatively small engagement, but counting the platoons from Cai Nuoc outpost there were close to 200 troops in the operation. That was a large percentage of Dai-uy's available force and he must be able to defend the District Town (Dong Cung) and Cai Nuoc Outpost come nightfall. Additionally, the VC had not broken contact but appeared to be maneuvering against 371 Company. They only did that when they thought they could overcome the government forces or they were protecting something. That something was the supply bunkers!

CHAPTER 42

MEETING ENGAGEMENT GOING WRONG

"371 Company has two dead and three wounded," Dai-uy Hy announced, while still on the radio. "Wounded are in sampan going to Dong Cung." "Notify Province," I called out to Sgt. Blair.

"Yes, sir, will do," he replied.

"526 Company also have contact and casualties," the District Chief continued. "What about the platoons across the canal?" I asked waving toward the east. "No contact with 521 Platoon," said the Dai-uy pointing at the radio, "518 platoon coming to canal close to here."

Suddenly, we heard the crack of a rifle round passing overhead, followed by several more. Everyone began hitting the ground or squatting down. A yell came from behind the house where a couple of soldiers were posted for security. "VC, VC!" was heard, and then the sound of carbines firing rapidly. I and Blair ran to the rear of the house. There in a small yard formed by a berm of mud between the house and the open area lay the soldiers behind a berm firing off to the west. I flopped down beside one and asked, "Where VC?"

He pointed directly out to the west across the open area to a tree line which appeared to be maybe 400 meters distant. The soldiers were all armed with the .30 caliber carbine and firing in that direction, but the possibility of placing accurate fire on a target at that range with the carbine would require an expert marksman and a lot of luck. The incoming rifle rounds snapping overhead were most likely from either U.S. M1 Garand or the German Mauser, both World War Two standard infantry rifles with an effective range of 400 meters or more. VC Local Force Units and Village guerilla squads were mainly armed with either or both weapons. The Garand and the Carbine were the main individual weapons in use by the government forces at this time. (Later they would be upgraded to the M16.)

Staring at the tree line, which I surmised to be the Rach Dong Cung, I could see several huts in the trees. I knew that the Rach was a route much used by the VC for the movement of supplies from the Nam Can District northward. Then I saw a VC running from one hut to another, followed by two more. Our soldiers fired at them excitedly, but there was no evidence of any hits. I heard Dai-uy speaking and looked to see him standing behind me.

I scrambled to my feet and asked, "What do you think is going on? Are they part of the VC unit the 371 Company is facing?" "No, they VC guerilla squad. They shoot because they see us, hope to hit someone, they not Local or Main Force VC." "Maybe we can fire a few mortar rounds over there," I suggested. "No, I must keep mortar ammo to support 371 and 526 companies." I nodded that I understood and agreed.

While we spoke, the sporadic small arms fire continued without any damage. The rounds were too high. "They fire at sky," Dai-uy said holding his arms as if he was firing a rifle up in the air. He then walked back to the front yard of the house and resumed talking on the radio.

As I followed him, one of the soldiers said "More VC!" I looked back across the open paddy fields, and sure enough there were four, perhaps five individuals moving laterally between the huts. I thought that the District Chief was probably correct and they were just trying to distract us. We needed to return the fire and I saw no one in the Command group with an M1.

A shout from the canal bank announced two things: sampans with wounded on the way to Dong Cung had pulled in to the small landing by the front yard, and soldiers from the 518 platoon appeared

309

on the opposite canal bank. Blair, a medic, and I ran over to look at the wounded. There were five, of whom two looked pretty serious. The medic examined them and punched some morphine into them. As I stood there, a thought struck me. I reached into one of the sampans and picked up an M1 rifle and a couple of bandoliers of ammo from one of the wounded and headed for the rear of the house where some soldiers were continuing to fire at the VC on the other side of the open paddy field. I called Sgt. Hai to me and asked him to check and see if the 472, which was now our reserve, had a machine gun with them. If so, I asked him to see if we could use it to engage the VC harassing us from the west. I then announced, "I'm going to do some shooting."

I was an expert shot with the M1 rifle. I had grown up in the Army with it. Several years past, when as a sergeant and attending a Light and Heavy Weapons Leadership Course at The Infantry School in Fort Benning, Georgia, I fired a perfect score, ten bull's eyes with seven in the X at 600 yards from the prone position. My second set of ten were nine in the bullseye and one in the nine ring. I could shoot. The sights on the rifle were set clear down in the receiver and on zero windage, which I had found to be common among the troops.

I raised the elevation on the rear site 20 increments and loaded a clip of all tracers that was in the bandolier (normally the rounds would be all ball ammunition). I dropped down on the ground between two soldiers and rested my rifle on the berm. I fired several rounds, watching the trajectory of the tracers carefully. I knew it would differ slightly from the ball ammunition. I ejected the tracers, inserted a clip of all ball ammunition and waited for a target. The wait was not long. In a couple of minutes two figures broke out running from right to left. I tracked the lead one and on the fourth shot saw him cartwheel and go down. The second runner also went down but was just getting out of harm's way. The soldiers stood up and cheered while emptying their weapons at the treeline. I don't think they had ever seen an enemy killed at that distance with a rifle.

310

I got up off the ground and walked over to where Dai-uy Hy was standing. I heard the 60 mortar firing and before I could ask, Dai-uy pointed to the north and said, "Support 371 Company."

I then noticed several soldiers, one with a BAR and the others carrying a .30 caliber machine gun with a tripod and ammunition cans, approaching the rear of the house. An NCO waved them into position at the berm where they could join the soldiers firing on the VC across the open paddy. I handed the M1 to one of the soldiers standing by the District Chief, who pointed to the canal in front of the yard to troops wading chest deep across from the other side.

"I bring 518 Platoon across, join us here. 526 Company cannot contact their platoon." That meant there was no one on our right flank and the 526 Company had no radio contact with their left flank. There might not be any friendlies on the east side of the road and canal.

This was the situation as I saw it: both the 371 and 526 Companies were exchanging fire with the VC, who were attempting to flank 371 Company. One platoon from the 472 Company was reinforcing 371 on the west to counter the VC movement. 472 Company "minus" was in reserve, with their mortar firing in support of 371 Company. The platoon from 518 Company had crossed the canal and was in the area of the Command Group. They were available to assist 371 Company or to clear the area to our west from where we had been receiving the ineffective, harassing, small arms fire. We had casualties in both lead Companies. A medevac was on its way.

I had been told that 526 Company did not have their mortar with them. They had left it in the outpost for defense and to cover the return of the company to the outpost if in contact with the VC. Additionally, Dai-uy Hy said that 472 Company had only 20 mortar rounds with them. He said he would use 10 of them in support of 371 Company but must keep remaining rounds to cover the return to Dong

Cung, if needed. The firing I had just heard was the 10 rounds fired in support of 371 Company. What an example of fighting on a shoe string! Some artillery or heavy mortar support would make all the difference in the world.

We could hear intermittent small arms fire and an occasional explosion of grenades or enemy mortar fire. I knew that 526 Company had casualties also. It was now past noon and the light rain had stopped, but there were heavy clouds on the horizon, which could interfere with any air support we might get. We heard a helicopter pass over and assumed our wounded were now being medevaced out to the Province hospital. The District Chief informed me that the 526 Company Commander had requested permission to break contact and begin movement back to Cai Nuoc Outpost. He had heard from his "lost" platoon and they were confused as to their orders and were returning to the outpost. Well, I thought, 20 less men in the field if they ever were there.

Dai-uy Hy told them to hold their position for one hour then begin falling back. He instructed the 371 Company to hold fast until he gave further orders. Neither company had reached the VC bunker area.

The machine gun crew and the BAR team were taking up positions on the berm line when I heard some shouting and then the cry, "Medic!" That inaccurate, constant, harassing fire from the west had finally hit someone. One glance at the face of the District Chief revealed his frustration. His operation was stalled, one of his units was retreating without making any contact with the enemy, and another had asked permission to break contact with the VC and withdraw. There were casualties, ammunition was low, and now enemy fire that had been just a nuisance had finally become effective. He called out to several soldiers and waved them to him. I joined him to see what action he was going to take. He sent one NCO to the berm to direct the machine gun crew to begin sweeping the tree line with fire. The

312

soldiers with the M1s joined in. You could see tracers arcing into the trees (one of every five rounds in the ammo belt for the machine gun was a tracer to enable a gunner to adjust his aim). He directed the NCO commanding 528 platoon to prepare to cross the open paddyfield and clear the tree line along the canal bank. He would place fire on the tree line for five minutes, and then the 528 platoon was to cross and clear the area.

After a moment of thought I said to Dai-uy Hy, "I'm going with them."

"You should not go, stay with me."

"I will be OK. Sgt. Hai, you will come with me. Blair, stay with the Dai-uy."

"Yes sir," Blair replied. "Be careful."

I retrieved the M1 rifle and bandolier from the soldier I had handed them to previously. I checked to insure the rifle was loaded and joined the 528 platoon leader. He seemed confused when I said I was going with him, and then grinned and nodded. I waved the Lieutenant who had assumed control of the firing from the berm to me and told him to shift his machine gun fire to the flank of the platoon skirmish line and the BAR to other flank as we moved out. "Have the other soldiers stop firing and be prepared to join us at the objective area (tree line)," I ordered.

I asked Sgt. Hai to tell the Lieutenant to repeat my instructions back to me to be sure he understood. The firing stopped, and the platoon moved forward of the berm and started across the open paddy field. Including Sgt. Hai, my radio man, and I counted 22 men on line. There was some scattered firing from our side, intended to keep the enemy down as we approached. We no longer saw any movement

313

between the huts as before, and the enemy fire decreased to only an occasional round or two.

We could see now that there were five huts in a line, about 150 meters from south to north. I motioned to the platoon leader to keep his men spread out so as to reach each house at relatively the same time. As we neared the huts, we could see that we were facing the back side of the structures without rear entrances. The fronts obliviously faced the Rach (Canal) Dong Cung. The soldiers began running toward the huts now firing rapidly. As they reached them they fired into the huts. The one the group I was with were targeting the second one from the left or south end. It had no rear entrance and the soldiers raked the hut with fire then circled to the front and after firing several more rounds through the doorway, they entered ,firing as they went. I followed in and saw that there was no one in the hut. There were some items scattered around on the dirt floor-- bowls, a pot, and some rags, indicating recent occupation.

I heard some firing and a couple of explosions coming from the other huts. There was yelling going on and more shots. Sgt. Hai and I left the hut we were in and went out and up to the right to where the firing was. I saw two VC bodies on the edge of the canal bank, apparently shot while trying to escape by jumping in the canal. Two other bodies were dragged out from one of the huts. Skid marks on the canal bank and muddied water indicated that some of the enemy fled by sampan. As the troops continued to search the area, one of the NCOs beckoned me to follow him. He led me back behind the huts to where several soldiers were standing, looking down at a body on the ground. The NCO pointed to it then back across the paddy while chattering excitedly.

Sgt. Hai said, "Sergeant say this man you shot." "Really?" I said. I glanced back across the open area and, yes, it looked like it was the right angle and line of sight.

314

"He shot in chest once, Tieu-ta number one shot!" Sgt. Hai exclaimed. Well, I thought, that might be the most important thing I did all day.

CHAPTER 43

OPERATION A FLOP

After some conferring with Dai-uy Hy on the radio, we started back across the paddy to join him and the Command Group. He told me that 526 had broken contact and were returning to Cai Nuoc Outpost. I'm not sure they were even still in contact with the VC. He had also ordered the 472 minus the platoon with 371 Company to start toward Dong Cung. He was holding the mortar squad until 371 reached the Command Group. They would pass through us and then we would follow. The 518 platoon would move out last and act as the rear guard.

As we rejoined the Command Group, I noticed a single column of soldiers moving down the old road toward Dong Cung and asked, "472 Company?"

"No," I was answered, "371 Company."

"Major, David Two Five is on the horn," said Sgt. Blair as he handed me the handset.

"This is Oscar Six, over."

"Oscar Six, David Two Five, I am en route to your location with some air support. Are you still in contact, over?"

"Negative Two Five, what do you have?"

"Two A1Es, they were on another mission but it was aborted."

"What do they have aboard?"

"A full menu, I think, 500 pounders, rockets maybe, and their 20 Mike Mike (millimeters) cannons."

"Great, I still have a target for them."

"What's the target?" David Two Five asked.

"A bunker complex with a concrete bunker," I replied.

"A concrete bunker, no way."

"Yes a concrete bunker. It's a box culvert under the old road where the VC blocked the upstream entrance and diverted the stream to give them a reinforced bunker with at least two meters of overhead cover. And there are supposed to be several normal mud and log ones nearby," I continued.

"Give me the location. I want to take a look before the A1Es arrive."

"Roger, Two Five, I am going to pop smoke which will be the closest friendlies to the target, which is about two klicks from my current position," I replied.

Dai-uy Hy was monitoring my conversation with the help of Sgt. Hai and nodded to me that he understood. He spoke on his radio briefly and nodded again.

Sgt. Hai said, "Dai-uy give order to pop smoke."

A moment later Sgt. Hai gave me a thumbs up. "Red smoke."

"Smoke out," I relayed to David Two Five.

317

"I see cherry, over."

"Roger, cherry," I confirmed, "about two and one half klicks up the road from the smoke you should see a man-dug canal crossing the roadbed. It will seem to disappear as it goes under the road."

"Runs from southeast to the northwest?" David Two Five asked.

"That's a Roger, Two Five."

"I got it. I am going down to take a look," he responded.

We could hear him but could only catch a glimpse of the plane through thickening clouds.

"Crap! I'm drawing fire! There's some stuff down there. What's there?"

"I have not been on the ground there, but my counterpart believes it is a major supply point. He thinks mortar and artillery ammo. Plus possibly a headquarters," I replied.

"Well, there is something down there," David Two Five mumbled. "I'm going off your net (changing frequency) for a minute. My guys are coming on station… OK, I'm back. I was wrong; they don't have any rockets aboard but 250-pound bombs and ammo for their 20 Mike Mike cannons. I'm going to put them in on the roadbed and from east to west of the road."

"Roger, we can see a little through the clouds and we can hear you," I stated.

"OK, Oscar Six. I understand no friendlies in the strike area. Is that right?"

"That's correct, you have a target clear of friendly troops," I responded.

"Roger, I'm off your net."

We could hear the deep throaty sound of aviation piston engines. The A1E was a model of the Skyraider A1H dive bomber built for the Navy that had proved very effective during the Korean War. It could carry 8,000 pounds of a wide variety of bombs, torpedoes, and rockets, plus four 20 mm cannons, and stay in the air up to 10 hours. The U.S. Air Force provided close air support with them in the early years in Vietnam. Later they were transferred to the South Vietnamese Air Force (VNAF).

We saw one of the planes roll over into a dive and disappear into some light clouds, then heard the roar of an engine as the plane recovered from his dive. The sound of two explosions followed in seconds. The same sequence followed three more times. We could then see the planes circling higher and further to the east. They then peeled off in a long sloping dive, strafing with their 20 mm cannons. We watched them climb out again, align wing tip to wing tip and disappear to the north.

"Oscar Six, there was sure something down there. We got a secondary explosion and they even returned fire before they were strafed," reported David Two Five.

"That's great!" I replied. "Give our thanks to the A1Es. I will try to get some troops in there to see what you tore up."

"I am going to make a pass over the area to make a BDA (Bomb Damage Assessment) if I can. The clouds are pretty low now and some rain is starting to fall. If I spot anything, I will let you know."

"Roger, and thanks again," I said and handed the handset to the soldier carrying the radio.

It was now late afternoon as Dai-uy Hy, myself, and the rest of the Command Group followed the column of troops down the foot path heading back to Dong Cung. The platoon that had crossed the paddy with me was behind us as the rear guard. The rain had increased to a moderate downfall, limiting our vision somewhat, but it wasn't the tropical downpour we often experienced. As we trudged along, I tried to assess the day's activity. Well I thought, it certainly was not a successful operation. We never even reached our objective. We lost contact with one of our units, the platoon from 526 Company that was east of the canal. We had casualties. The count I had was five KIA and nine wounded. I was certain we inflicted casualties on the VC, but the only ones that I was sure of were the five we had killed across the paddy. The results of our air strike was unknown as yet but hopefully had produced some favorable results. Still, as a successful offensive operation it was a flop!

I then discussed my thoughts with Dai-uy Hy. He nodded his head in agreement as I touched on each point, but when I ended he looked at me and said. "It was not a loss. We had almost 200 men on the operation, first time in weeks. VC know we will come after him. VC know we have advisor support now."

"You may be right," I said. "We are not being attacked as much as we were a few weeks ago."

"I plan we go up river soon. When we get new mortar and soldiers from Ca Mau, we go into Nam Can. Siege fini!" Dai-uy pronounced.

"Great," I responded and then thought, we will see.

We had now passed through the wire and defensive wall and the troops began scattering to their individual quarters. The District Chief turned and said to me, "518 Company have security tonight, other soldiers rest," then saluted and walked off in the direction of his bunker.

In the early hours of the morning, I was awakened by the crash of incoming mortar rounds. Blair and I rushed out from our quarters toward the bunker under the roadbed when I noticed that some of the exploding rounds sounded different from the normal mortar attack we were used to. Then I heard the rushing sound associated with artillery. We were receiving both mortar and artillery fire for the first time since my arrival. I guess the VC wished to show us that our air strike had failed to affect their ability to increase their attacks on the government's position. Fortunately we had only one person wounded.

As we were cleaning up the debris from the attack,we found an unexploded artillery round. It was a Japanese 70 mm that had been reloaded but failed to detonate. This confirmed the rumor that there was artillery in the area: A short time earlier, Hai Yen was hit with an attack consisting of 75mm rounds presumed to be from a captured U.S. Army Pack Howitzer. That was more of a surprise than the Japanese 70. It looked like the District Chief's comment that the siege environment was "fini" may have been premature.

CHAPTER 44

FRIENDLY FIRE

It was near 2300 hours when Sgt. Blair and I walked into the District Headquarters building from our nightly check of the perimeter and guard posts. A Lieutenant, the night duty officer, and six or seven soldiers were there--the relief for those on duty. They were gathered around a table where a large sea turtle was lying upside down on it back. It had been boiled in a large pot and one of the soldiers was removing the cartilage from the soft underside while the others stood waiting with knives, chopsticks, and bowls to take part in devouring the turtle for their midnight meal. I politely declined their offer to join them, and after a few words with the Lieutenant, Blair and I went on to the shed-like addition to the building that served as our quarters.

After placing our weapons so they could be picked up in a hurry, we pulled off our boots and lay down on our cots. The team radio, a PRC 25, sat on our ammo crate table along with an oil lamp flashlights, my pistol, and a small AM/FM commercial radio on which we listened to the Armed Forces Radio. The team radio was left on so we could monitor the traffic between the Province and Districts and any other station on the net. Normally we took turns on radio watch while the other got a little sleep before we arose at daylight. Unless there were attacks on friendly positions, radio traffic was hourly checks from the Province TOC to ensure contact was maintained with all teams. Transmissions from aircraft in the province were always monitored ,as they were the lifeline between the Districts and the Province team. It was our way to keep abreast of what was happening.

On this particular night, Blair and I were lying there talking when we heard an aircraft that sounded like it was approaching our area. An Army Mohawk aircraft, radio call sign Delta Hawk, that was fitted with night surveillance radar equipment, flew our area once or

322

twice a week. We would always contact them and ask them to tell us if they observed anything of interest in our general vicinity. Whenever they had something, we would then plot it on our maps to see if it was anything for which we could take action. As we listened, the aircraft sounded strange. "Is that Delta Hawk?" asked Blair.

"I don't know, I guess so, they sound to be flying lower."

As the engine noise became louder I said, "They are really low. I'm getting up to see if I can spot them. You see if you can raise them on the net."

At that moment a loud explosion rocked the building, and immediately small arms fire broke out. I thought, the VC have breached the wire and are in the perimeter. I pulled on my boots, grabbed my carbine, and ran out the door. Firing had increased and I could see flames toward the northwest side. Soldiers were running about and yelling. I grabbed one and asked "Dai uy o dau? (Where is the captain?) " He shrugged, pointed towards the bunker under the bridge abutment, and ran off.

Blair came up behind me with the radio I told him, "Tell Province we are under ground attack."

"Right, will do," he replied.

A soldier pulled on my arm, "May bay, may bay!" he shouted and pointed up in the air to the east. I looked up and saw red blinking lights. Navigational lights; it's an airplane!

"Blair, see if you get that plane on the net!" Several soldiers and the Deputy District Chief had gathered around me. I could see the plane making a turn.

323

Blair shouted "I can't raise any aircraft."

"Call Province and tell them we are being bombed!"

The plane was coming back on a straight line to us.

I turned to the Deputy District Chief and said, "Fire up some flares so they can see who we are."

He ran off. A moment or two later a flare went up, then another.

Sergeant Blair yelled to me, "Province says there are no friendly aircraft in the area."

"What? Give me the mike. "This is Oscar six. What do you mean there are no friendly aircraft in the area? There's a God damn two engine prop plane dropping bombs on us! Who in the hell is it, the Russians?"

"Here Sgt. Blair, take this and keep on the net and near me. I'm going to find Captain Hy."

The plane was almost overhead and a little to the north side. The flares lit up the town, and perimeter like daylight.

Captain Hy came running up. "No VC!" as he pointed up, "Airplane!"

"I know, but Province says no friendly aircraft in the area!" Another explosion, another bomb, and the plane droned on to the west. "It's in the wire, I thought. "Thank God the bomb landed outside our perimeter wall in the barbed wire."

Blair tapped me on the shoulder, "The plane is circling again."

324

I looked up, and sure enough it had turned 180 degrees and was coming back on a westward course right toward us. "Dai uy, fire our machine guns straight up. Fire the 50 caliber."

Hy yelled out to one of his NCOs and a .30 caliber machine gun opened up, firing in the air over the town perimeter. Another one joined in; you could see the tracers arcing up and then falling back as they reached the limit of their trajectory. Then the .50 caliber started firing with the tracers looking like flaming beer cans punching up through the sky past the altitude at which the plane appeared to be flying. The plane veered sharply to the south crossing over the river. We saw a burst of flame on the other shore and then heard the blast. They had dropped a third bomb on the opposite side of the river from the District Town. The plane continued on southeast, gaining altitude until it was out of sight.

The District Chief began redirecting his men, pulling them off the perimeter and putting them to work extinguishing the fires. The confusion and near panic had subsided as work parties were organized and control was established.

"Major," Sgt. Blair called to me, "Province wants to talk to you."

"OK," I took the handset from him. "This is Oscar Six, over."

"Oscar Six, this is Island Five (Lt. Col. Culpepper, the Deputy PSA). I have some unpleasant news--that was a friendly aircraft in your area."

"I didn't think the damn VC had bombers," I replied.

"It was a USN Neptune flying on Market Time patrol."

325

Market Time was a Navy operation to detect and intercept surface commercial traffic along the coast and in South Vietnam waterways. The District Headquarters of Cai Nuoc lay on the Song Bay Hop, a major river emptying in the Gulf of Thailand and mainly controlled by the VC.

"Apparently the plane's crew was given a set of four coordinates forming a rectangle and was told there were no friendly forces in the area. Unfortunately, you were located right in the middle of what was considered a free fire zone."

"Who gave them the coordinates? Didn't they know we were there? Did your TOC know?" I asked pointedly, trying to restrain the anger in my voice.

"No," Culpepper replied. "We did not receive any traffic on Market Time missions in the Province. Let's set that aside for a moment. What is your damage? Do you have any casualties?"

"I don't have a count on casualties yet. There are several houses burning. Ammo was stored in some houses, and I can hear some small arms ammo popping off in the fire and some heavier stuff, probably grenades and M79 rounds. They dropped three bombs, one in the center of town, one in the wire, and the last one across the river after we opened up with our machine guns."

"You fired on them!" he exclaimed.

"We fired up in the air after the second bomb."

"Well," said Culpepper, "keep us informed. The PSA or I will get down there tomorrow if we can. It is almost tomorrow now, so it will probably be the next day. Out here."

326

I handed the handset back to Sgt. Blair and turned to the District Chief, "it was the U.S. Navy, a mistake."

Dai- uy Hy said, "It seems we have many enemies," and then smiled and walked away.

An NCO approached me and said, "We have only two wounded. Eleven houses burned, one full of ammo, all gone."

"Get me an account of the ammunition loss please."

"Da Tieu-ta (yes, Major)" he replied and trotted off.

"Well, Sgt. Blair, not as bad as it could have been," I said. "Let's hope there is not a repeat."

Blair just grunted. It was now about two hours to daylight. I went to lie down for a while; tomorrow--or actually later today--was going to be busy.

After a breakfast of chicken soup and coffee, I joined Dai-uy Hy to look at the previous night's damage. One house was destroyed, and nine were damaged, four of which would have to be completely rebuilt. The loss of ammunition--mainly mortar rounds and grenades-- was critical, as we were normally always short. . One of the two wounded required medical evacuation. Damage by the other two bombs was minor; they just tore up some of our defensive wire. While we were assessing the results of the bombing, a radio message was received informing us that the PSA and party were en route to our location. I told Dai-uy Hy of the impending visit and he immediately dispatched some men to form a loose perimeter to secure the landing pad from mortar, rocket, or sniper fire. As the word spread that someone was coming to see the results of the friendly fire incident, residents and soldiers began to gather at the landing pad. I saw two

327

soldiers carrying what appeared to be a piece of aluminum. The District Chief walked over to where they were standing and then motioned for me to join him. As I approached he pointed to the piece of metal. I could see some black lettering that spelled out USN Mark IV 500 lb Fire Bomb. Proof positive that the U.S. Navy had bombed us! A muttering began among the people standing nearby, which was quickly silenced by Dai-uy Hy.

An NCO in halting English asked me, "Why Americans bomb Vietnamese soldiers?"

"I don't know. I am here with you; they bombed me, too," I responded.

I could then hear the approaching helicopter and said to Sgt. Blair "I am going to try to hold them here long enough for us to take out those who need to go and bring in a lift for us. If I get their OK you notify the TOC."

"Yes sir," Blair nodded.

CHAPTER 45

THE NAVY VISITS

The single Huey helicopter came into view, circled the hamlet, and then dropped onto the landing pad. The skids were barely touching the ground when a figure jumped out the side door and in a crouch came bounding toward us. As he neared, we could see that he was Asian and wearing the rank of a Lt. Col. Although I had not met him, I knew that he was the new PSA who had replaced Lt. Col. Gilland. His name was Nagota.

I stepped forward to meet him, saluted, and said "Major Dagenais, District Senior Advisor, glad to see you sir."

He returned my salute and offered his hand in greeting, saying, "I'm glad to meet you. I wish it was under other circumstances."

I then motioned to Dai-uy Hy, who saluted Lt. Col. Nagota and greeted him in perfect unbroken English. "Welcome to Cai Nuoc District. I am Captain Hy and I am very glad to meet you."

Nagota acknowledged his salute, and smilingly shook hands with Hy. He then turned to three others who had now off-loaded from the chopper and were waiting for instructions or a direction to move away from the pad. Two of the passengers were officers from the Province Team, and one, a rather tall man in jungle fatigues, was wearing the insignia and the rank of a U.S. Navy Captain.

Lt. Col. Nagota beckoned him forward and said, "This is Captain Davis from the Navy Headquarters in Can Tho. He has come down to ascertain if the Navy was involved in last night's attack."

I looked at him, saluted, and snarled, "I'm Major Dagenais and I think you have a hell of a nerve showing up here."

"Well, we are not sure the Navy was involved."

At this moment Dai-uy Hy waved forward the soldiers holding the piece of the bomb they had recovered. They set the metal fragment down in front of the Navy Captain so the lettering on it was in plain view, USN Mark IV 500 lb Fire Bomb.

Captain Davis bent down staring at the fragment intently, then straightened up and said, "Can I now see the damage?"

"Of course," I said.

With a few words, Dai-uy Hy dispersed the group of soldiers and civilians that had gathered at the landing pad and prepared to lead the Captain off in the direction of the bomb-damaged structures.

"Colonel Nagota, leaving the chopper on the pad for any length of time will probably draw some VC mortar fire. I suggest that you allow me to evac some people to Ca Mau and return with a lift of supplies or personnel. By that time you should have finished your visit here," I suggested.

"That's a good idea. I want to see the hamlet, your quarters or operational area, and have a brief look at your defense posture," he agreed. He called one of the Province Team staff officers that had accompanied him over and instructed him to have the chopper pilot make a supply run for us and said he would be ready to leave for Ca Mau upon the pilot's return.

Our inspection party consisting of Lt. Col. Nagota, Captain Davis, and one of the Province staff officers and myself followed the

330

District Chief to examine the previous night's damage. Sgt. Blair took the remaining staff officer to our quarters to await us there. The area where the bomb exploded was mostly ashes with twisted sheets of aluminum scattered about. Several nearby houses were charred and only partially standing. Some soldiers and civilians, including children, were busy cleaning up the debris.

"There's no crater," commented the naval officer.

"It was a fire bomb, remember?" I reminded him.-

"Ah yes, it would leave only a minimal crater."

"The troops have already filled it in. There is a crater over there," I said pointing to the remains of another building. "It was caused by exploding ammunition that was stored there."

"What about the other two bombs?" asked Lt. Col. Nagota.

"One landed in the wire," I said pointing to the north, "and the other on the south side of the river after we fired up in the air with our .50 caliber machine gun."

"Yes, the pilot of our aircraft reported that the enemy had fired on him," commented Captain Davis.

"Well, Dai-uy Hy and I are not the enemy," I retorted sharply.

"I think we have seen enough to support that it was an unfortunate case of a mistaken target and friendly fire on our own troops. Thank God the casualties were light. I understand it was only two," said Lt. Col. Nagota.

"Yes, sir, they were evacuated out on your chopper a few minutes ago," I answered.

"Good," Nagota replied.

"I believe we are done here. Dai-uy Hy will you please give me a brief tour of the hamlet or town and your headquarters so that I have mental picture of Cai Nuoc District Headquarters when discussing it with the Province Chief?"

"Yes sir, we go this way," Dai-uy Hy replied, leading off through the jumble of houses to what I called the main street.

We proceeded up the street toward the old roadbed and bridge where the headquarters, communications, and Dai-uy's bunkers were located, pointing out points of interest along the way: the aid station , midwife's office, the only store, and a couple of eating places. Upon reaching the bunkers under the roadbed and entering through the tunnel, Captain Davis found that he had to both stoop and crouch to be able to enter the Dai-uy's quarters. I guessed that he had to be at least six foot six.

On the table where we normally joined Dai-uy Hy for our evening meals was spread a hand-drawn map of the hamlet and the District Headquarters with the surrounding defensive perimeter. It was drawn to scale and beautifully done. I had never seen it. Obviously it was used only for briefing high ranking and important visitors. Dai-uy Hy, in English assisted by Sgt. Hai, briefed Lt. Col. Nagota on the defensive posture of the District, being careful not to make comments that would lead Nagota to believe that the Province Chief was not supporting him appropriately. I knew that Dai-uy did not want Lt. Col. Nagota questioning the Province Chief on complaints from the District.

332

The PSA thanked Dai-uy for the briefing and said to me, "Let's look at your Headquarters now, and I need to discuss some items with you. My chopper should be here soon."

"Yes, sir, please follow me." I replied.

I led Lt. Col. Nagota and the party out through the other end of the tunnel into the square in front of the District Headquarters Building and our shed-like quarters. He looked at it for a moment and then walked over and entered its doorway. Sgt. Blair and the other Province Team Officer that accompanied the PSA were inside, blocking the entry of another person.

"This is the only space you have for the team?" asked Lt. Col Nagota.

"Yes, sir, there are only the two of us, and we will have to make some adjustments as additional team members arrive."

Nagata shook his and said, "Let's talk some. What did Dai-uy not tell me?"

"Shortage of ammo and personnel, there are 90- plus troops at Ca mau awaiting transport down here. I have been promised a 4.2 mortar; we need it now. We have no M79 ammo at all. And far as the team, I need one or two more people. Blair and I can't stay awake 24/7 forever."

"I understand," he said. "Things look pretty bleak here. I'll see if I can break things loose. The TOC reports that you have casualties almost every day."

"That's correct, sir, and we don't have enough men to conduct offensive operations. I have never been able to get to Cai Nuoc

333

Outpost. And there is a platoon outpost less than two klicks up river from here that I have not visited," I replied.

"Your living conditions appear to be pretty primitive," he remarked.

I explained our eating arrangements, personal hygiene, and sanitary conditions, which caused him to shake his head in what I think was disbelief. Sergeant Blair interrupted our conversation to announce that the Colonel's chopper was arriving.

I walked with the PSA and his party to the landing pad. He assured me that he would try to accelerate the movement of supplies and personnel to us. I asked that I be informed of the reason for or where the error occurred that resulted in the Navy bombing us. Sergeant Blair and I saluted as the chopper lifted off and Blair asked, "Do you think the Colonel will get that bunch cracking up there?"

"I don't know. I sure as hell hope so."

CHAPTER 46

MOVE OR DIE

I finally received long overdue help. During the morning following the VC artillery attack, a radio message from the Province Team TOC was received stating that our 4.2 mortar would be delivered that day and that Lieutenant Harris would be moved from Hai Yen to join Sgt. Blair and me in Dong Cung. That increased our advisory team by 50 percent, from two to three!

I notified my counterpart that the mortar was on its way. He assembled the soldiers designated as the crew for the 4.2 at the chopper pad to receive the mortar. They would move it and the ammunition to the sites that had been prepared. There were two lifts of two Hueys; Lt. Harris and a trickle of replacements were on the second lift. Dai-uy Hy joined Sgts. Blair and Hai, and me in greeting Harris as he arrived. Blair helped Harris gather his gear and led him off to our quarters. I told Blair to get the new lieutenant settled and show him around, and that I would join them later. I wanted to watch the emplacement of the mortar and discuss its use with Dai-uy Hy.

At 1115 hours, the VC fired four 82 mm rounds into the hamlet, scattering everyone and wounding two civilians. Both wounds were minor and did not require medical evacuation. At almost the same time, a patrol less than 1,000 meters east of our position had an encounter with an unknown number of VC, who broke contact after an initial exchange of fire but not before one of our soldiers was slightly wounded. We fired a few 81 mm mortar rounds in the general direction that the patrol leader thought the VC went. Just another normal day at the office!

I caught up with Lt. Harris and Sgt. Blair as they were returning to our quarters. We sat down and had a lunch of C ration crackers and cheese plus some rice balls Sgt. Blair had bought from a soldier's wife. Harris seemed a little dazed from Sgt. Blair's initial briefing on our daily routine and living conditions. Comparing Hai Yen, where conditions were already below U.S. Army standards, with Dong Cung was like the difference between daylight and dark. The team house at Hai Yen, originally built by the CIA, had an indoor latrine, a shower (albeit cold water only), electric power, and lights four hours a day, a freezer , separate sleeping quarters for each team member, and a large enough area for eating and other team activities. At Dong Cung, we were crowded into our small shed-like addition to the District Headquarters building. We had built a double bunk arrangement to accommodate the arrival of Lt. Harris and drove a few more nails in the wall so that he could hang up some of his gear.

Harris looked at the small table, the chairs, and ammo boxes and asked in a slightly stunned voice, "Is this it?"

"That it is," I replied, "but it's going to get better soon. Did you see the latrine and shower arrangements?" I asked.

He just nodded and then grinned. Use of the latrine by Lt. Harris would be a source of amusement for us at a time in the future.

I followed up with Harris on Blair's briefing, directing him to watch, listen, and ask questions when unsure of what is going on. I had a feeling that he was going to attract a lot of attention from the local population. They probably had not seen a man so tall (over six feet) and red headed. As predicted, he became a favorite of the children and young women. He wasn't too pleased with the idea of eating with the Vietnamese, including the evening meal with the District Chief, but I thought he would get used to it. He had his first meal with us that evening consisting of the normal fare--rice, greens (rau mung), and an unidentifiable meat, and tea. He concentrated on the rice and sampled the meat and greens sparingly. Dai-uy Hy was concerned that the

336

lieutenant was not eating enough and kept urging him to eat more. I assured him that Harris would be OK.

The following morning, the Deputy District Chief Lt. Hong informed me that Dai-uy Hy was sending him out with two platoons. They were to investigate rumors that the VC had visited some nearby families a couple of klicks north of town. The VC were said to be collecting taxes and planting mines along the foot path on the old road. He expected to be out only four or five hours. I decided it would be a good time to take Lt. Harris out for his first time with the troops. We weren't going far, risk was minimal, and it was an opportunity for both the new Lieutenant and the soldiers to see each other in the field. I told Lt. Hong that Harris and I would go along, joining him at the strong point guarding the north exit from the hamlet. Blair would stay behind and mind the radio traffic from Province and could relay any important messages. (Radios in the field using a short antenna often could not always reach the Province TOC.) An hour later we joined Hong, who had about 40 men with him, and passed through the wire in single file heading north up the foot path.

The troops moved slowly. Lt. Harris, Sgt. Hai, a soldier detailed to carry our radio, and I were two-thirds the length of the column from the leading squad, along with Lt. Hong and one of his platoon leaders. We had gone less than a kilometer when small arms fire erupted up ahead; there was nothing for a moment or two, and then three or four single shots. Hong was on the radio talking to the lead Platoon Leader.

Sgt. Hai listened to the conversation and said, "Soldiers see three maybe four VC on the path, fired on them. They run away. Maybe VC put traps in path."

"Yeah," I said, "installing a mine or some grenade traps."

337

The column stopped moving and the soldiers had turned and were facing out toward each flank, squatting down or in a crouch. A few minutes went by and then word came from the front that they had found an improvised mine made from an artillery shell. I motioned the radio man over to me and took the handset from him and transmitted back to Sgt. Blair, "Oscar Three, this is Oscar Six, over."

While waiting for Blair's response, I noticed that Lt. Harris was moving around nervously and motioned to him to be still. He did not understand what I meant and kept shuffling around. With the radio handset in my right hand and up to my ear, I swung my carbine by the barrel left handed at Harris, hitting him on the arm, and yelled, "Stand still!"

He looked at me stunned.

As I finished my conversation with Blair and put down the handset, Harris exclaimed to me with a note of surprise in his voice, "Sir, you can't strike another officer or any soldier!"

"You are right," I replied, "but I was trying to get you to stand still! If you kept stomping around, you might set off a mine and kill us all, Goddamnit!"

Harris, red faced and angry, turned away from me. Lt. Hong motioned that we were moving forward and I started off with him. When we reached the area where the VC had placed the mine, we found that the troops had cordoned it off with a fence of sticks with bits of rags attached. I walked over and looked at it. Sure enough, it was an artillery shell with something wrapped around it plus some wires disappearing into the dirt of the roadbed. Some brave soul had cut the wires. Lt. Hong looked at me and with his hands pantomimed an explosion.

338

Sgt. Hai said to me, "No one here knows how to disarm VC mine. District Chief send someone later to blow it up." Well, it was marked; however, the VC might return and move it somewhere else. It had happened before.

We moved on and reached the objective, a cluster of four houses on the edge of the footpath facing the canal. Several small sampans were tied to stakes driven in the water. No nets or other fish traps were evident. The only crops growing were a few rows of peppers close to the back of the houses. How do the people who live here feed themselves, I wondered? Three men were standing together in front of one of the houses. Several women with children were huddled off to one side. Lt. Hong began a conversation with the men while soldiers searched the houses. Sgt. Hai gave me a running interpretation of the exchange between Hong and the civilians.

"They say VC come and want money. Want young men to join them. Two boys go with them. VC say they will take Dong Cung so men must help them. They leave this morning. I believe these men here VC," Sgt. Hai added.

Lt. Hong's voice rose as he spoke sharply and pointed to the men and then in the direction of Dong Cung. The three villagers nodded, bowed, and backed away toward the women and children.

Apparently we were done here. The soldiers began to form up and return down the foot path back toward Dong Cung. I walked over to Lt. Hong and began walking with him. "Trung-uy (Lieutenant), I did not see any fish, rice, or any food growing. Are they farmers, fishermen, or what?"

"They VC supporters, they watch Dong Cung, they watch soldiers, they tell VC."

"Lieutenant, tell civilians they must move to Dong Cung. If they here next time he comes, he burn down their houses," Sgt. Hai interjected.

"Would he really do that," I asked?

"Da phi (yes!), he ordered so by Dai-uy Hy," Sgt. Hai replied.

I glanced at Lt. Harris and said, "Did you get all that?"

"Yes, sir, but what would he do with the people?"

"Take them prisoner, I suppose."

"No, sir," said Sgt. Hai. "He kill men, let women, babies go."

"Well, there's your answer Lieutenant."

The return trip was uneventful and we arrived back at the District Headquarters shortly past midday. That night was quite different. A VC bombardment at 0200 hours of both mortar and artillery fire, estimated at 60 rounds or more, indicated that they were still intent on driving the government forces out of Dong Cung and Cai Nuoc District. A damage assessment at first light revealed minor damage to structures, but we had seven wounded--six soldiers and one civilian. The VC added a new mode of attack as well. Two B40 rockets had been fired at the machine gun on the bridge, but both had missed. We thought they were fired from a sampan on the river. The gun would be a difficult target to hit with an RPG. I made myself a mental note to fire flares over the river during the next night attack so we could see anyone on the river, although a flare might also help the VC to hit the gun position.

Later that morning after the wounded were evacuated and clean up and repair was under way, Dai-uy Hy told me he was convinced that a major attack was imminent. He had been receiving reports from civilians of increasing visits and sightings of VC to our north. There was no unusual VC movement reported on the south side of the river in the Nam Can District, commonly referred to as the Nam Can Jungle. After discussing our ability to increase our patrolling efforts, I again queried the Province Team's DPO on when we were going to get our soldiers down from Ca Mau. The few we had coming in on a supply lift barely equaled our losses. The answer was always the same: "We're working on it."

I felt that it was necessary to talk with Lt. Harris concerning the incident on the foot path. We sat down outside our quarters and I said, "Lieutenant, you have the right to file a complaint against me for yesterday's action. You are correct. I do not have the right to strike any soldier."

"Sir, I realize now the reason for what you did. I should not have been shuffling around. I could have set off something like what was found further up the foot path," he admitted.

"Yeah, Lieutenant, I was busy on the radio trying to hear a message and couldn't stop and explain why you should be still."

"I understand, Major, I consider it a lesson learned the easy way."

"Good, that's settled. Now Dai-uy Hy says he is sure we are going to have a major VC attack soon."

"Based on what, sir?"

"Info he is receiving from the civilian population. He is increasing the number of patrols he has out. I ding donged Province again about our troops sitting at the airfield in Ca Mau."

"And?"

"Same story, they are working on it. I guess they have to coordinate with the Province Chief, and his priorities may not be the same as ours. We must not be high on his priority list. You may have noted that he didn't visit us after the friendly bombing."

"I did wonder about that."

"OK, I'm going to chat with Dai-uy Hy. You give Sgt. Blair a hand in whatever he's doing."

CHAPTER 47

OUTPOST OVER RUN

It was in the middle of the afternoon when rifle shots were heard close in and up-river, which precipitated a partial alert. Dai-uy Hy appeared in the yard in T-shirt and shorts, apparently awakened from a midday nap. The radioman emerged from the communications bunker and spoke with the District Chief. Sgt. Hai and I hurried over to join Dai-uy Hy, who turned and spoke to me rapidly in Vietnamese. Sgt. Hai interpreted

"Dai-uy say patrol see three men, one have rifle. They kill man with rifle, other two run away. Patrol coming back here."

About 30 minutes later, five soldiers entered through the wire and reported to Dai-uy Hy at the Headquarters building. The patrol leader, a Sergeant, was brandishing the rifle taken from the VC they had killed: It was a U.S. Army issue M1 Garand. The patrol, whose mission was to visit the platoon outpost up the river and return, encountered the three VC on their way to the outpost but turned back without going further. The defense posture of the hamlet returned to its normal daytime level alert status.

We didn't have long to wait to find out the enemy's next move. At approximately 2300 hours, a barrage of mortar and artillery fire was poured into the platoon outpost. The exploding rounds lit up the sky and were easily seen from our location.

"I cannot help them with troops from here," announced Dai-uy Hy. "Can we get air support?"

I immediately contacted the Province TOC and requested air cover. I told them that we would probably lose the outpost if we didn't

343

get some help and instructed them to be sure the PSA knew of my request. Meanwhile Dai-uy was on the radio with the outpost commander, who reported that many rounds were falling in the outpost. He already had casualties. Dai-uy Hy began assembling a small force to relieve the outpost if the VC followed up with a ground attack.

"We will go up the river by boat. I will lead."

I looked at Harris and Blair, "You know what that means, don't you?"

They both nodded, understanding we were all going.

Blair then said "Major, Province wants to talk to you," handing me the radio handset.

"This is Oscar Six, over."

"Oscar Six, this is Seaforth Six, understand you have an outpost in danger of being overrun."

"Yes, sir, only about two klicks up the river from us. You probably passed over it when making your visit here the other day."

"Well, I have good news for you. There is a Spooky gunship en route to your location. You will have to put him on the target."

"Roger, we can do that."

"Good luck, Seaforth Six out."

I quickly briefed the District Chief, Lt. Harris, and Sgt. Blair on the gunship and asked Dai-uy Hy for exact coordinates for the outpost.

I was sure, however, that the gun ship would be able to spot the outpost by the VC barrage that was taking place.

"What kind of plane is it and what kind of armament do they have on board?" asked Lt. Harris. "It's a C47 cargo plane converted to a gunship and now known as an AC 47. They have three 7.62 mm Gatling guns on board, each capable of firing 6,000 rounds a minute. They also have parachute flares. When they fire, it looks like a solid sheet of flame from the plane to the ground," I replied.

"Wow!" Harris exclaimed.

"I have lost contact with the outpost," Dai-uy Hy interrupted.

"We can still see flashes of light and hear explosions," said Blair.

"Maybe it's the platoon," ventured Harris.

"No, must be VC. Outpost have only rifles, grenades, and two BARs," reported Dai-uy Hy.

"Damn!"

Almost simultaneously, I heard the drone of an aircraft and a voice on the radio, "Sea Forth Oscar Six, this is Puffy One Three over."

"Puffy One Three, this is Oscar Six, you are coming in loud and clear, and we can hear you, over," I responded.

"Roger, understand you have an outpost under attack."

"Correct, I can give you coordinates of its location."

345

"No need to, I have you located. Can you direct me from there? If they are under attack we should be able to spot them."

"This is Oscar Six, yeah they are up the river to the east of us about two klicks on the north side of the river."

"One Three here, we are swinging that way now. OK, I got 'em. I can see some explosions and some tracers, both red and green (Chinese tracer rounds were green). Tell you what, I'm going to make a circle over the area and drop a flare and see what's going on."

"Here we go."

We were standing on the bridge abutment where we had an uninterrupted view up the river and could see the plane began its circle. Suddenly there was a flash that lit up the sky, bathing the area below in a light brighter than daylight.

"Puffy One Three here, I can see people running to the east and some inside the outpost or what's left of it. There may be some in the river also. Hey, I see a flaming arrow! They must have just lit it. It is being pointed to the east and north. I can make a run about a hundred meters outside the outpost walls from the river bank to the east around to the north and back to the river on the west side. Permission OK?"

I briefed Dai-uy Hy on the pilot's suggestion. He nodded in agreement and then said, "Do not fire in river, maybe soldiers swimming away."

"One Three, permission granted, but do not fire in the river"

"Roger, understand do not fire on people in the river."

"That's affirmative."

346

"Stop stop, no fire, no fire," Dai-uy yelled wildly, "VC in outpost, soldiers outside!"

"One Three, abort, abort, The VC are in the outpost, friendlies outside.Stand by."

"Roger, standing by."

"A soldier from outpost on radio, not commander, say platoon overrun, some soldiers killed, rest leave. Try to get away," said Sgt. Hai who was standing by the radio man.

Dai-uy Hy was now on the radio, seemingly listening and then giving orders. He called to me. "Have plane fire in outpost, all VC, no soldiers there, all out."

"Are you sure," I asked?

"Da, fire in outpost."

"Puffy One Three, this is Oscar Six, my counterpart says the VC have overrun the outpost and all our guys are dead or outside the outpost walls. He thinks the VC have lit the flaming arrow and are pointing it toward the friendlies, hoping we would kill our own."

"Wow, we almost did. He wants us to fire on the outpost?"

"That's affirmative, over."

"OK, will do but only the interior, only inside the walls. It will only take a few minutes."

I relayed the pilot's comments to Dai-uy Hy, who nodded that he understood.

We watched the plane bank into a tight circle and then saw a sheet of flame extending from the aircraft to the ground, followed by a roar that sounded like a raging waterfall. The gun fire stopped for a moment, and then there was another few seconds of fire and thunder. I was sure no one could survive such an onslaught. I could see the amazement on the faces of those around me.

"Oscar Six, I'm afraid that's all I can do for you. I can't take the chance of firing on the friendlies."

"I fully understand that," I said, "I know you took out some bad guys and saved some of ours. Thanks for your help."

"Any time, Puffy One Three out."

We watched the blinking navigation lights of the AC47 fade out in the northeast. I asked Dai-uy Hy how many men were assigned to that outpost.

He replied in Vietnamese, "Co Le Khong Hai Muoi Lam (perhaps 25)."

"We must go there at first light," he continued in English. "I send scouts in boat. If clear, we follow."

"OK, I will be ready."

I walked over to where our radio was sitting on a box, contacted the Province TOC, and updated them on our situation. I then told the Duty Officer that I wanted him to remind the PSA on how critical it was to get the troops waiting there at the airfield down here. At 0700 hours Lt. Harris and I were with the District Chief in one of three small boats chugging up the river, keeping about 200 meters from shore to discourage some VC marksman from trying to earn a "Hero Medal."

The squad that had gone up the river earlier picked up four soldiers who were along the river bank, having fled from the outpost. They thought there were others who also had managed to escape from the VC assault.

As we approached the outpost, sited at the mouth of the Cai Muoi Canal, Dai-uy sent the other two boats forward while we waited to see if there was any enemy activity on shore. A wave from an NCO in one of the boats after they had beached indicated that it was clear and we could join them. The outpost, a standard triangle-shaped fort with bunkers at each of the three corners, was a shambles. The walls and the bunkers were mostly completely destroyed. Debris, which included sheets of aluminum roofing, articles of clothing, broken ammo boxes, and other personal gear, was scattered both inside and outside the walls. Two unexploded RPGs were found. Smears of blood were everywhere. We had no way of knowing whose it was, our men or the VC--probably both.

One body was found outside the wall and determined to be one of ours. Two ladders were found that were sometimes used by the VC to scale over the walls but were not in a location that indicated they were used for that purpose. They were also used by the VC to carry wounded or dead bodies. We only spent 30 or 35 minutes at the site before we loaded back up and started back down the river to Dong Cung. I asked Dai-uy Hy if he was going to re-establish the outpost. He didn't answer, just shook his head no, and remained silent the rest of the trip back. The final tally on casualties was 9 KIA or missing of 23 that were reported to be in the outpost. Most of the survivors had made their way down to Dong Cung, swimming or wading along the river bank. Also important was the loss of weapons. Both BARs were missing, plus some rifles that had been discarded by the fleeing soldiers.

I reported the results of the attack to the Province TOC and to the new Deputy Province Senior Advisor. The PSA was out of the province and I asked to talk to Lt. Col. Culpepper. I didn't know that he had rotated out and was replaced by a State Department Foreign Service Officer by the name of Moore. Moore was a retired Army Lt. Col. I stressed with him the need for more troops. Just sang the same song but to a new audience.

CHAPTER 48

MANNA FROM HEAVEN

One of the definitions in the dictionary for manna is "something of help given unexpectedly." I was unexpectedly surprised by some much appreciated help.

"Seaforth Oscar, this is Hillclimber Two Two, over."

"Hillclimber," I exclaimed, "that's a Chinook! Jim, answer him,"

Lt. Harris grabbed the handset and answered, "Hillclimber Two Two, this is Seaforth Oscar Five, over."

"This is Hillclimber Two Two. We are en route to your location with a load or actually half a load. We don't have an escort. What's the situation there?"

The Chinook was the largest helicopter in the Army inventory; because of its size, it was a prime target for the VC. They usually flew high out of small arms and RPG range and many times were accompanied by gunships. I had never seen one this far south in the Province.

"Give me the horn and go ask Dai-uy Hy to join me most ricki tick (hurry)," I said to Lt. Harris as I held out my hand for the handset. "Yes, sir," he replied, handing me the mike and hurrying out toward the District Chief's bunker.

"Hillclimber, this is Seaforth Oscar Six. Our area has been pretty quiet the last day or two. Our pad is small and on the north side

351

of the settlement. I'll have the troops on the perimeter put on alert and a crew standing by to unload."

"Hillclimber Two Two, OK that sounds good. What we have for you can be off loaded and we can be on our way in zero five over."

"This is Oscar Six, roger that, can I backload?"

"Negative, negative, I will have a half load still on when I leave you and I have full backload commitment on my next stop."

"OK, I understand. What's your ETA?"

"'Bout three zero minutes."

"This is Oscar Six, understand three zero minutes. If you need smoke or anything let me know."

"Roger."

Dai uy Hy arrived, followed by Lt. Harris who was grinning broadly. Hy was wearing his broad brimmed hat, a white T-shirt, white boxer shorts, and flip flops. I briefed him quickly on the Chinook and what I had discussed with the pilot. He nodded, turned to two soldiers who always seemed to be with him, and snapped out what appeared to be orders. The two trotted off, shouting out to others that were nearby. Dai-uy Hy looked at me and said, "I go now, meet you at the landing pad."

"See you there," I replied.

When he joined me a few minutes later, he was wearing a fatigue uniform, boots, and a patrol style cap--quite a quick change.

352

We heard the Chinook before we saw it. It was flying much higher than we were accustomed to seeing aircraft in our area. "Hillclimber Two Two, we have a visual on you, over."

"Roger Oscar Six, do you have a flag flying at your pad?"

"That's affirmative, over."

"OK, I've got you. We will be coming in high and descend rapidly."

The helicopter seemed to center over us and then descended almost vertically to the landing pad. The rear was open, and as soon as the Chinook touched down, cargo was shoved off. I had no idea what we were getting; neither the District Chief nor I were expecting anything other than our normal requests of ammo, weapons, and other military sundries. You can imagine our surprise when we saw lumber, sheets of aluminum, cement, crushed stone, sandbags, and spools of barbed wire being dumped on the pad. In a matter of minutes the unloading was complete and the pilot was pulling pitch, rising off the pad.

"Oscar Six, we're done here. Good luck with your cargo."

"This is Oscar Six, many thanks for the load. Didn't expect it but sure have use for it. Oscar Six out."

We were like kids on Christmas morning looking at what Santa brought us. There were two by fours, two by sixes, one by sixes, and several six by six inch posts included in the lumber; a keg of nails and a coil of electrical wire was also noted. As we were admiring our wind fall, the radio came alive with a call from the Chinook pilot.

"Ahh, Seaforth Oscar Six, are you Hai Yen, over?"

"Negative, we are Cai Nuoc District Headquarters located in Dong Cung Hamlet. We were at Hai Yen and relocated here a month ago or so."

"So you are not Hai Yen?"

"No, Hai Yen is west of us. Has an air strip, might be Binh Hung on your map. Why, is there a problem?"

"Yeah, that stuff was for Hoc Tien, not Hai Yen."

"Well, if you had dropped it at Hai Yen you still would have been wrong. It was a good drop though, we need it badly. I'm going through Province and thank some body for the delivery."

"OK, this is Hillclimber Two Two out."

"Well," I said to Dai-uy Hy, Harris, and Blair, "our gain, Hoc Tien's loss. We need to get it off the pad and guarded until it's put to use." "Yes," agreed Dai-uy Hy, "many soldiers take to use on their houses, must guard, talk on where to use."

"Dai-uy, let's meet in one hour in your bunker, have coffee, and decide how to use the material we just got. I have three small projects I would like you to consider." "Da, one hour," agreed the District Chief.

Harris, Blair and I returned to our quarters and sat down to discuss my projects. I wanted to see if they agreed with them before I presented them to Dai-uy Hy.

354

CHAPTER 49

CIVIC ACTION

An hour later, Lt. Harris and I were huddled around a table in the District Headquarters with Dai-uy Hy and several of his staff. A list had been prepared of the material that we had fallen heir to, and we were discussing how best to use this unexpected treasure trove. The barbed wire and sand bags could easily be used to repair and strengthen our defensive positions. The interior of the communication bunker and the Headquarters building could be improved with some of the lumber. I had three projects that would improve the quality of life for the Advisors. They were: enclosing the shower point to provide one taking a shower a degree of privacy, constructing a latrine so that the advisors would not have to squat in the open out over the canal along with the hamlet residents, and lastly a walkway between the District Headquarters Building/Advisory Team's Quarters and the Command Bunker area. The open area between the two points was, during the wet season, normally two to three inches deep in mud, which was tracked inside all points. Mud was frequently an inch or more deep in the Advisors' sleeping area no matter how careful we were in coming and going.

The projects would use only a small amount of the material received. For the shower, just a few two by fours and three or four sheets of aluminum would enclose it. There was no need for a roof, and a floor already existed. The latrine was another story. I drew a sketch of a one-holer outhouse that would be constructed out over the canal, near the community one in place. It would, like the shower stall, be constructed of aluminum sheets on a framework of two by fours. The civilian workmen assigned to do the construction of the two structures seemed perplexed when I tried to explain the bench-like seat upon which one would sit to relieve one self.

The walkway would require using some of the cement and crushed stone. That project would benefit everyone passing back and forth between the bunker area and the District Headquarters and Advisory quarters. Dai-uy Hy agreed to the three projects and ordered that they be started without delay.

After some further discussion, it was agreed that the bulk of the remaining material be used to repair the school building and accompanying bunker. There was no school operating in Dong Cung. The school building was vacant and needed some repair to the damage resulting from mortar and artillery attacks. It was a wooden building, perhaps 5meters wide and 20 meters long. On the side facing the main street, was an identical-sized bunker with several low doorways that corresponded to ones in the school. If the VC launched a bombardment while school was in session, the children could exit the building into the bunker, staying there until the attack was over.

The bunker walls were built of two rows of small tree trunks a half a meter apart and filled with mud mixed with rice straw. The roof had been built in a similar fashion, with a layer of tree trunks covered with a layer of mud. The maintenance of both the school and bunker had been neglected because there were no teachers available, and the priority of work was channeled to the defense of the hamlet. The timber, lumber, and sand bags would enable the District to bring the school and the bunker up to an acceptable level. Dai-uy Hy said that three teachers standing by in Ca Mau were assigned by the Province to Dong Cung. We just needed a school. The decision was made, and Dai-uy Hy ordered that the work begin at once.

Two incidents somewhat humorous to some of us but not to all occurred prior to the construction of the latrine. The community latrine was used by both sexes at the same time if the need was evident. Individuals using the facility were visible to those on shore who cared to look in that direction. Someone using the latrine would be exposed

356

except for a portion of their body that was hidden by a screen of woven palm leaves. Because I was the senior officer, I was afforded privacy when I used the facility. Lt. Harris and Sgt. Blair did not receive that courtesy, and it was not unusual for someone to squat down on the logs only a short distance from you to take care of their needs.

The first time Lt. Harris used the latrine, he drew a small crowd of female watchers on the canal bank. Harris was well over six feet tall, red headed, and young. Most of the inhabitants of the hamlet had never seen a man that tall or one with red hair. The women would gather and point at him and smile and giggle to one another. He was terribly embarrassed and did not want to use the community latrine.

So what was the answer? He could relieve himself while out of the hamlet in the brush, but what was he to do if in the hamlet for several days? He decided that he would try to hold off until dark and then go out to the latrine over the canal. The first time went OK. The second time he returned to our quarters in agony; he had been eaten up by the hordes of mosquitoes that were always present.

The next time he had a nighttime call to nature while wearing shorts only, he doused himself liberally around his buttocks and groin with mosquito repellent and set off for the latrine with a flash light. He returned in a few minutes and stood by the doorway. He had fallen off the logs into the area under the latrine and was covered to the waist with mud that was the recipient of residue from above. Blair and I thought it was hilarious. Lt. Harris did not. He above all appreciated our new latrine, although there was one hitch in its design. I could never convince the workmen to build the bench seat with a hole in it to sit over. We ended up with a hole in the floor over which one squatted, Japanese/Vietnamese style. At any rate, it was better than a log over the canal.

Work began on the school project at once. The civilians in the hamlet, both male and female, turned out to work on the bunker. Inside the school building, minor repairs were made on tables and benches to be used as desks. The interior walls were whitewashed and the floor scrubbed.

While inspecting it one morning I said to Dai-uy Hy, "We must get some teachers now. How long will that take?" He pointed to two young women cleaning inside the building. "There teachers." I looked at the women he referred to and recognized them as the two who got off the chopper the other day dressed in ao dais. The ao dai is the traditional Vietnamese dress for women; it was seen mostly in the towns and cities but seldom worn by the women working in the countryside. It was an attractive two-piece garment consisting of floor length trousers and a sheath-like long overdress from the neck to well below the knees.

"They from Ca Mau?" I asked.

"Da phai," he replied, "and one more come by river boat. Hide in water vat. VC no find."

"We have three teachers here now?"

"Da bat thay giao (yes, three teachers)."

These were very brave young women. The Viet Cong, in their campaign to eliminate any government influence on the population, targeted the education system, particularly in the contested areas across the country. In towns and cities where the Government had strict control, education existed. Elsewhere, the VC made a concerted effort to destroy the last vestiges of learning sponsored by the government. Educational material was confiscated, schools were burned, teachers were abducted or killed, and as a last resort students in some areas were

358

stopped on the way to school and had a hand amputated by the VC. This brutal attack on students was effective. Parents stopped sending their children into harm's way.

The District Chief had closed the school in Dong Cung mainly because of the frequent mortar and artillery attacks. Although they still occurred, they were fewer since we had acquired the 4.2 mortar and the .50 caliber machine gun. With the ability to repair the school and with teachers on hand, he was determined to afford the children an opportunity to learn.

As Dai-uy Hy and I walked back up the street from the school, he motioned a young man over to us. He was wearing a polo shirt and dress trousers. I had not seen him before. He was introduced to me as Mr. Lee, the District Health Technician. "Where did he come from?" I asked.

"Province send him. He join with midwife. Run Health Station," replied Dai-uy Hy. I had met the young woman who was the District Midwife and had a small treatment room midway down the street. "They also treat wounded soldiers," Dai-uy announced.

I shook his hand and welcomed him to Dong Cung. He smiled and nodded deeply.

As we moved on I asked, "How did he get here?"

"On supply chopper. He not take much room," Dai-uy Hy said with a smile.

Well, I thought, we are making progress, however small. Opening a school and a District Health Facility was a move toward what MACV termed as "Nation Building." Before leaving the District Chief, I again brought up the subject of more offensive operations, but I agreed that until we increased our troop strength we could do little more than continue our patrolling and small raids. We needed the replacements waiting at Cu Mau.

Sgt. Blair met us at the street, and as we were walking back to our quarters I noticed three geese in the yard by the Headquarters.

"Where did those geese come from?" I asked Blair.

He smiled and said, "They are government geese, anti-VC geese."

"What are you talking about?"

"Sir, those geese were at the outpost that was overrun. They left there and swam down the river and came ashore here."

"Really, are you are kidding me?"

"No, sir, that's the truth!"

"Why would they come ashore here?"

"I don't know; perhaps they thought they would be fed."

"More likely will be eaten," I said.

There was a large gander, a smaller one, and a goose. We were to find out that the large gander was very possessive of the goose and frequently beat up on the smaller gander. Also he would attack women by running at them, flapping his wings and pecking them. Well, I thought if no one eats them, we have some pets.

CHAPTER 50

RIVER OPERATION

At last! We received a message from the TOC that the Vietnamese had finally come up with a plan to move our troops and supplies in Ca Mau down to us, not by air, but by the river!

What? Move troops and supplies from Ca Mau to Dong Cung by the river? I immediately got on the horn with the TOC and asked for the DPO, Lt. Col. Wright. When he came on the net I asked, "What in the world is this? Resupply us by the river? Whose bright idea is this?"

"Now calm down, this is the Province Chief's plan. I am sending a chopper in an hour to bring you up here to be briefed on the operation."

"Has my District Chief been made aware of this?"

"I don't know," replied Lt. Col. Wright. "A Province staff officer will be on the chopper coming to pick you up and will brief your counterpart and then return to Ca Mau on the chopper when we send you back to your district."

"This is really going to be interesting, I can't wait!"

"We will be picking up the DSA at Cha La also," interjected Lt. Col. Wright. "Save all your questions for the briefing. See you in a couple of hours, out."

I checked with Dai-uy Hy to see what he had been told. He said that he had just heard from the Province Headquarters that an operation plan was approved and that someone was coming to brief him. We agreed to meet as soon as I returned and to compare what we had been told and begin preparing for whatever it was we must do.

As scheduled, in about an hour later a chopper arrived. A Vietnamese major and two hospital returnees disembarked, followed by several crates that were thrown off by one of the crew. The major was greeted by Dai-uy Hy and went off toward the Headquarters Building. I boarded along with three soldiers, two of whom were ambulatory (commonly referred to as "walking wounded"). Major Simpson, DSA from Cha La, was already aboard. An hour later, we were walking into the Province Team Compound and shaking hands with the PSA, Lt. Col. Nagota.

It was now mid-day, and we joined Lt. Colonels Nagota and Wright for lunch in the Team's Mess. It was not a standard Army Mess Hall but a Mess Association. Each individual assigned to the Team contributed to a mess fund, which was used to purchase food stuff from the U.S. commissary in Saigon and on the local economy. The Army had not yet seen fit to establish a ration system to feed the Advisory Teams in the field. At the Province level, the team population could be anywhere from 50 to 80 plus; it was the center for support to the District Teams and any MAT teams assigned out with RF units. Yet no system was in place to feed the Advisors. Providing a method for supplying rations to the isolated advisory units was under study and by the time I rotated stateside a rudimentary supply arrangement had been initiated. I was frustrated that the Advisors at our level were neglected, but we learned to survive by purchasing on the civilian market and scrounging from U.S. military units whenever possible. On a subsequent tour in Vietnam, I found this new supply system for advisors to be an improvement.

Harris and I paid the charge for transit consumers and actually enjoyed a meal different from what we were accustomed to in Cai Nuoc. Afterwards we retired to Lt. Col. Nagota's office to discuss the resupply operation. We were joined by the S3 (Operations Officer) and the S4 (Supply Officer). With a nod from Lt Col. Wright, the S3 began briefing on the Vietnamese plan for resupplying Cai Nuoc. The operation was to be in two phases: first, movement of personnel and supplies by air from Ca Mau to Cha La District Headquarters for Dom Doi District, then from Cha La down the Song Bay Hop to Dong Cung by river packets. Supplies would go as cargo on the river, with some troop accompaniment. The remaining soldiers would go by land along the north side of the river. Cha La would be responsible for transport on the river and securing the north bank of the river to an agreed location; Cai Nuoc would take responsibility for securing the remaining distance to Dong Cung. I had a barrage of questions, but before I could speak Lt. Col. Nagota cautioned that this was the Province Chief's plan and we were to do our best to support it. I was then given the go-ahead to ask my questions.

"Why can't they gin up enough aircraft to do this right?"

"It's the Province Chief's plan, I have discussed with him and we must support him. We will see if they can pull it off."

"Is the Vietnamese Navy going to supply gun boats for security on the river?"

"No. They don't operate on the Song Bay Hop. Neither does the U.S. Navy, as you well know," responded the S3. "Cha La will commandeer the needed number of boats, the river packets that you see going up and down the river now."

"The VC frequently stops and taxes them," I stated.

"Yes, we know. You are going to have air cover, A1Es, for the entire operation." (A1E Skyraiders were propeller-driven dive bombers proven very effective in the Korean War and used by U.S. forces in Vietnam and the South Vietnamese Air Force.)

"A1Es!" I exclaimed, "Great, they carry a hell of a load of armament and can stay with us all day!"

"Well, not all day, but they are committed to cover the operation," replied the S3.

"How much cargo, how many soldiers are there?" asked Major Simpson, the DSA for Dom Doi and located at Cha La.

"I don't have an exact number; the figures change every time I ask the Vietnamese Staff," replied the S4.

"The last count I have on personnel is 91, and that's counting both hospital returnees and replacements," I interjected.

"What's the cargo?" Simpson questioned.

"Small arms and mortar ammunition, grenades, medical supplies, and some stuff for the District Civil Staff, I'm not sure what it is," he said.

"I need to know how much there is so I can be sure that they get enough boats," Major Simpson said.

"I'm sure that the District Chiefs will work out the details of the Province Chief's plan. Our job is to help them get it done on their own as much as possible. We will provide some chopper support in the move to Cha La and air cover on the river. You two DSAs need to coordinate the efforts of your counterparts. Any other questions?" asked Lt. Col. Nagota. "If not, we're done here. Col. Wright, any idea when this is going to kick off?"

"In a couple of days I understand, depends on Cha La getting the boats lined up," Lt. Col. Wright replied.

"OK, gentlemen, dismissed, good luck."

We filed out of the PSA's office and Lt. Col. Wright stated, "The S3 has a chopper standing by to transport you DSAs back to your Districts as soon as you are ready, Keep me posted on any problems that may arise."

"That may arise--you mean that DOES arise, don't you?" I asked.

"Think positive," he grinned as he walked off toward to his office.

Major Simpson and I had a few minutes to chat before we took off. We had never met before although we had talked to each other on the Province radio net. Our pilot dropped Simpson off first and then Harris and me at Dong Cung before continuing on to Hai Yen and back to Ca Mau.

We were walking across the yard in front of the District Headquarters building and our quarters when we met Sgt. Blair, who said, "Watch the geese!"

The three geese were in the middle of the yard and two women were passing by them while approaching the Headquarters. The large gander began honking loudly, and while flapping his wings ran at the women pecking them. The women retreated a few steps waving their arms and yelling. A soldier emerged from the Headquarters and drove the gander off with a stick. The women then entered the building to conduct whatever business brought them there.

"This has been going on all morning," said Sgt. Blair. "A number of women have been coming to the Headquarters and leaving with papers in hand. The big gander has been after them all."

While we were standing there, the wife of the District radio operator came out of the communications bunker under the roadbed and proceeded across the yard toward the Headquarters building. She was very small, even for a young Vietnamese girl. The big gander spied her and came running, flapping his wings and hissing. When he stuck his neck out to peck her, the girl grabbed the gander's neck with both hands. She picked him off the ground and swung him around in a circle several times, then releasing him to end up four to five meters away. The gander got up, shook himself, and ran to join the other geese at the end of the yard. There he stood honking but not moving toward the young girl. We were to note in the future that he continued to attack the women who came into the area but that girl never again!

I briefed Lt. Harris and Sgts. Blair and Hai on the river resupply operation and noted concern on the faces of the NCOs. They were experienced enough to realize the obstacles that we might encounter. I advised them that we would accompany the troops securing our portion of the north side of the river and meet the Cha La (Dom Doi District) Advisors at the location selected by the two District Chiefs for turning over the troops traveling on foot. The responsibility for coordinating with the air cover would move from Dom Doi to Cai Nuoc Advisors at approximately the halfway point on the river or as might be dictated by the situation at the time.

Sergeant Blair asked how many soldiers would be in the group coming by foot. I told him based on the last count we had of 90-plus, I thought it could be 60 to 70, depending on how many would be on the boats. I told them to hold any further questions until after I discussed the operation with Dai-uy Hy, which I wanted to do as soon as possible. Sergeant Hai ran over to Dai-uy Hy's bunker to see if he was available, returning quickly to announce that the District Chief was anxious to discuss the operation now. Taking Sgt. Hai with me, I joined the District Chief in his quarters, where he had a map and some papers spread out on his table.

Dai-uy Hy pointed to a spot on the map and said, "We meet our soldiers there." I bent over and studied the rendezvous closely. "We meet the troops at Rach Nha Thinh where it joins the river?" I asked. "Da," replied Dai-uy Hy. "It is wide, but people live there, have boats. We can cross OK."

"How about between here and there? I count 11 canals or streams we must cross."

"No problem," replied Dai-uy Hy shaking his head. "They have foot bridges or not deep, can walk across."

I noticed several small red circles drawn with a grease pencil on the map on the north side of the river and one on the south side. "What are these?" I asked. Sergeant Hai looked at the Dai-uy, who nodded assent and then said, "They are locations from which VC fired on river boats before."

Except for the vicinity of Dong Cung, which was within the range of their small arms and automatic weapons, the river was basically open to the enemy's use. Civilian commercial river boats plied up and down the river almost daily and stopped at various river communities. They carried an assortment of goods such as cargo, passengers, and also mail. They were frequently intercepted by the VC, who then taxed the goods they didn't confiscate. Any passengers they determined to be related to the government were abducted. Cargo believed to be intended for the government was taken plus any of the mail they found interesting or government related. At this particular time, the VC had almost free rein of the river. This would change in a few months when the U.S. Navy began a program to open the rivers and main waterways, but at this time the Song Bay Hop was "Indian Territory."

We went on discussing the coordination between us and the District Chief and Advisors from Cha La. We were told that there would be four river packets moving the cargo. Four to six of our soldiers would be on each boat. That would leave about 70 to go on foot plus some troops from Cha La to secure or scout ahead of the main party. Dai-uy Hy stated that we would use 472 Company for that mission from the rendezvous point to Dong Cung. We were advised that the operation would kick off in two or three days. Ca Mau had to first move the supplies and troops to Cha La. The following afternoon we received word the troops and supplies were being moved the following day.The next morning I met with Dai-uy Hy at his bunker. It had been a quiet night, with no incoming and only a little small arms fire directed at our strong point at the north; there had been no casualties. Dai-uy Hy had been on the radio with the District Chief at Cha La, who reported that the movement of our troops and supplies from Ca Mau was ongoing. There was one bit of bad news: it appeared that 11 of the soldiers had deserted, reducing our replacements to 80. I was not surprised desertions were high among the Vietnamese, and the long wait for transport to Dong Cung provided an opportunity to just walk away.

The 472 Company had an effective strength of 60 and would be parceled out for security along the route from our rendezvous back to Dong Cung. The points along the river bank that were known to be used by the VC to fire on boats in the past would be reconnoitered to be sure that they were not presently occupied. I was taking the entire advisory team--all four of us!--as I thought there was a possibility that there may be a need for us to be more than one place at a time, perhaps on a boat. If necessary, I could split Lt. Harris and Sgt. Blair off and keep Sgt. Hai with me. We were hoping that the cargo could be loaded on the boats today or tomorrow and we could jump off the following morning. We wanted to get our soldiers and freight down to Dong Cung as soon as possible. The VC would know that troops and supplies flown into Cha La were in excess of normal resupply and determine that something was up. Besides, we didn't want our men and much needed supplies lying around Cha La any longer than necessary. Later in the day, I was on the radio with Major Simpson and he was sure the boats would be loaded by tomorrow and the operation would be a go for the next morning. I so informed Dai-uy Hy, who concurred.

CHAPTER 51

ON THE RIVER

Our normal morning shower of rain was ending as the leading squad of men crossed over the canal on the east side of the hamlet heading up the river. The well-worn foot path was muddy but not enough to impede movement, and the column moved along at a reasonable pace. Our intent was to arrive at Rach Nha Thinh by noon, which was expected to be no problem unless enemy activity caused a delay. A fair number of houses were scattered along the river bank, many of them at the confluence of small streams and the river.

The first one we approached was spanned by the normal foot bridge constructed of poles and was slippery with mud from use. American Advisors frequently slipped and fell off these bridges, causing amusement among the local troops. However, they themselves were not immune to falling, especially when burdened with equipment and weapons. If the stream was narrow and shallow, many just chose to wade across. I noted that Dai-uy Hy directed some of the houses we passed to be looked into and at several locations waved soldiers off the path to scan the area. A radio transmission from Major Simpson revealed that their column was also on the move. The boats had not yet departed but were soon to do so.

I had not heard from the Province TOC or a FAC concerning our air cover. I was about to check on it when Dai-uy Hy informed me he had just been told that the A1Es scheduled to provide cover were VNAF (Vietnamese Air Force) planes, not U.S. Ground-to-air coordination would be conducted by the District Chiefs, not the Advisors. This was something new to me. I had heard that the A1Es were being turned over to the Vietnamese but didn't know the transfer had started.

We had being moving without any delay when several rifle shots were heard at the front of the column. We were in our normal position about a third of the way back from the lead squad. Forward movement stopped. Several soldiers turned to face inland from the direction of the river. Dai-uy was on the radio listening and then speaking rapidly. Sergeant Hai approached and said "Soldiers see two men with rifles, think may be Cha La soldiers, but they run away, so soldiers shoot at them."

"Hit them?" I asked.

"No, sir, I no think so."

The column started moving forward again but at a slower pace.

"Sergeant Blair, check with Cha La and see if they have seen any VC."

"Yes, sir, their call sign is Lima, right sir?" he queried.

"Right."

"Seaforth Lima, This is Seaforth Oscar, over," called Blair.

"Oscar, this is Lima Six, over."

"Lima Six, this is Oscar three, my six would like to know if you have seen any VC, over."

"Oscar Three, this is Lima Six. Tell your boss that's a negative except we rounded up a couple of suspicious looking characters hanging out where we were loading the boats."

"Wilco, Lima Six, you have anything else for us at the moment, over?"

"Lima Six here, yeah you have lost some men. This morning the count of replacements is 73, down 7 from last night. Looks like 7 don't like Dong Cung or are VC."

"Roger Lima Six, I'll tell him, Oscar Three out."

Blair turned from the radio, and reported, "Major Simpson said no contact but picked up a couple of VC suspects. He also said to tell you that seven of our replacements went AWOL last night. We are down to seventy three."

"What! Damn! Dai-uy did you know that seven men deserted last night?" I asked the District Chief.

"Da," he replied, shrugging his shoulders. "What can I do?"

"I don't know. We will never get enough men to eliminate the VC in Cai Nuoc District!"

It was nearly noon and we were closing in on the Rach Nha Thinh when we heard a thunder-like noise. Two A1Es bearing the emblem of the Republic of South Vietnam on their wings came roaring down the Song Bay Hop at tree-top level. They banked sharply and climbed rapidly to the east.

Dai-uy Hy called out to me over the roar of the aircraft, saying "Cha La has contact with airplanes." I nodded to him that I understood as I watched them doing a 180-degree turn and leveling off, coming down the river again a bit slower. Sergeant Hai tapped me on the arm pointed to the river and said "Boats pass us now going down river."

"That's great. At least our supplies are halfway there."

I watched the two aircraft approaching when they suddenly went into a steep climb with one plane winging over and into a shallow dive, dropping two bombs on the opposite side of the river. The second plane followed, strafing with its four 20 mm cannons.

I asked Dai-uy Hy, "Was that one of the sites used by the VC to fire on boats?"

"Da phai," he replied.

The two planes made another turn down the river and then flew off to the north, out of sight.

"Is that the end of our air support?" I asked.

"I don't know. I will ask Cha La District," replied the Dai-uy.

I radioed Major Simpson at the same time. "What's the deal on the air support, do you know?"

"I think it is over,. My counterpart is checking on it now, but I think that's it. You know the problems the Vietnamese ground commanders have with the VNAF. If we get in trouble we will have to contact our TOC for help."

"Yeah, I'm afraid you are right. Well, we are on the move again. We should join up with you in 30 minutes or so."

"Great," said Major Simpson, "I am sitting on a log on my side of the Rach. Your guys are crossing in a couple of sampans. The Rach is pretty wide and there is no bridge."

"OK. I will meet you on your side. See you shortly."

I briefed the team on my conversation with Major Simpson and told them we all would cross over and visit for a few minutes. Then I told Dai-uy Hy of my intentions. He said he would cross over also and talk with the District Chief from Cha La.

Houses lined both banks of Rach Nha Thinh with small docks where a number of boats, some motorized, were moored. As we approached the Rach, we noted a group of soldiers sitting about, apparently having just crossed from the other side. Several more were unloading from a sampan, and Dai-uy Hy hailed the civilian operating it and told him to transport us to the other side. I saw Major Simpson sitting on a bench in front of a large house with a canteen in one hand and a cigar in the other.

"Join me," he invited, waving the cigar.

We walked over and shook hands all round as we introduced each other. Dai-uy Hy was greeted by a Vietnamese Major, whom I surmised to be Major Simpson's counterpart.

"Well, looks like my part of this operation is about over," said Simpson.

"Yeah, I guess so," I agreed.

"Do you know what the A1Es hit?" I asked.

"There were three boats with about a dozen guys in them. My counterpart believed they intended to attack our river boats and requested the A1Es to hit them."

"Did you get a report from them on the results of the strike?"

374

"No," replied Simpson, "they just flew away."

"I thought they were to cover our entire operation," I ventured.

"So did I," laughed Major Simpson, "but I guess the VNAF had other plans."

"So it appears, but the mission is only half over, I just hope we can get these troops and stuff to Dong Cung. We need it all badly," I stated.

"And with saying that, I'd better get moving. I see that all the troops have crossed and my counterpart is waiting on us."

"Well, good luck," said Simpson, standing up and offering his hand.

Thanks, I'll see you around, perhaps at Province."

"Yeah, perhaps so, take care."

I never saw him again, which was not unusual under these conditions

We had left Rach Nha Thinh only about 40 minutes or so when gunfire broke out up ahead. There were a couple of shots, rising quickly to a substantial rate of fire, and then decreasing to an occasional two- or three-round burst.

"What's going on?" I asked Sgt. Hai.

"I don't know," he replied, running over to Dai-uy Hy who was on the radio.

The Dai-uy waved him off and started up toward the front of the column. I immediately followed. The firing was still going on and sounded closer. I could determine that there were several different weapons being used. I was really concerned because the hospital returnees may not all have had weapons, and the replacements would be mostly green troops. The security provided by 472 Company was scattered thinly along the column. The firing stopped and in a few minutes, another hundred meters or so, we came up to where a VC attack had taken place. There on the foot path lay two dead replacements. Crouched a few meters away was a soldier from the 472 Company holding his arm from which a trickle of blood was dripping. In some nearby brush lay a dead VC, an unexploded grenade trap nearby.

In a few minutes the column was on the move again, two soldiers were bandaging the wounded man's arm, and the two KIAs were being carried to the river bank.

I looked at Dai-uy Hy and all he would say was "Ambush."

The speed of the march quickened. The enemy surely knew now, if they didn't before, what we were up to and had had time to plan some actions against us. Dai-uy Hy wanted to get the new troops to Dong Cung as soon as possible. We had heard from the DDC (Deputy District Chief) Lt. Hong back at Dong Cung that the boats were in sight. He had the responsibility of unloading the supplies and getting them stored. Hospital returnees would report to their unit and the replacements would be assigned by the District Chief later. In the meantime, Lt. Hong would use them to help unload the boats.

The column reached Dong Cung without further incident at 1830 hours. We had been out 12 and a half hours and covered approximately 25 kilometers. Of the 91 soldiers that were at Ca Mau, only 69 arrived safely, 16 of them on the boats. Desertions at Ca Mau and Cha La had cost us 20 men.

Getting the boats through was easier than I expected. I believe the air strike by the A1Es discouraged the VC from attacks on the river. Parceling out the returning wounded and the replacements among the three companies still did not bring them up to authorized strength. In fact, we were at not much more than when I had arrived two months prior. I got on the radio with Lt. Col Wright and gave him an oral report, complained about the desertions and the air support, and promised a written summary of the operation in a few days. It was difficult to keep a positive attitude under these circumstances. We seemed to be spinning our wheels, going nowhere. Whatever small gains we made were overshadowed by the lack of ability to take the initiative, only defend ourselves.

CHAPTER 52

STRONG POINT OVER RUN

Two days after our river operation, Dai-uy Hy came to me and said, "We did not get M79 ammunition."

"None at all?"

"None," he replied shaking his head. "I think District Chief at Cha La take. I report to Ca Mau. They say Cha La major say he no take."

"Well, I am going to contact the TOC and demand some M79 ammo be on the next chopper."

"Gio Lam (very good)," said Dai-uy as he nodded and walked off toward his bunker.

I was able to reach Lt. Col. Wright on the radio and he promised to see that we had M79 ammo on the next flight. Pilfering of supplies by one Vietnamese unit from another was not unusual .

The following night I was awakened by a loud explosion followed by small arms fire. It seemed to be on the north side near the Strong Point on the old road. I then heard the machine gun in the bunker directly behind the Strong Point open fire. Sporadic rifle fire began all along the perimeter wall. Harris, Blair, and I began moving toward the Strong Point roadbed when we were joined by the District Chief and several soldiers. The .50 caliber machine gun on the bridge then began firing over our heads out in front of the Strong Point. It was now obvious that there was some type of an attack directed at the Strong Point.

378

As we neared the position, I noticed several soldiers standing at the rear of the below-ground emplacement. The position was about three and one half meters square and dug down into the roadbed chest deep with a parapet for protection from direct fire. Four posts supported a thatched roof overhead. Ten meters in front (north) of the emplacement were five fighting positions (fox holes) in a semi-circle, spanning the width of the roadbed. This defensive position was designed to deny the enemy the most vulnerable avenue of approach from the north. It was manned at night by 15 to 18 soldiers and usually included automatic weapons (BARs). Five soldiers occupied the foxholes and rotated with the others in the main position.

It was the dark of the moon and cloudy, so visibility was limited to a few meters at the most. We elbowed our way through the soldiers, peering into the sunken pit-like position. Flashlights were produced and their beams revealed the most horrible sight I had ever seen. The dugout was splattered with blood and pieces of flesh. Mangled bodies lay in unnatural positions, some even missing limbs. One soldier standing near me turned and vomited. Pieces of equipment could be recognized and part of the wall on one side had partially collapsed. A Lieutenant from one of the companies reported to Dai-uy Hy that the five men in the forward fox holes were all dead.

Firing around the perimeter had ceased. As I watched, the District Chief motioned several men to him and spit out orders so rapidly that I could not catch even a single word. After waving them off, he turned to me and said, "I order all soldiers on defense to daylight. I send out patrols now. I order no touch this. I will inspect in daylight. Then remove bodies and clean up." I nodded that I understood. I knew that he wanted to determine how security was breached and how one of our strongest defensive positions was overrun.

It was still about two hours to daylight when we returned to our quarters. I radioed the Province TOC and gave them a preliminary report on the incident.

Sgt. Hai joined us and reported, "Sixteen soldiers dead, five in fox holes and eleven in bunker. Many were new replacements."

"What company?" I asked.

"In 518 Company." Sgt. Hai replied.

Damn, I thought, that's the worst I've seen since I got here. Our overall strength increased by 49 two days ago, but after tonight our net gain was only 33. Not enough to upgrade our offensive operations.

Later in the morning, Dai-uy Hy asked me to join him to discuss the VC attack. He had formed an opinion on how the assault was carried out. He believed that some or all the soldiers in the foxholes were asleep, as were some in the dugout. He thought that the VC party was small in numbers and bypassed the sleeping soldiers in the foxholes. He was sure that the VC, once past the foxholes, had gathered behind the dugout and had simultaneously pitched five or more grenades into the sleeping troops. At the same time, others shot the soldiers in the holes from behind. A BAR and 10 rifles were missing, and the others destroyed in the grenade assault.

"Nine soldiers were new replacements," said Dai- Hy. "Too many in one place. I tell Province Chief," he continued. "He say I waste men. That not so."

I agreed with Dai-Hy, but knew that assigning that many new replacements in the strong point was a mistake.

CHAPTER 53

R & R

The Army's R&R (Rest and Recreation) program was designed to give the soldier a brief respite from combat duty during a year long tour in Vietnam. R & R sites were included in-country at Vung Tau and China Beach. R&R away from Vietnam was allowed in Bangkok, Tokyo, Singapore, Hong Kong, Australia, Manila, and Hawaii. Many servicemen met up their spouses or sweethearts in Hawaii for a week-long break from the war.

My wife and I discussed meeting in Hawaii but decided that we would forgo the opportunity. We did not want to go through the agony of saying farewell any more than we needed to. This was my second hardship tour in a little over two years. It had been only 17 months since I had returned from almost 14 months in Korea. We decided that another emotional parting in six months was more than we wanted to go through. Two years later when I going off on my third hardship tour, our attitude changed and we met whenever it was possible.

I had delayed my R&R several times and finally decided to go to Bangkok, Thailand. It was now in the middle of July and I received orders to report to Saigon for transport to Thailand before the end of the month. I had selected Thailand based on my memory of a song popular a few years earlier. The song was titled "Far Away Places" and a line that I remembered was "Going to China and maybe Siam, I want to see for myself the places I've been reading about in a book that I took from a shelf." Siam was now Thailand, and I was going to see it.

Three days later I choppered to Ca Mau and left the next morning for Saigon on an Air America C47. I retrieved a duffel bag that I had left in storage at the Province Team Compound and took with me a wrinkled khaki uniform, a pair of mildewed low quarter shoes, a belt, and cap--I knew that I could not fly to Bangkok in faded jungle fatigues as it was against regulation to travel in fatigues outside Vietnam. Upon arrival at Tan Son Nhut airport in Saigon, I caught a military taxi to a section of what became Camp Alpha that managed the R&R Program. The area consisted of several wooden buildings and a large number of general purpose tents housing double-decked army cots. I in-processed, received a Flight Number, time of departure for the next morning, and a tent and bunk assignment for the night. I then proceeded to another building where I turned in the uniform and boots I was wearing for laundering and cleaning. I would recover them upon my return from R&R before going back to the field. After checking my pistol in an arms room, I headed for the largest building there, which was an all ranks club.

The building was packed with men waiting for their flight to somewhere better than here. Some were going to meet their loved ones, and others were hoping to meet someone to love. The noise was deafening. Everyone was in a festive mood and the alcohol was flowing. As I was shoving my way toward a long bar at one end of the building, I spied a Master Sergeant sitting at a small table up against the wall. I knew him from when I had served with the 1st Battalion, 6th Infantry, 1st Armored Division, Fort Hood, Texas. I waved at him; recognizing me, he beckoned to me to join him.

As I reached the table, he stood up and offered his hand, saying, "Good to see you Major. The last time I saw you, you were a Captain."

"Yeah, even a blind hog finds an acorn once in a while. How have you been?" I asked, shaking his hand vigorously.

"Oh, you know how it is, been here and there, mostly here for a while," he responded.

His name was Moss and he had been the Battalion Motor Sergeant and, as I well remembered, a damn good one.

"Let me get some drinks. What are you drinking?"

"Scotch and water. Better get doubles—it takes a while to get their attention at the bar," he advised.

Upon my return with the two drinks, we toasted each other and started the ritual that soldiers who have not seen each other for some time go through. Where have you been, who have you seen from the old outfit, where, what friends were promoted, what friends had been killed or wounded. The afternoon passed, well watered by fresh rounds of drinks. Finally I realized I must get some sleep, and after swearing to look one another up some time I staggered out of the club searching for my tent and bunk. I don't remember how I got there, but at first light the following morning I awoke on the bottom bunk in the tent where I had been assigned.

The tent held eight double bunks and appeared to be full. As I put my feet on the concrete floor, my head began pounding as if it was going to split open. I was now paying a price for my bout of drinking. The past several months I had been, because of the need to be sober and alert, a virtual tee totaler. My system was currently not used to large quantities of alcohol. As I sat there holding my head in my hands, a voice said, "A little too much of John Barleycorn last night?"

I looked up and saw a young Lieutenant standing there.

"I was in the upper bunk when you staggered in last evening, you were not feeling any pain," he said. "Well, go wash up. I have some aspirin here if you want some, you will feel better," he continued, pointing to a long metal trough between the rows of tents.

383

"Yeah, thanks," I mumbled as I stumbled over to the trough. It was about three feet off the ground and had spigots every few feet. I joined several soldiers who were shaving or brushing their teeth and turned on a spigot and stuck my head under the stream of water. After a few minutes I shaved, shakily, brushed my teeth, and returned to my tent.

I said to the Lieutenant, "I will take those aspirin now if you are still offering."

"Sure," he replied, handing me a bottle. "My name is Jim Stevens."

"What unit are you with, Stevens?" I asked.

"Company C, the 6th of the 31st Infantry, sir," he replied.

"Are you going to Bangkok?"

"Yes, sir, I think everyone in this tent is Bangkok bound. The flight is at 0900 and there is a bus to take us to the plane leaving at 0730."

"Just enough time to find a cup of coffee," I mumbled.

"There is a mess tent over there. I already had breakfast there."

I stumbled over to the mess and after two cups of coffee and the aspirin felt human again.

Lieutenant Stevens had sat down and was chatting with me about the R&R in Bangkok. "Have you made reservations there?" he asked.

384

"Yes, through the Majestic Hotel in Saigon. Have you?"

"No, sir," Stevens replied.

"Well, if you have not made any other arrangements we can hang out together. I want to do some shopping, sightseeing, and eat a lot!"

"That sounds good, sir."

"Look, Jim, let's knock off the sir stuff for the duration of the R&R. We can pick up the military courtesy when we get back."

"OK, sir. I'll try."

Right on schedule, an Army bus pulled up and stopped in front of the mess tent just as I had finished drinking my coffee. A trim young officer dismounted and announced loudly, "I'm Captain Brown. Everyone bound for Bangkok please board the bus."

Jim and I walked over and boarded. The configuration of the seating was not the normal rows of seats but was a long bench down each side of the bus. We were the first aboard and sat down at the front of the bus with our bags between our feet. Other passengers boarded and sat down in about the middle of the bus. Two officers, one a Lt. Col. Chaplain, sat down opposite Jim and me. They were talking loudly, especially the Chaplain, when the officer overseeing the loading stepped aboard and addressing the Chaplain said, "Sir I have a full colonel coming aboard .Will you make room and save him a seat right up front here for me?"

"Yeah, I will," the Chaplin responded turning back to his companion and continuing his loud conversation.

A few minutes later a Korean Army Colonel in full uniform stepped up into the bus. He looked around for a moment, noting a space on the bench at the front when the Chaplain looked up and said to him, "Move on down the aisle, this seat is saved."

The Korean Colonel looked at him then moved down the aisle and quietly sat down. Five minutes later Captain Brown appeared at the front of the bus and announced, "OK gentlemen we are off to the air terminal where you will board a Pan Am chartered flight to Bangkok. It will take about two hours and there is a one hour time change, so you will gain an extra hour on your R&R."

He glanced down at the front of the bench seat and asked, "Where is the Colonel?"

"He never showed up," said the Chaplain.

"Yes he did," I interjected, "The Chaplain sent him on to the back of the bus."

Captain Brown looked at the Chaplain with disgust and walked back to where the Korean officer was sitting. It was easy to see that the young Captain was apologizing to the colonel and offering him a seat up front. The colonel shook his head smilingly and stayed seated where he was. Captain Brown returned to the front, gave another disgusting look at the Chaplain and waved to the driver to start the run to the terminal. Fifteen minutes later we were loading on a Pan Am jet liner destination Bangkok, Thailand.

After becoming comfortably seated, a stewardess came down the aisle offering coffee, tea, or sodas. I asked for some aspirin along with coffee. She smiled and reached into her pocket and produced a small tin of aspirin that she handed me. "I get a lot of requests for aspirin on this run. It must be something you soldiers eat." "No," I replied, "Something we drank too much of!" She laughed, handed me a plastic cup of coffee, and moved on to the next row of seats. The plane soon took off, and in two hours we were landing in Bangkok.

A young man in civilian clothes appeared at the front of the plane and announced, "I'm Captain Spencer from the Bangkok U.S. Army R&R Reception Center. Welcome to Bangkok. We are going to be loading on a bus in a few moments, and after a 20-minute drive will arrive at the Reception Center. There you will receive a short briefing on Bangkok and the Thai people." A collective groan greeted the captain's welcome. "I know," he continued, "You just want to get going, but believe me the briefing will be short and some worthwhile information will be passed out. So let's get loaded and on our way."

Good as his word, 30 minutes later we were seated in a classroom-like briefing area in the Reception Center. Captain Spencer, standing at the front of the group, was joined by another Captain. I immediately recognized him as a fellow student at the Civil Affairs School and the Vietnamese Language Course at Biggs Field, Texas.

"Leonard Jones," I yelled out from the back of the room where I was sitting, "What are you doing here?"

He looked up and spying me in the audience, waved and smiled, and then alternated with Captain Spencer in the briefing. We were warned about the dos and don'ts and courtesies concerning the Thai culture. Lists of recommended hotels, restaurants, clubs that were accustomed to GIs on R&R, and nightspots with entertainment in English were passed out. Schedules of Thai activities such as Thai Boxing and Dancing were provided plus warnings of schemes designed to fleece the GIs out of their money. For the shoppers, names of retail shops that specialized in items such as jade, silk, ivory, and traditional Thai curios and that were considered to be honest were provided. A tour of the Holy City was strongly advised. A report time for our

387

departure back to Saigon was given and lastly we were requested that any problems we encountered during our visit be reported to the R&R Reception Center. They were open 24 hours a day.

A van was standing by to transport personnel to the various hotels. Jim and I were dropped off where I had reservations and he was able to get a room on the same floor as mine. The hotel was a western-style modern one and had a number of long-time patrons that were families of personnel assigned to the British Legation; it was very similar to a hotel one might see in New York or London. Our next move was to get some civilian clothes.

The front desk directed us to a British men's shop within walking distance. A few minutes later we entered the shop and were greeted by a young round-eyed woman wearing the shortest skirt we had ever seen. (Round-eyed was a term used by GIs for non-Asian women). The young woman had a pronounced British accent and was very attractive. Jim and I had a difficult time keeping our eyes off her legs. The miniskirts had been around for a while in England and were becoming popular in the U.S., but for a number of months neither of us had seen few if any female Caucasians, and the women in Vietnam wore trousers or dresses at floor length. The woman seemed to take our ogling in stride and was soon assisting us in selecting some trousers and shirts. We each purchased two pair of trousers and two pullover knit shirts. We were told the trousers would be altered and ready for pick up in only an hour. We spent that hour in a coffee shop eating and planning our R&R. We had five nights and six days, including the day we arrived. We wanted to visit the Holy City one day, spend two days shopping, and the rest just seeing the sights.

We both wanted to eat. I had lost more than 35 pounds, and Jim had a strong appetite. So we planned to hit a top restaurant each night. From the list given us at the Center we selected a Japanese, a Chinese, a Thai, and an American one, leaving one night open. We would eat

388

breakfast at the hotel and during the day would eat where ever we found something. We actually ended up eating four to five times a day!

With the basic plan in mind, we picked up our clothing purchases and returned to the hotel. Our first evening out was to the Japanese restaurant. There we ate Kobe steak for the first time. We didn't care for the music, so after dinner we moved on to a night club that had an Australian show. There I heard for the first time the songs "Blowing in the Wind," "Where Have All The Flowers Gone," and "Love Is Blue," all of which were very popular back in the U.S. Before turning in for the night, we made another stop to eat in the all-night coffee shop in our hotel.

The follow morning we were off to shop. The weather was cooperating; it was clear and warm but not oppressively humid like Vietnam, so we were able to walk to the shop we had selected. It was a pleasant and interesting stroll along the streets of what we considered downtown Bangkok. The shop we found was owned and run by a Chinese family. As we entered, we were approached by two young Chinese, brother and sister we were to find out later, who were pleasant and not aggressive in their salesmanship. We actually spent several hours there browsing through all of the wares. Our stomachs began to growl; we were hungry for lunch and discussed leaving to get something to eat. Immediately the siblings invited us to join them and their whole family for a meal. It was a wonderful invitation that we accepted, but I suspected they wanted to keep us there for fear of losing the sale if we left the shop for lunch. Their ploy worked, as the both of us purchased jewelry, jade, silk, and some artwork. Later we visited other shops but returned to this one to finish buying items to ship home to our families.

The days rolled by. We spent more than a day seeing the Holy City, including the massive reclining Buddha, the 365 Buddhas, and the Emerald Buddha reputed to be worth millions. We had hired a guide

389

who spoke English exceptionally well, and he provided an interesting dialog on the history and background of Thailand. We experienced both ends of the spectrum of Thai culture by attending Thai Kick Boxing and also Classical Dancing.

During the day we ate where ever we were when the pangs of hunger hit us. One day, we were walking down a street and ducked into a sandwich shop to get some lunch. It was a narrow shop with a counter and stools on one side and booths on the other, much like you might find at home. Jim and I took a booth midway back from the front and ordered club sandwiches and lemonade. Customers were coming and going; at one point, as a customer left, a little white dog that we had noted sitting outside came in. It proceeded down to the last booth, which was empty, and lifted his leg and urinated against the wall. When finished he padded back up to the entrance and sat down. When the door was opened by a customer coming in, he went back out and down the street. We thought it was hilarious. Contrasting what we were used to, this little guy came in to "use a facility" and then went back out on the street and on his merry way. I have no idea if this was common, but it was the first and only time we saw it while there.

At last the final day of our R&R had arrived. After an afternoon steam bath and massage, we had a final sumptuous meal that evening. The next morning found us boarding a plane for our return flight to Saigon.

It was early afternoon when we arrived back at Camp Alpha. After retrieving my uniform, boots, and pistol Jim and I shook hands, promising to keep in touch but knowing that we wouldn't. He was off to find transportation back to his unit and I hopped a military shuttle bus to downtown Saigon to the Army Transit Billeting Office, located in the Carvelle Hotel. I got a room in the MacArthur BOQ (Bachelor Officer's Quarters), a leased Vietnamese hotel on Tu Do Street and within walking distance.

Tu Do Street was well known to the GIs for its bars, tea rooms, massage parlors, jewelry, and souvenir shops, and it held a somewhat nefarious reputation. The sidewalks were covered with mats holding trinkets and black market U.S. items being hawked by old women, children, and ex-Vietnamese soldiers--mostly with missing limbs. Young women in short dresses standing in doorways called invitingly to passing GIs. A variety of hotels were located on Tu Do Street, from the reknown and upscale Majestic to local flop houses and brothels.

The MacArthur was located near the upper end of Tu Do Street near the square. I checked in, was assigned a room, showered, and started out to walk up to the Rex Hotel to have dinner and a few drinks in the Officer's Club. On my way out I noticed a bar off of the lobby. I decided to stop in, have a drink, and see if I might see someone I knew. It was now around 1700 hours and I expected a few transits like myself might be in this early. I was surprised to see a number of Naval Officers in undress whites and several round-eyed women. The women all appeared to be middle-aged and well dressed. They probably work at the Embassy or other U.S. Government Headquarters, I guessed. I bellied up to the bar and ordered a drink and then turned and greeted a Navy Lieutenant standing to my right.

He nodded and commented, "We don't see those in here very often," pointing to my faded jungle fatigues. I glanced around and realized that I was, with the exception of the women, the only non-Naval person in the room. The Lieutenant moved on down the bar to talk and I turned to the bar tender and asked, "Is this a private party?"

"No, sir," he replied, "but mostly only Navy people hang out here."

"But it is a club run open bar, right?"

"Yes, sir."

391

I now felt out of place and decided to down my drink and get out. But before I could, a tall Navy Captain in an impeccable white uniform approached me and said, "Good evening Major, how are you?"

"Fine, sir," I replied.

"We don't often see Army personnel in here," he continued. "We have kind of taken this club over."

"The bartender told me it was an open club bar," I responded.

"True, but I expect you would be more comfortable at the Rex or the Brinks. That's where the Army people usually gather. Enjoy your drink," he smiled and walked back to a small group who were laughing at something. I hoped it was not me.

Well, I thought, I have just been diplomatically ordered out of the bar. No way! I called out to the bartender to give me a refill. I was not going to be forced out. However, after getting my drink guzzled down, off to the Rex Hotel I went; it was not going to be any fun staying where I wasn't wanted. . There I ate dinner, had another drink, and then returned to my room to get some sleep. In the early hours of the following morning, I was at the 8th Aerial Port, Tan Son Nhut, trying to get down country to Ca Mau.

CHAPTER 54

RETURN TO THE WAR

Trying to get a flight out of Saigon was always a chore. There were all types of aircraft belonging to the U.S. Air Force, Army, Navy, Air America (CIA), Vietnam Air Force plus the Vietnam Civilian Airline, going everywhere. Grabbing an open seat on anything flying in your direction was many times the quickest way to get where you were going. Luck was with me; I was able to get a seat on a scheduled Caribou flight that made a daily run to all the Province Capitals in the delta. Ca Mau was their fifth stop, and I was in the Province Team Compound by noon.

Reporting in, I found that the PSA, Lt. Col. Nagota, and Capt. Berti, my replacement at Hai Yen, were both in Saigon attending a conference for recently arrived Advisors. Lt. Col. Wright welcomed me back and updated me on events that had occurred during my absence. There were no major incidents in Cai Nuoc reported by Lt. Harris and Sgt. Blair, and enemy activity in Hai Yen appeared to be normal. However, Wright wanted me to go to Hai Yen until Capt. Berti returned. There was no replacement yet for Lt. Harris since I had moved him to Cai Nuoc, and there was no officer present at Hai Yen until Berti's return, placing an additional burden on Sgt. Brown, the senior NCO on site. I readily agreed. I looked forward to being with my old team and the Chinese for a few days. While waiting for Lt. Col. Wright to arrange for a FAC to transport me to Hai Yen, I made the rounds with the Province Team Staff to discuss the status of supplies, replacements, and ammunition for Cai Nuoc.

Late in the afternoon, one of the FACs, Shotgun 42, flew me to Hai Yen, where I was met on the air strip by Sgt. Brown and Major Thinh. Almost like being home, especially when greeted by Bake the cook and Poke the housekeeper as I entered the team house. Since I

393

would only be there a couple of nights, I did not plan to participate in any major operations.

That evening I met with Major Thinh and discussed the general situation at Hai Yen. Enemy activity was about the same. Support from Province had improved mainly in the area of food and building materials for the civilians. A considerable number of families had moved from the VC-controlled area around Cai Bot Lake. Thinh said that the status of the troops was OK but needed motivation. He also was not sure that the Chinese were always following his orders. He believed that the Chinese officers always consulted Lt. Niep, Father Hoa's brother, before carrying out Major Thinh's orders. I thought this was probably true and was a carryover from when Thinh's predecessor was in command. I told him that they would always obtain Lt. Niep's opinion on any matter in which they were required to be engaged if it was not in their established routine, combat operations or otherwise. Their loyalty was to Father Hoa through his brother, and not to the Vietnamese.

I got on the radio with Dong Cung and was updated by Lt. Harris. There was not much new--a couple of night bombardments both mortar and artillery involved. There were a couple of soldiers wounded while on patrol, and both had been medevaced. One piece of good news: the bunker for the school was completed and school was now in session. Only about 20 children were attending, but more were expected. I told Harris that I was coming back in three days and if he wanted he could go up to Ca Mau and spend a few days relaxing with the Province Advisory Team. He could get some good meals (compared to what we ate in Dong Cung), drink some beer, and talk to someone different. He jumped at the suggestion, and said he would be ready to go out on the chopper when I landed. True to their promise, three days later the Sector Swing Ship (helicopter used by the Province Advisory team to routinely transport supplies and personnel between the Province and outlying teams) arrived and Captain Berti stepped off.

394

We exchanged greetings and a handshake, and I boarded. Twenty minutes later I was standing on the landing pad in Dong Cung, Cai Nuoc District Town. My home away from home.

After settling down in our primitive abode, I passed out some goodies that I had brought back for the team. There were cigarettes, cigars, soap, some candy bars, a bottle of cognac, and some coffee for Dai-uy Hy. Lt Harris, who had changed his mind about going out to Ca Mau (why, I don't know), brought me up to date on events while I was gone and suggested that I go and look at the school. Dai-uy Hy agreed and led the way down the street to where the two young women were holding classes. The students had notebooks and pencils that had been supplied by the Province Refugee Office. There were a few texts or workbooks available plus some pictures on the walls. It looked like a real school.

"Well," I noted, "We are making progress: a school and a health station."

"And that's not all," said Harris.

"We get generator," interrupted Dai-uy Hy.

"Generator!" I exclaimed. "How large?" "Thirty KW (kilowatts)," replied Lt. Harris.

"When?"

"Soon, Province says," responded Harris.

"Wow, we are entering into the modern world," I observed.

The District Chief then said to me, "Come, we have tea and plan."

395

I walked with him to his bunker.. His orderly appeared at once with a pot of tea and glasses. Dai-uy Hy said, "I have information where VC artillery may be."

The night attacks, normally mortar fire, were including more and more artillery rounds. The attacks were not as frequent and seemed to be alternated between Dong Cung and Cai Nuoc Outpost to the north. Cai Nuoc Outpost received some 60 mm mortar fire, which had been almost eliminated at Dong Cung because of the addition of the.50 caliber machine gun. The artillery fire we were receiving appeared to be from a Japanese 70 mm howitzer.

"Artillery Nipponese, perhaps here," stated Dai-uy Hy, stabbing his finger on a map. "Somewhere here, can fire at Dong Cung and Cai Nuoc Outpost," he continued.

The area that Dai-uy Hy was pointing to was about halfway between the two government positions and was in the range to fire on either. The howitzer (commonly known as a *pack howitzer*), was designed to be transported by six men or three horses. In our area, that meant either by sampan or on the back of enemy soldiers.

"They need hard ground," I commented.

"Maybe VC build firing position. I have agents looking, they report soon."

"Great," I replied. "If we get a location, I can request a bomb strike."

"No," said Dai-uy Hy, pointing at his chest. "Dai-uy capture, look good to Province Chief."

"Ah, OK, I understand," I said, smiling.

He now pointed to another area on the map, upstream on the Nam Cam District side of the river. Rach Cai Trang canal entered the Song Bay Hop about two kilometers from Dong Cung. The waterway split two large abandoned coconut plantations near the river before disappearing into a mangrove area to the south. "Much VC activity there," he noted, indicating a spot on the map which included a number of buildings. "What kind of activity?" I asked. "Don't know perhaps we go see. Artillery problem, this no problem," Dai-uy replied.

Our discussion ended with a final cup of tea, and I left to join Harris and Blair. In a few minutes I had briefed them on the meeting with the District Chief. I warned them to be prepared, since it looked like we were soon going somewhere, either into the Nam Can or on a mission to capture an old World War II Japanese artillery piece.

It was two days later at 0200 in the morning when I was awakened by Sgt. Hai. "Dai-uy wants you to meet him now." "What's up?" I asked him, sitting up and reaching for my boots.

"Dai-uy go capture VC gun," he replied. "He wait for you in bunker."

"OK, go tell him I'm coming." "Yes sir."

"Lieutenant Harris, Sgt. Blair, better get stirring, looks like we are going somewhere soon," I announced. "We're up, sir. What's going on?" asked Harris.

"I don't know, but I think that Dai-uy Hy has some info on the VC artillery location. I'll be back shortly," I answered.

A light rain was falling as I crossed over to the Command Bunker. A group of 30 to 40 soldiers were standing nearby and appeared to be equipped, armed, and prepared to move out at a moment's notice. Entering the bunker, I was waved to the table where the Dai-uy was studying a map. He looked up and pointing to a spot with his finger said, "VC artillery there."

"Firing position?" I asked. "No, VC camp, they stay there. Hide, have one cannon, Nipponese. I attack before light. We go now."

I looked at the location he had pointed to and noted to myself that it was north of us, close to the old road, and west about 800 meters in light growth along a minor stream.

"We must go now, morning come soon. You go, too?" Dai-uy Hy inquired impatiently. "Yes, Lt. Harris, Sgt. Hai, and I will go. Sgt. Blair will stay here to contact Ca Mau for support if necessary. We will meet you by the troops on the roadbed," I answered as I started back to our quarters to pick up my gear. I was not taking a radio but would use one of the District Chief's and just change frequencies to the Province net. Since this appeared to be an ad hoc night mission with minimal planning, I advised Harris and Hai to carry extra ammo and grenades both smoke and frags), I chose my carbine rather than the M1 I had been carrying since the successful long range shot I had made on a VC a few weeks ago (he troops wanted to see me with it). The carbine did not have the range but it had more firepower and I expected we might be in close quarters and poor light. I, of course, routinely carried my pistol and knife.

We caught up with Dai-uy Hy at the Strong Point as his men moved out heading north. The Dai-uy had only a radio operator and two soldiers for security, so our command group totaled only seven. The rain was still falling, we were soon soaked, and although visibility was limited we moved rapidly and were soon past the location where we had the firefight on the previous operation. Thirty or forty minutes later we left the roadbed, moving west between some huts and onto a faint trail along a narrow stream. Our speed slowed considerably and

398

included frequent five- to ten-minute stops to rest and recon. . Finally Dai-uy huddled with the two soldiers that were on the point.

I joined him as he waved the soldiers off and said to me "They see VC camp, few guards, everyone asleep." "How many?" I asked. "Hai muoi (20), perhaps," he replied.

The troops began moving in single file, disappearing into heavier foliage that partially hid the narrow trail. Harris, Hai, and I fell in behind Dai-uy Hy. The column moved slowly, the rain now only a drizzle. It was still an hour or so before first light and visibility was only a few feet. I had no idea what the assault plan was. There was a Lieutenant and several NCOs with the troops. I hoped they had instructions for the attack. Suddenly I could see a soldier a step or two off the path standing over something at his feet. "VC guard, soldiers capture," Sgt. Hai whispered. I could now see a man trussed up hand and foot and with a bag over his head, lying on the ground. As the column passed by, soldiers would kick the captured VC or strike him with their rifle butt.

A few minutes later, the column stopped. Dai-uy Hy motioned several soldiers forward. He then crouched down and gestured to us to do the same. A few minutes passed and as my legs began to cramp, there was a shout followed by a fusillade of rifle fire and grenade explosions. I jumped up but Dai-uy Hy pushed me back down, ordering, "Wait!"

Then the snap of small arms fire passing overhead caused me to crouch even lower.

The initial crescendo of fire decreased. Dai-uy Hy rose and started off in the direction of the firing and was soon out of sight. Harris, Hai, and I followed. Shapes appeared out of the darkness and I went into a crouch again, preparing to fire; I didn't know if they were

399

our men or the enemy. I could hear soldiers yelling and then Dai-uy Hy calling to me. We moved in the direction of his voice and almost knocked him down as he appeared out of the darkness. He was standing by an object on the ground. I bent down to see what it was.

"It's a wheel?" I asked. "Da, from Nipponese cannon." "Where is the rest of it?" I inquired. Hy shook his head, "Soldiers look for, I think it is gone. VC carry off."

The sky began to lighten in the east and I could see soldiers searching through the meager gear abandoned by the VC and also noted three bodies.

"Do we have any casualties?" I inquired.

"Yes sir we have two wounded," replied Sgt. Hai.

A soldier approached with a canvas bag and dropped it at our feet. It contained several rounds of ammunition for the Japanese artillery piece.

As the morning light improved, the search for any signs of the artillery piece failed to produce any results. It appeared that the VC managed to escape our attack and the capture of their artillery. I was sure they had a withdrawal plan that involved having the Japanese howitzer disassembled and located in different locations so it could be rapidly moved. Perhaps even parts of it were in a sampan on the stream close by.

The results of our raid were three known VC KIA, one captured plus the artillery wheel, some 70 mm ammunition, and two friendly wounded. I could see that Dai-uy Hy was disappointed; capture of one of the enemy artillery pieces would have been a feather in his cap and offset the Province Chief's rebuke concerning the loss of 15 men in the VC attack on the Strong Point.

It was now full daylight, and the combing of the VC bivouac area was finished. Troops were gathered in small groups, resting and eating. The wounded were being moved toward the canal paralleling the roadbed where they would be loaded in sampans for transport back to Dong Cung. Any further medevac from there would be by air.

Lieutenant Harris, Sgt. Hai, and I joined Dai-uy Hy where he was sitting with his Lieutenant and NCOs and apparently giving orders.

As we approached, he waved his men off and said, "We move in one hour." "Back to Dong Cung.?" I asked.

"Da, I have other duties to which I must attend," he replied. I then radioed Sgt. Blair that we should be back in Dong Cung before noon and briefed him on the results of our raid. I asked him to check on the wounded when they arrived and request a medevac if necessary.

As we departed the area, I watched soldiers placing a number of grenade traps in the hope that the VC would return to the site. Once out of the heavy brush and out onto the old roadbed, the return gained speed and we closed in Dong Cung by noon, as expected. Our ad hoc attempt to capture an enemy artillery piece was unsuccessful and I had a feeling that we could soon expect a retaliatory response.

CHAPTER 55

A MAN FROM "THE COMPANY"

"Major, there is a message for you, don't recognize the call sign," announced Sgt. Blair. It was two or three days since our unsuccessful raid and VC activity had been light.

I took the mike from Blair and said, "This is Oscar Six, over."

"Oscar Six this is Slippery Elm Four, I am in route to your location and request some time with you, over."

"Slippery Elm Four, who are you?" I asked.

"I will identify myself upon arrival," responded the unknown station.

"OK, I'll be here. What's your ETA?"

"About 20 minutes, over."

"Roger, I will meet you on the pad. Oscar Six, out."

I told Harris to come with me to see who was coming to visit; I guessed it must be some civilian agency. A few minutes later an OH-58 Air America helicopter came into sight, circled the area, and settled down on the landing pad. A man in civilian clothes with a belted sidearm and carrying a canvas bag and an attaché case jumped out. "Hi, I'm Phil Jones and am here to talk to you about establishing a DIOCC," he stated, extending his hand. He turned to the helicopter and motioned to a middle-aged civilian pilot to shut down. The pilot nodded, cut the power, and gestured that he would stay with the chopper.

I introduced Lt. Harris and Sgt. Blair. As they were shaking hands, I asked, "Do we need the District Chief to join us?" "No, just you and Harris," Jones replied. "Can we sit down in your headquarters?" "Follow me," I answered, leading off.

Upon arrival Jones said in an incredulous voice, "Is this your headquarters?"

"Yep, what you see is it," I replied. "Grab a seat at the table. Tell you what, Sgt. Blair, how about going out and keeping the pilot company, take him down in the ville for a cup of coffee and I will update you later."

"Yes sir, glad to," said Sgt. Blair.

Jones sat down at the table, opened his attaché case, and withdrew some papers and a bound booklet. I joined him, and Lt. Harris pulled up an ammo box to the table and settled down on it.

"You have heard of the Phoenix program, haven't you?" Jones inquired.

"A program run by the Company (a pseudonym for the CIA) to seek out and destroy the VCI (Viet Cong Infrastructure), am I correct?"

"Yeah, but jointly with the Vietnamese Intelligence people. I'm here to help you set up a DIOCC," responded Jones.

"A DIOCC, what's that?" "A District Intelligence and Operations Coordinating Center."

I had received a briefing on the program some months earlier. The DIOCC was the lowest rung of a nationwide effort to collect, analyze, and provide information on the Viet Cong shadow

403

government. It was a brainchild of the CIA, but the shortage of personnel resulted in MACV furnishing 250 officers to operate the program at the district level. A CIA agent directed the efforts at the Province, which was initially known as the ICEX (Intelligence Coordination and Exploitation). In1968, the establishment of the program in the districts was underway, and by 1969 most districts had a DIOCC in place.

After a brief discussion Jones agreed, somewhat reluctantly, that we were probably not ready to operate a DIOCC. We had neither the personnel nor the equipment needed to take on the mission. Jones informed us that he could provide material such as desks, typewriters, chairs, radios, paper, pens, and money.

"Money?" I asked. "Yes, piasters to pay for intelligence, also for elimination of known Viet Cong officials."

"You mean I can pay them to kill the enemy?"

"Well, for information that results in their elimination," Jones replied.

He then opened the booklet that was among the papers he had removed from his attaché case and opened it, revealing lists of names on each page. Each name had a brief paragraph, some with photos.

"These individuals have been identified as Viet Cong officials operating in Cai Nuoc District. I am sure that your counterpart is aware of them," explained Jones. "We would like to know the status of them, any of them. Are they active? Perhaps some may have been eliminated or captured. Intelligence collected on a particular leader or official may be sufficient to conduct a mission to destroy them with assets that are not available to you and your District Chief."

"So you want me to discuss these VCI suspects with Dai-uy Hy to see if they are alive and well or are six foot under, am I correct?"

"Yeah, that's about it," replied Jones.

"Any intelligence that I have developed in the past I have forwarded to the Operations Section in the Province Advisory Team and I expect to continue to do so until I hear different from my boss," I stated.

"Oh, I understand, my job here today is to only update you and to offer any assistance we can provide toward preparing to implement the program at the District level," Jones quickly responded.

"OK, you can tell your supervisor what our conditions are here and that I will attempt to carry out any orders pertaining to the Phoenix program that I receive from my Headquarters," I announced.

"Good enough," responded Jones. "I recommend that you and your counterpart review the info I have here for you and let us know, through your intel people at Province, of course, anything that you believe to be of interest to us."

"I can do that. What about the money you spoke of?"

"You may be authorized to pay between two and ten thousand piasters for intelligence leading to the capture or elimination of anyone on the lists in that booklet. I can't give you that authority today but you will hear more about it," assured Jones.

"All right, I guess we are done here. Lt. Harris, see if you can round up Sgt. Blair and Mr. Jones's pilot and meet us at the pad."

"On the way, sir," replied Lt. Harris as he went out the door.

"Please call me Phil, major," requested Jones.

"OK, Phil it is," I said smilingly.

We were joined by Lt. Harris, Sgt. Blair, and the pilot at the landing pad where, after a shaking of hands and a warm-up of the helicopter, Jones soon disappeared from sight.

"What did you think of Mr. Jones, "Harris asked me?

"I think you will never see him again," I replied.

I then sought out Dai-uy Hy, who I found at the Headquarters building and told him that I wanted to discuss the Phoenix program with him. He knew of it and the Vietnamese version called Phung Hoang (the name of an all-seeing bird from a Vietnamese legend similar to the occidental phoenix). We proceeded to his bunker, where we were less likely to be interrupted. I briefed him on Jones's visit, and he showed little interest until I opened the booklet listing the VCI in the District. He reached under the bedding of his cot and produced an old Caterpillar Equipment Company yearly planner. He opened it, displaying on left and right pages what appeared to be individual family tree diagrams.

"VC families," he announced as he flipped through the pages.

Some names had lines drawn through them with notations. I soon realized the notations represented the demise of the person and the date it occurred. Upon comparison of the two documents, we found that several on the lists Jones had left me were marked as dead in Dai-uy Hy's book. Referring to the cash payment for intelligence leading to the elimination or capture of VCI officials, he asked if he could receive payment for those his records indicated as dead. I told him I didn't think so but would check to see if it was possible. The answer to that question when passed to Province was no way! However every VC we killed thereafter during the remainder of my tour was identified as someone on the list of VCI officials.

CHAPTER 56

MEDIVACED

The following night, the VC retaliated for our raid on their artillery position with an attack of both mortar and artillery fire, the artillery probably the one piece we almost captured. Their firing data were better than usual, with most of the rounds impacting near the center of the hamlet and bridge. Several rounds were close to our quarters and the District Chief's bunker.

I was on my cot when the first rounds hit, and I jumped up and ran toward the bunker. Harris and Blair were ahead of me, both being already up when the attack started. As I ran across the yard, a mortar round exploded to my right rear several meters away. I was pelted with dirt and small stone fragments and felt a stinging sensation down my right leg. I ran faster, falling into the tunnel entrance. I regained my feet and joined the others in the bunker. The enemy attack lasted only a few minutes longer. Not being sure of the VC firing position, our mortars began some counter-fire directed toward the site we had raided but stopped after a few rounds. A damage assessment began at once, and additional troops were directed to the defensive line on the north side. We had only three wounded and no one killed.

Standing in the yard outside of the bunker, I began cleaning off mud that had been splattered on me from the round that hit close behind me. As I wiped off my trousers on my right side, I realized that the wetness was not just from mud but also blood. I dropped my trousers and found half a dozen small lacerations not much bigger than a pinpoint, all oozing blood. There was a small cut and lump close to my knee. Wow, I thought, that was close! Then I noted that my right foot was throbbing. I looked down and there was no cut visible on the boot, only a sort of scuff mark. I pulled off the boot and my foot began swelling at once. A Vietnamese medic looked at it and shrugged his shoulders and left to treat some real wounded.

By morning, I had decided that it must be broken. I radioed Province and reported the attack and my bad foot. I told them it would be OK and that I would just stay off of it for a couple of days. Lieutenant Colonel Wright, insisted that I be medevaced. I was picked up a couple of hours later and taken to Soc Trang, where a medical detachment x-rayed my foot, washed my leg with an antiseptic, gave me some pills, and sent me to get some sleep. The next morning I returned to Ca Mau and the Province Team, where my foot was looked at again and determined to be not broken, just badly bruised. The next day found me in Dong Cung and back to duty.

CHAPTER 57

UNSUCCESSFUL OPERATION

The morning shower of rain had slackened to a drizzle and raised our hopes that an expected supply chopper would be arriving as scheduled. As the hours passed, the sun broke through the clouds and everyone's shirt was soon black with sweat from the unrelenting humidity. We were three quarters of the way through the rainy season (May through October) in our location, and heavy continual rains were less frequent but days without some moisture falling had not yet arrived. As the weather improved, we could expect increased enemy activity. However, it also allowed the friendlies to conduct more productive reconnaissance patrolling.

Just before noon, a helicopter came into view, circled the hamlet, and settled down on the landing pad. Two soldiers jumped off and the crew began shoving crates and boxes out onto the ground. They were quickly gathered up and carried away from the pad. The pilot handed me the usual packet of correspondence from the Province Team and mail.

He then handed me a bag and announced, "From us." I reached into the bag and pulled out a large salami and a bottle of cognac.

"Hey, thanks a lot! We will enjoy them both," I yelled above the engine noise. The pilot smiled, gave me the thumbs up sign, and then lifted the chopper off the pad and was soon out of sight.

Sgt. Blair announced, "I know where I can get some bread," and hurried off to get a loaf. No matter how small the Vietnamese community, they always seemed to have good French bread and coffee, and Dong Cung was no different. Later for lunch we enjoyed salami sandwiches, a real treat for us. The salami lasted for a few days; it

410

became kind of green and a little slimy for the lack of refrigeration, but we ate it anyway!

Among the documents in the packet from the Province Team were orders for my return to the United States. I was to report in to the Infantry School at Fort Benning, Georgia. My port call at Tan Son Nuit Airport was the 17th of September. I had to be in Saigon at the Kolpher Compound on the 15th. The excitement of the anticipated return to the "land of the big PX," as the U.S. was known by many GIs, was somewhat dampened by the thoughts of leaving the people that I had grown close to. Living without the normal conveniences of the American way of life and the frequent exposure to enemy action had created a relationship with the local troops and their families that is hard to explain to those who did not experience such duty.

There were two things I needed to do: first, find out if my replacement was on hand or identified, and second, notify my counterpart of my departure. I had only about two weeks left in Cai Nuoc. An inquiry directed to the Province Team concerning my successor was not promising; he was in the pipeline but not identified nor in country yet. I went to inform Dai-uy Hy of my departure date and found him in the District Headquarters building with his deputy, studying some papers and the usual map.

He greeted me with "I plan two operations." "Where?" I asked, approaching the table and looking at the map. "Here and here," Dai-uy answered, pointing at two locations that were marked with a grease pencil. One was east and north of us along the Rach Cai Muoi, and the other was the old plantation area across the river in Nam Can that he had mentioned before.

"We attack here first, maybe tomorrow or next day.VC unit there. Maybe Nipponese cannon," indicating the Rach Cai Muoi target.

"Lt. Hong will command. You will go, yes?" "Yes, we will go," I assured him.

I knew that the Districts were required to notify the Province Headquarters of their operations, but I wasn't sure if Dai-uy Hy did so. I knew that Hai Yen, a Chinese enclave, did not feel obligated to inform the Province of their military operations despite having a Vietnamese Commander. In fact there were instances where individual companies did not always tell the Hai Yen Commander when they were out on a mission.

I, however, always informed the Province Team when we were on an operation so they would know that we might request air or medevac support. After leaving the District Building, I returned to our quarters and told Harris and Blair that we would be going on an operation in a day or two. Lt. Harris had been feeling poorly the last few days, so I decided that I would accompany Lt. Hong and leave both Lt. Harris and Sgt. Blair back at Dong Cung, a violation of an unwritten rule that advisors will not go on a combat operation alone—a hard rule to follow on a two- or three-man team. I frequently ignored this rule both at Hai Yen and here in Cai Nuoc.

While discussing the two operations with Dai-uy Hy, I had forgotten to tell him of my impending departure. When I returned and so informed him, he expressed regret, saying "You are my first Advisor." He then asked about a replacement and announced that we must have a farewell party. I said a party was not necessary but he insisted that it was appropriate. I acquiesced, my mind on the operations we had discussed.

Two days later at 0500 hours, we crossed the canal on the east side of the hamlet and moved on a diagonal line intending to intercept the Rach Cai Muoi canal approximately two kilometers from where it emptied into the Song Bay Hop. The route of movement was terrible;

412

the swamp was knee deep at times, thick brush limited our line of sight to a few meters, and there was an ample crop of leaches. On the plus side, it was not raining and a heavy cloud cover diminished heat from the sun; however, the humidity was high and we were all soon dripping wet.

The objective, I finally found out, was a small settlement of huts on the west side of the canal, almost directly east of the VC bivouac area we had recently raided. Information received from farmers indicated that there were VC camped out there the last several days. The plan was to reach the canal a short distance downstream from the suspected VC location, enter the canal, and wade upstream to the objective and conduct a surprise assault out of the canal. The banks along the canal were heavy with brush and vines and any footpaths were sure to be guarded. Our attacking force was 60-plus including the PF (Popular Force) Platoon. Not the D-Day Invasion but at least an offensive operation.

We reached the canal a little after daylight. I had fallen back toward the rear of the column; shortly after leaving Dong Cung, I had begun to feel a little ill and nauseated, causing me to stop and rest a few minutes, hoping I didn't have whatever Harris had. Fortunately the nausea passed and I rejoined the column a hundred or so meters behind Lt. Hong. The troops had begun entering the canal, hugging the west side bank. I slid down the slippery bank and tried to move up the column to rejoin Lt, Hong but was not able to do so until the forward movement stopped. When I caught up with Lt. Hong, he was talking quietly with an NCO.

"What's up?" I asked, as I joined him.

"Hooches not here, over there," he replied, waving to the other side of the canal.

413

"The map shows…" I started to say.

"Map wrong, too old. Houses new," Hong interrupted. "And VC not there I think," he continued.

Several soldiers had crossed to the other side, finding the water chest deep in the center of the canal, and were climbing up the bank when a shout was heard and then rifle fire. Well, that's nice, I thought, we have been spotted and are still in the canal. We gotta get out of here!

Some soldiers started up the bank on our side of the canal. One was nicked on the ear by a round and another had a finger shot almost off. It was then that we realized that the VC were not in the hooches on the east side of the canal but on the west side. The ground on the west side had opened up into what was an uncultivated rice paddy. Soldiers were now peering over the edge of the bank and firing out across the paddy. A tree line was visible 300 meters or more from the canal, and Lt Hong was directing his men to fire on it. The incoming small arms fire kept us in the canal. Suddenly I heard the distinctive sound of a BAR firing in short four- to six-round bursts. Then a second one began firing, alternating with the first. The steady hail of fire only a foot or two above the top of the canal bank kept our men down. The individual rifle fire decreased to almost nothing.

"They are moving out of there," I yelled to Lt Hong. "The BARs are covering their withdrawal!"

Hong nodded in agreement; he recognized what the VC was doing. I rose up enough to see over the edge of the bank and could see VC running laterally, apparently gathering their gear and moving away to the northeast. The two enemy BARs continued their grazing fire. I saw some of our men going back down the canal.

414

Sergeant Hai, who had been by my side all morning, said, "Lt. Hong send soldiers down canal then over bank, try to flank VC."

I nodded that I understood; we sure couldn't go over the canal bank right into the face of those BARs. Suddenly one of the BARs stopped firing, and then the other. It became quiet for a few moments. Lt Hong began urging his men over the bank. A few sporadic shots were heard, then nothing. The enemy had broken contact and made their escape. Our raid was a failure.

Reviewing the morning's action, it appeared that the VC had expected a raid on the group of hooches and therefore did not occupy them but were prepared to defend themselves and to attack the raiding force if it was to their advantage. I believed our numbers were enough; I didn't think there were more than 30 or so VC in the engagement. I don't think the artillery piece was there. There was no indication of any enemy casualties. We were lucky in that our losses were minor. No one was killed and only four were wounded, all hit trying to exit the canal. In discussing the raid with Lt. Hong I saw that he was ashamed to report to the District Chief that they had failed their mission. I assured him that Dai-uy Hy would understand.

Our return was anti-climatic. We moved directly west, crossing mainly abandoned rice paddies and reaching the old roadbed about four klicks north of Dong Cung with the column closing in by 1400 hours.

After cleaning up and writing a report on the operation to be forwarded to the Province Team TOC, I then sought out the District Chief to discuss the day's operation and the one into Nam Can that he had mentioned. I found him wearing only a T-shirt and white undershorts, sitting on a folding chair in front of his bunker and quarters. He greeted me by waving me to a second folding chair beside him. I started to discuss the day's activities, but he shook his head and said "Lt. Hong already report to me," and then asked, "When must you leave?"

It was now the first of September and I had to be in Saigon on the 15th. I needed at least a day, preferably two, in Ca Mau with the Province Team.

"In ten or eleven days," I replied.

Dai-uy Hy looked thoughtful for a moment and then said, "I must go and look at old plantation in Nam Can, then have farewell party for you." I again said that a party was unnecessary, but he waved his hand dismissively saying, "It is necessary!" I then resigned myself that there was to be a party no matter what I thought.

CHAPTER 58

A WALK IN THE SUN

I was puzzled at the District Chief's intent to conduct an operation across the river into the Nam Can District. We had only crossed over once or twice since I had been in Dong Cung, and that was only a short distance, a hundred meters or so, searching for VC mortar positions along the shore. Now he intended to conduct an operation five or six kilometers deep into the abandoned plantations. If he had some intelligence concerning some VC target, he was not divulging it to anyone.

The Nam Can District contained a number of large coconut plantations. The area that Dai-uy intended to visit encompassed approximately twelve square kilometers, three kilometers wide and four kilometers deep, running almost due south from the Song Bay Hop. A large canal, the Rach Cai Nhap, bisected the plantations, flowing from the south to the north and emptying into the river four kilometers upstream from Dong Cung. Few houses or structures appeared on the map, but according to Dai-uy Hy there were at least two plantation houses with accompanying out-buildings located within the area sited along the main canal. One of those was the objective. Well, this could be interesting, I thought; the VC controlled the entire district. There was no government position anywhere since the Vietnamese government had abandoned the District Town some months prior.

I briefed Lt. Harris and Sgt. Blair on what I knew of the District Chief's plan and added it must be soon if it was going to happen before I departed. Harris's condition had not improved, and I decided if there was not a change for the better by morning, I was going to request a medevac for him. He looked awful.

417

In the morning we had two wounded, one shot in an encounter the prior evening while on patrol and one hit by some mortar fragments during a VC attack during the night. Harris was no better, and I informed the Province TOC that I had an Advisor to be evacuated plus two wounded soldiers. The need to evac an American raised the priority and I was assured a medevac chopper was on the way. I asked where he would be taken and was told probably Can Tho, where there was a U.S. military medical facility. Within an hour a medevac chopper arrived, loaded Lt. Harris and the wounded soldiers, and departed.

Preparation for the operation into the Nam Can plantations became obvious. Sergeant Hai told me that the District Chief was in the process of securing boats that could go on the river but were small enough to travel on the canals into the plantations. The canals were wide and deep enough to accommodate most of the river packets seen on the Song Bay Hop. They had been improved or dug by the plantation owners to transport their copra crop to market. Dai-uy Hy had no watercraft except a few small sampans, so he had to hire or commandeer enough boats to transport the troops he planned to take on the mission. River boats stopped at Dong Cung almost every other day. He had to negotiate the time, date, and number of boats needed. I had no idea how long it would take to round up the boats required.

The wait was not long; I was informed by Sgt. Hai that four boats would be available in two days. Each boat could carry about 20 individuals, so the operation was limited to 80 troops, about a third of our available force. Once briefed on the course of action by Dai-uy Hy, I planned to notify the Province TOC for possible air support. I then realized that this may be the last operation I would be on prior to departure for home. I hoped it would be a quiet one, "a walk in the sun."

The following evening, one of the soldiers that acted as an orderly and bodyguard for Dai-uy Hy approached me and announced

418

that the District Chief would like me to join him in his quarters. It was not mealtime, so I suspected he was ready to brief me on the Nam Can operation. As usual, he waited as late as possible before providing the details of an operation plan to myself and then his subordinates. As I entered his bunker, he greeted me and waved me over to the table covered with the normal map and papers. The map was marked with the route up the river and into the canal that traversed almost through the center of the plantations for several kilometers. There were several small circles and one large one marked with grease pencil along the main canal. "Perhaps VC there," Dai-uy stated, pointing at the circles.

"How about this one?" I asked, indicating the large one.

"Old plantation house, maybe VC headquarters," he replied.

"The map doesn't show any buildings," I noted.

"Map not correct, old French map shows plantation houses, I know they there."

The area circled was at a split in the canal forming two arms of a Y, each proceeding on to the south. According to the map, the coconut groves in the Y area thinned and then ended at what appeared to be swamp and mangroves.

Pointing again to the map and at the small circles the District Chief said, "These may be warning, observation posts, tell VC Commander if Government soldiers on canal." "Yeah, you may be right. Let me request a VR flight tomorrow morning of the area and see what they can tell us." Day-uy Hy nodded his agreement and said, "We leave 0700 tomorrow. Four boats, tow some sampans." "We'll be ready," I assured him, and left to brief Sgt. Blair on the next day's activities.

419

The following morning arrived without the normal shower of rain but with a light cloud cover. The first hitch in the day's operation was that one vessel had engine trouble and had to be scratched, reducing our troop count to around 60. The boats appeared to be quite old but seemed to be in reasonable condition. They were ten or twelve meters long, rather narrow with above-deck sides and roofs. Benches lined each side for passengers, with an open area in the stern for large items of cargo. The center of the passenger area was frequently filled with smaller items, animals or poultry.

The arrival of Shotgun 46 to conduct the requested VR was timely. After providing coordinates and description of the area we were concerned with, he warned me that the foliage was so heavy in the old coconut groves there was little he could see. He could scout the canals we were going in on and any structures that he could spot. I acknowledged the difficulty in reconning the old coconut groves and swamp areas but asked him to make a sweep of the area and tell us of what he observed. He rogered me and flew off. He could be over the area in ten minutes and I expected a report while we were chugging up the river toward the mouth of the canal.

I was correct; in 30 minutes, Shotgun 46 came back up on the net and reported that the waterways were clear with only one or two small sampans sighted. Only one person was spotted in each. They made no effort to hide. A few individuals were spotted near some houses along the canal. They also made no attempt to hide or run. He noted what appeared to be a group of buildings or a larger structure partly hidden by trees near where the canal split, approximately three kilometers in from the river. He did not see any personnel or structures in the old groves but did say he did not make a low pass over the area so as not to tempt any VC that might be anxious to down an airplane. I thanked him as he flew away in a northerly direction.

We were now on the river and I relayed to Dai-uy Hy Shotgun 46's report. He responded with a nod and said, "Think no VC camp there, they use canals for travel, not have units there, maybe stopover for VC boats passing through."

Our boat was second in line and about 200 meters from the lead vessel, with the third trailing the same distance. We were in the middle of the river, to discourage any small arms firimg. As we approached the mouth of the canal, the first boat turned in and slowed to almost a stop. It then moved forward at a reduced speed. I found this odd and also noticed that the troops did not appear to be as alert as usual. I had a feeling that something was going on that I was not aware of. When we made the turn into the mouth of the canal, I noted that some soldiers had loaded into the sampans being towed by the lead boat. They had untied the sampans and were paddling to both banks. As I watched, they disembarked and moved away from the canal toward the trees and what appeared to be an overgrown rice paddy. On one side, a couple of old dilapidated huts located 50 meters or more from the canal seemed to be the objective. The others were just moving away from the canal. They appeared to be in a relaxed mode, not the normal alertness I had seen on other operations. I turned to Sgt. Hai and pointing at the troops ashore and said, "Soldiers rear guard?"

"No sir, they gather," he replied.

"Gather? Gather what?"

"Coconuts, maybe pineapples, maybe other food," Hai responded.

Ah, it hit me like a ton of bricks, they are foraging! The centuries-old military supply system. I knew that small parties scavenged supplies that included rice, chickens, bananas, and a yam type tuber, but on a small scale. This appeared to be a major plundering

421

of the countryside. I approached the District Chief where he was standing in the bow of the boat and asked, "Are we looking for VC or food?" He looked at me and smiled. "Both," he answered. "We are taking food from the civilians." "We take from people in Nam Can. People here all VC or help VC. VC take food and young men for soldiers. These people not support Government, we take and give to soldier's families and people in Dong Cung," explained Dai-uy. "Then this operation is not to find and kill VC," I stated. "If we find VC, we kill," he retorted.

A few soldiers on our boat had climbed into the towed sampans and were paddling to the canal banks to, I assumed, search for food stuffs for "gathering." At a slight bend in the canal, the lead vessel had moved close to the bank and stopped. I could see a couple of soldiers jump off and take up guard positions. Our craft eased past and was now in the lead. The third boat was pulling over to the opposite side from the one stopped and I could see troops preparing to land. We were the only one still moving up the canal. The men still on board now appeared more alert, scanning the canal banks ahead with weapons at the ready.

I approached Dai-uy Hy again. "Where are we going?" I asked.

"There," he replied, pointing to what appeared to be a dock up the left bank a couple hundred meters. Looking to where he directed I could see what appeared to be a large rambling structure back from the canal and under the trees. "Old plantation villa, Phap (French)," he announced. "VC capture years ago. Drive French out. Not stay but use canal for movement north."

I had noted on the map that the left leg of the canal connected upstream with a manmade canal that ended at the Song Cua Lon, a large river that emptied into the Gulf of Thailand about 25 kilometers from the southern end of the country and the South China Sea. The district town of Nam Can, which was now in VC hands, lay on the Song Cua Lon ten kilometers west of the juncture of the canal and river. The combination of the river and canals provided a supply route from the open sea for VC boats up to the size of 20 meters. Three months after my departure, in December 1968, the U.S. Navy began operations in the rivers and canals of the southern end of the Delta and established a base on the Song Cua Lon at the old District Town of Nam Can, thus interdicting enemy traffic on the river.

After landing at the old dock, we made our way toward the plantation house. A few individuals near the house fled. I was surprised; the villa was built partly from stone and stuccoed masonry which must have been transported in from some faraway area. It was definitely not local material. It appeared that there were people living in parts of the house. It reminded me very much like the abandoned plantations I had seen in the Quan Pho area when at Hai Yen.

Dai-uy with two of his men was questioning three civilians that appeared to be far past the age for military service. One was pointing to an area of coconut trees behind the rear of the house. After a few minutes he waved them off, they bowed slightly, and hurried away.

Sergeant Hai who had been standing near the District Chief came over to me and said, "Farmers say VC were here a few days ago, stayed in house. They also stayed in coconut trees. Farmers no know why, Dai-uy going to look at tree area."

Dai-uy Hy was now walking toward the rear of the villa, preceded by a half dozen soldiers, and motioned to me to join him. As I did so, he pointed to one row of coconut trees that appeared to have a path along it. The trees were planted in rows with a ditch between each row, which I assumed was for irrigation. The ditches contained water covered with a green scum, algae I supposed, and like the trees appeared to be neglected for a long period of time. We followed the path for a short distance to where it widened into connecting paths crossing to adjacent rows. There the vegetation appeared to be trampled down.

"VC sleep here, not in house, maybe think house be bombed," announced Dai-uy Hy. A closer look at the area appeared to support Dai-uy's comment. "Return now, mission complete," he continued.

We began walking back up the path toward the villa when one of the soldiers cried out, pointing to a spot in the adjacent ditch. There I saw what appeared to be the back of something in the water--a crocodile? There are no crocodiles in the delta! Two soldiers jumped into the ditch and grabbed at what was a large lizard. A third soldier jumped in and assisted in wrestling the creature out of the water, tying a piece of commo wire around its jaws and looped behind the front legs. My God, I thought, it is six or seven feet long!

"What is it, is there a name for it?" I asked, astounded by its size. "Ky-da, I see before in Nam Can, not this big," said Dai-uy Hy.

The soldiers had now tied a rope on it and were dragging it along the path toward the house and boat where, after securing it further, it was placed in one of the sampans.

"What are they going to do with it?" I asked. "Don't know, perhaps keep," Dai-uy answered. "Maybe eat," Sgt. Hai suggested.

My attention was now directed toward the boats. The lead one had joined us at the dock and the soldiers were climbing aboard both. The sampans were loaded, in addition to the lizard, with coconuts in their green outer husks, yams, and what appeared to be very large pineapples. A number of poles or small logs three or four meters in length were stacked in the middle of the boats. After maneuvering around, we started down the canal back toward the Song Bay Hop. The lead vessel was now trailing. I could see the third boat now in the lead, with us in the middle. A short time later we entered the river and motored back to Dong Cung without a shot fired. I could not believe it. A real "walk in the sun."

CHAPTER 59

BACK TO THE WORLD

The next day I queried the Province TOC on my replacement and the status of Lt. Harris. He was still in the hospital in Can Tho, doing well, and expected back to duty in a few days. There was no new word on my replacement except he was en route. I was told that I would be picked up on the 10th, only four days away. The mixed feelings that I had experienced earlier returned.

I was finding that leaving Dong Cung was difficult. I It must have been evident, because later that day while discussing my departure with Dai-uy Hy he said "You are sad to leave here but will be happy to see family." I nodded in agreement. "I have party day before you go." I again said a party was not necessary. Dai-uy smiled and repeated, "Party on day before you leave, wear good uniform."

The next two days passed without incident except for the usual couple of VC mortar rounds at our evening mealtime and an exchange of rifle fire on one of the squad patrols. I spent some time visiting and taking photos of the civilians in the hamlet who I had come to know. I had a tape recorder on which I listened to the tapes that my wife had sent me and I gave to Sgt. Hai, and my radio to Sgt. Blair. The day before departure came, and I was informed that the party would be in the District Headquarters at 1400 hours. I entered the Headquarters to find a table large enough to seat 20 or more and covered with food and drink. As I entered, I was greeted by the District Chief clad in a neat camouflage uniform, his deputy, and the leading civilians in the hamlet and District Staff.

Several young women in traditional Vietnamese or Chinese dress were present. Apparently the school teachers, the midwife, and daughters of the Chinese merchant were drafted to attend the party. The Company Commanders and several of the NCOs were there but returned to their duties after shaking my hand and saying farewell. As requested by Dai-uy Hy, I was wearing a camouflage uniform, unauthorized in that the U.S. Army wore a plain olive drab jungle fatigue. Group photos were taken of me with the officials and also with the women. Several small gifts were presented. All in all, I was very moved emotionally by the event, especially when I thought that many of them had so little and would never live to see a normal life.

It was a quiet night but I did not sleep well. I found myself worrying about what would happen after I left. It was hard to accept that it was over. Someone else would take my place. I would probably be soon forgotten. The chopper arrived on time, kicked off some cargo, and waited while I said good-bye to Sgts. Blair and Hai. My last farewell was with Dai-uy Hy. We shook hands, and he gave me a cane that he carried at times. I gave him my watch even though he had a much better one. His last comment to me was, "You like brother." With that I climbed aboard and lifted off, never to see Dong Cung again.

My spirits rose when I arrived at Ca Mau and reported in to the Province Team. I spent several hours with Lt. Col. Wright discussing the problems facing my replacement. I also briefed the Captain from the S3 Section who was taking my place until Lt. Harris returned and my turtle showed up. [2] I did not get to see the PSA, as he was at the Embassy in Saigon. I had only seen him twice before and that was concerning the friendly fire incident and the river operation. I spent the following day writing reports and gathering up my personal gear that

427

had been left in storage at the team compound. I weighed myself and found that I had dropped from 165 pounds to 129, a loss of 36 pounds and 22 percent of my body weight. At 1000 hours the following morning I boarded an Army Caribou bound for Can Tho, where I would hopefully catch a flight to Saigon. Fortunately, a seat was available on an Air America C47 bound for Tan Son Nuit after lunch.

While waiting for the flight, I met a medevac pilot who had evacuated a number of my wounded from Dong Cung. I told him I was on my way home, and while we were chatting he noticed a VC weapon I was taking home as a souvenir. It was a German Army issue Mauser rifle of World War II vintage. There were a lot of them in the hands of the VC. Mine was captured when I was at Hai Yen. It was in perfect condition and Phong my bodyguard had refinished the stock. It was a beautiful weapon. The pilot admired it and said he wished he could find such a souvenir. I handed it to him and said, "It's yours."

I could think of no better use for it than as a gift to one who so many times had risked his life saving the life of others.

I caught my flight and by 1800 hours had checked into the Majestic Hotel at the end of Tu Do street downtown Saigon. The next day, after morning coffee and some French bread, I walked back to the Rex Hotel. There I caught a shuttle bus to the Kolpher Compound to begin my out-processing. They made it as painless as possible: I turned in my weapons and field gear, and threw away my uniforms. I visited the medics, where I received some ointment for the fungus

2 — The term turtle was often used to refer to replacements, ndicating that they were always slow in arriving.

that I had on my feet and groin, pills to continue to take for malaria, and a couple of immunizations. Along with others leaving, I had to attend a short briefing, collect my personnel and pay records, my orders, the flight number, and the time to report at Tan Son Nuit. On the way out of the supply room there were two boxes on a table in the hallway. One contained Vietnamese Service Medals and the other Vietnamese Campaign Medals. We were told to pick up one each on our way out, a real "thank you" for our service. They could have at least presented them to us, instead of picking them up like a mint on your way out of a restaurant.

After that, I was free until departure time. I spent that time visiting the PX and hanging around the club at the Rex Hotel, where I saw several officers that had in-processed the same time as I had the previous year. On the day of departure, I had to be at the airport at 0800 hours. I barely slept the night before, afraid I might somehow miss my flight. After arriving at the airport, going through an inspection of our luggage by the military police and verification of our orders, we were boarded. We sat on the runway for 20 minutes on a chartered commercial aircraft waiting for takeoff instructions. There were 160 passengers aboard, but it was strangely quiet, as if it was not certain that we were actually going home. But once the plane started moving and lifted off, a tumultuous shout of joy and relief echoed throughout the cabin. We were on our way to the United States, land of the big PX and home.

Above: Bridge across the Song Bay Hop from Dong
Cung hamlet to the Nam Can District.

Below: Wooden deck had been removed and used to
build bunkers. There were no roads remaining connected
to the bridge

430

Above: .50 caliber machine gun mounted on the bridge to provide supporting fire to the hamlet perimeter.

Below: The only street in Dong Cung from west to east, terminating at bridge abutement.

431

Above: The street from east to west. Note in the foreground entrance to command bunker under the bridge abutment, protected by mud wall on the river side.

Below: Entrance to command bunker from the east side and District Headquarters.

Above: Radio operators and soldiers with families assigned to the command bunker.

Below: 81 mortar position on the old road bed.

433

Above: Bunker supporting defensive positions on the old road.

Below: Mud bunker built adjacent to the school to protect schoolchildren. School reopened after the arrival of three teachers.

434

Above: Farewell luncheon held for departure of the author, the first District Senior Advisor assigned to Cai Nuoc.

Below: The teachers and local young Chinese women were drafted by the District Chief to attend the luncheon. Note women on the right were Vietnamese, the women on the left were Chinese.

EPILOGUE

It would be only another 30 months before I would again be bound for Vietnam. I spent that time assigned to the OCS (Officers Candidate School) at Fort Benning, Georgia, and six months Temporary Duty (TDY) at the University of Omaha to complete my studies for an undergraduate degree in history. Upon arrival back in Vietnam at Camp Alpha, I found that I was again assigned to MACV as an Advisor in IV Corps, the delta, as I had requested.

I had originally been assigned to USARV (United States Army Vietnam) but had asked for MACV. My personnel records reflected previous assignments as a S4, supply and maintenances staff officer. The drawdown of U.S. units had begun, and I was afraid that I might be stuck with assisting in the closing-out of units that were shipping stateside. I had written a letter to John Paul Van, the IV Corps Senior Advisor, requesting his support in being reassigned to the delta. I had received my letter back with a handwritten notation on it: "We will watch for you." Upon arrival, a Warrant Officer in the assignment section at Camp Alpha informed me that my orders were changed and I was on my way to the delta.

While waiting to process through one of the many offices, I was approached by a major who said, "I saw your name tag. Were you assigned to Cai Nuoc in An Xuyen Province?" I could tell by his gaunt appearance and faded jungle fatigues that he was out-processing, not one of the incoming replacements like myself. "Yes, I was," I replied.

"You were the first Senior Advisor?" "That's right." "You put the machine gun on the bridge?" "Yes, I did. Is it still there?" I asked. "No, it blew up but another one replaced it," he answered.

"You have just come from there?"

"Yes," he nodded.

We both had some time to wait, so we sat down. I asked many questions concerning the status of Cai Nuoc and the personnel who were there when I left. I asked about the District Chief, Dai-uy Hy. He told me he was assassinated by the civilian who owned the rice mill. It turned out he was the local VC Commissar.

"My God," I said, "I sat and ate with him!"

"Yeah, and he was never killed or captured either as far as I know," the major stated.

He updated me on the current situation in Cai Nuoc. The government controlled a bit more of the area. There was a four-man Advisory Team in place. Navy Swift Boats were now coming up the Song Bay Hop. In 1969, they established a base on the Song Cua Lon, the southernmost river in Vietnam, located in the Nam Can District. The Nam Can District town was re-occupied by government forces; however, there was no land route between Dong Cung, Cai Nuoc District, and Nam Can. He couldn't tell me much about Hai Yen; he knew the team assigned there but little more. We both had to continue our processing, he going home and I arriving. We shook hands. I never saw him again. I have long forgotten his name.

Two days later I departed for Can Tho, the largest city in the delta and IV Corps Headquarters, where I was to report to the Corps Senior Advisor John Paul Van. I found that Van had been transferred to II Corps and Mr. Wilbur Wilson (known as Coal Bin Willie) was the new Senior Advisor. During an initial briefing with Mr. Wilson, I was informed that I was being assigned as the Senior RF/PF Advisor on the Advisory Team in Vinh Binh Province, currently rated 38th of 44 Provinces for security and government control. The following day Mr. Wilson transported me in his personal helicopter to Tra Vinh, the capital of Vinh Binh and headquarters of the Province Advisory Team. There I would spend a second year in Vietnam--which is a story for another time.

GLOSSARY

A1E	Propeller driven dive bomber
AO	Area of operation
Ao dai	Vietnamese woman's traditional dress
ARVN	Army of the Republic of Vietnam
AWOL	Absent Without Leave
Bac-si	Doctor, Medic
BAR	Browning Automatic Rifle
Beaver	Dehavilland single engine cargo plane
Bird Dog	Light observation fixed winged aircraft
BOQ	Bachelor Officer's Quarters
Boston Whaler	Light outboard motor propelled watercraft
B40	Rocket Propelled Grenade
Caribou	Dehavalland 2 engine cargo/personnel plane
Chao	Vietnamese "hello"

Chinook	Two engine helicopter capable of transporting cargo or 30 personnel
Cholon	Chinese section of Saigon
Chopper	Helicopter
Chi Com	Chinese Communist Rifle
CIA	Central Intelligence Agency
CIDG	Civilian Irregular Defense Group
Claymore	Command detonated anti-personnel mine
CO	Commanding Officer
COMUSMACV	Commander U.S. Military Advisory Command Vietnam
Cords	Civil Operations and Revolutionary Development Support
Co-VAN	Advisor
CRP	Combat Reconnaissance Platoon
C4	Plastic explosive
Dai-uy	Captain Vietnamese Army
DC	District Chief

DDSA	Deputy District Senior Advisor
DIOCC	District Intelligence and Operations Coordinating Center
DPO	Deputy for Plans and Operations
DPSA	Deputy Province Senior Advisor
DSA	District Senior Advisor
FAC	Forward Air Controller
Grazing fire	Automatic weapons fire that does not rise above the height of a standing man
Guns	Armed Helicopters used in support of ground troops
HES	Hamlet Evaluation Report
Hill Climber	Chinook radio call sign
Hooch	House, hut
Horn	Radio hand set
ICEX	Intelligence Coordination and Exploitation, later renamed Phoenix
JUSPAO	Joint U.S. Public Affairs Office
KIA	Killed in action

Klick	Kilometer
Latrine	A communal type privy, toilet as in a camp
LAW	Light Anti-tank Weapon
MAC	Military Air Command
MACV	Military Assistance Command Vietnam
MEDCAP	Medical Civil Action Program
Mike	Radio hand set
Mike Mike	Millimeters
MPC	Military Payment Certificates
North Vietnam	Democratic Republic of Vietnam
Nungs	Vietnamese born Chinese
OD	Officer of The Day
OD	Olive Drab
Otter	Dehavalind single engine cargo/ passenger plane
PAVN	People's Army of North Vietnam

PCS	Permanent Change of Station
Phoenix	See ICEX
POL	Petroleum, Oils, Lubricants
Pop Smoke	Mark a location by throwing a smoke grenade
PFD	Present for duty
PRU	Province Reconnaissance Unit
PSA	Province Senior Advisor
PSP	Punched Steel Plate
Puff the Magic Dragon	C47/AC47 gun ship
Pungi stakes	Sharpened slivers of bamboo or hardwood used as an anti-personnel barrier
RF/PF	Regional Forces/ Popular Forces
Roger	A term used in radio transmissions meaning I hear you and understand
RPG	Rocket Propelled Grenade
RVN	Republic of South Vietnam

Sector	Military designation for Province
Sector Ship	Helicopter used by the Province Team for administrative and logistic support to sites within the Province.
Sub Sector	Military designation for District
Shotgun	Call sign for the 221st Aviation Company
S1	Staff officer/Office for Administration
S2	Staff Officer/Office for Intelligence
S3	Staff Officer/Office for Plans and Operations
S4	Staff officer/office for Logistics
S5	Staff Officer/Office for Civil Affairs
Spooky	C47/ AC47 gun ship
Sky Spot	Night bombing mission
Slick	Unarmed Huey Helicopter
TDY	Temporary Duty
The Company	CIA
Thieu-ta	Major, Vietnamese officer rank

TO&E	Table of Orgranization and Equipment
Turtle	Incoming individual replacement
USAID	United States Agency for International Development
USO	United Services Organization
VC	Viet Cong - Vietnamese Communist
Ville	U.S. slang for village or hamlet
VR	Vertical Reconnaissance (aerial)
Walks in the sun	Ground operations without enemy contact
Wilco	Term used in radio transmissions meaning will comply. Frequently used with Roger as Roger Wilco; understand, will comply.

Some Suggested Reading

Roberta Ostroff. *Fire in the Wind*. Annapolis, Maryland: Blue Jacket Books, Naval Institution Press, 2001.

Edward Geary Lansdale. *In The Midst Of Wars: An American's Mission to Southeast Asia.* New York: Fordham University Press, 1991.

Jim G. Lucus. *Dateline: Vietnam.* New York: Award Books, 1966.

Dickey Chapelle, "The Fighting Priest of Vietnam," *Reader's Digest,* July 1963.

Dickey Chapelle, "Helicopters over South Vietnam." *National Geographic,* November 1962.

Al Santoli. *To Bear Any Burden: The Vietnam War and It's Aftermath in the Words of Americans and Southeast Asians.* New York: E. P. Dutton, 1985; pages 78-81, *The Chinese Priest.*

"The Report the President Wanted Published." *The Saturday Evening Post,* May 20, 1961.

"With Marylanders in Vietnam," *The Evening Sun,* Baltimore, Maryland, May 3, 1968.

"Saigon and the 'Last Americans'," *Chattanooga Times,* Chattanooga, Tennessee, February 1, 1968.

Jottings by Joan, Joan Horsey, Chestertown, Maryland: Chester River Press, July 1968

Made in the USA
Charleston, SC
09 February 2014